M000218855

COMPLEX SERIAL DRAMA AND MULTIPLATFORM TELEVISION

This book examines the creative strategies, narrative characteristics, industrial practices and stylistic tendencies of complex serial drama. Exemplified by shows like HBO's *The Sopranos*, AMC's *Mad Men* and *Breaking Bad*, Showtime's *Dexter* and Netflix's *Stranger Things*, complex serials are distinguished by their conceptual originality, narrative complexity, transgressive lead characters and serial allure. As a drama form that continues to expand and diversify in today's television, HBO's *Boardwalk Empire* and *Game of Thrones*, Netflix's *Orange Is the New Black* and Hulu's *The Handmaid's Tale* provide further examples. Dunleavy investigates the strategies that underpin the innovations, influence and success of complex serial drama, giving students and scholars a nuanced understanding of this contemporary TV form.

Trisha Dunleavy is Associate Professor in Media Studies, Victoria University of Wellington, New Zealand. Her research focuses on television, in which the key areas of interest are TV drama, related institutions and industries, and national screen production cultures. Her earlier books include *Television Drama: Form, Agency, Innovation* (Palgrave Macmillan, 2009) and *Ourselves in Primetime: A History of New Zealand Television Drama* (Auckland University Press, 2005).

COMPLEX SERIAL DRAMA AND MULTIPLATFORM TELEVISION

Trisha Dunleavy

Routledge
Taylor & Francis Group

NEW YORK AND LONDON

First published 2018
by Routledge
711 Third Avenue, New York, NY 10017

and by Routledge
2 Park Square, Milton Park, Abingdon, Oxon OX14 4RN

Routledge is an imprint of the Taylor & Francis Group, an informa business

© 2018 Taylor & Francis

The right of Trisha Dunleavy to be identified as the author of this work has been asserted by her in accordance with sections 77 and 78 of the Copyright, Designs and Patents Act 1988.

Library of Congress Cataloging in Publication Data
Names: Dunleavy, Trisha, author.
Title: Complex serial drama and multiplatform television / Trisha Dunleavy.
Description: New York: Routledge, 2018. | Includes bibliographical references.
Identifiers: LCCN 2017032513 | ISBN 9781138927735 (hardback) |
ISBN 9781138927759 (pbk.) | ISBN 9781315682310 (ebk.)
Subjects: LCSH: Television plays, American–History and criticism. |
Television series–United States. | Cable television–United States.
Classification: LCC PN1992.65 .D85 2018 | DDC 791.45/6–dc23
LC record available at https://lccn.loc.gov/2017032513

ISBN: 978-1-138-92773-5 (hbk)
ISBN: 978-1-138-92775-9 (pbk)
ISBN: 978-1-315-68231-0 (ebk)

Typeset in Bembo
by Deanta Global Publishing Services, Chennai, India

CONTENTS

ACKNOWLEDGMENTS

This book owes much to the support and contributions of a number of individuals and organisations. Thanks first to my family – my partner, Derek Neal, and children, Liam and Trees. Of all academic colleagues who supported me in this project, I am most grateful to my American friend and colleague, David Lavery (formerly of Middle Tennessee State University) for his infectious enthusiasm for this subject and the many insights he provided. Very sadly, David passed away in 2016. I am grateful to American scholar Douglas Howard for his feedback on some key book chapters and to Danish scholar Eva Novrup Redvall for her encouragement in the final months of work. Thanks also to the many of my colleagues at Victoria University of Wellington, New Zealand, especially those in the Media Studies programme, for their support.

I remain enormously grateful to the group of American-domiciled individuals who gave their time to conduct interviews with me and generously extended their hospitality to a visitor from New Zealand. Aside from David, Joyce and Sarah Lavery, who hosted me in Murfreesboro, special thanks to American scholars Gary Edgerton, Robert Thompson, David Bianculli and Brian Rose, all of whom were attentive hosts and shared with me their own ideas about American television. Thanks to Ron Simon at the Paley Media Center for his many insights and to the Paley staff (in both New York and LA), who could not have been more helpful. I am especially grateful to writer-producers Alan Ball and Tom Fontana for their insights about conceiving and creating TV drama, and to cable network executives Gary Levine (Showtime) and Charles Shreger (HBO) for their ideas about original drama in a changing TV industry.

My employer, Victoria University of Wellington, has facilitated my completion of this book by providing research funding which ensured me the necessary resources and time in which to work. This book would not have been possible without this funding support. I am very grateful, as always, to the Victoria University Research Trust for the successive research grants it awarded. These allowed me to travel to the U.S.A. to undertake initial research and conduct the above interviews. Subsequent Research Trust grants allowed me to gather a comprehensive database of material, and to regularly update this as new developments required it. Thanks to the Trust's Philip Roderick for his ongoing assistance. I am also appreciative of the additional grants that I received from Victoria's Faculty of Humanities and Social Sciences, which helped get research started and also paid for some final pre-submission work. Final thanks go to those involved in seeing this book through to publication. Many people have contributed to this, Mia Moran, Jack Whelan and Rachel Cook among them. I am especially grateful to my Routledge editor, Erica Wetter, for and support throughout the completion of this book.

INTRODUCTION

The morning of the day I got sick, I'd been thinking. It's good to be in something from the ground floor. I came too late for that, I know. But lately I've been getting the feeling that I came in at the end, the best is over. I think about my father, he never reached the heights like me. But in a lot of ways he had it better. He had his people. They had their standards, they had pride. Hey, what have *we* got?

Tony Soprano, 'The Sopranos', The Sopranos (1:1)

In my first job (I was in-house at a fur company), this old pro copywriter, a Greek named Teddy, told me the most important idea in advertising, is, *new*. It creates an itch, he said, but put your product there, like a kind of calamine lotion. He also talked about a deeper bond with the product: *nostalgia*. It's delicate, but potent ... Teddy told me that, in Greek, nostalgia literally means 'the pain from an old wound'. It's a twinge in your heart, far more powerful than memory alone.

Don Draper, 'The Wheel', Mad Men (1:13)

My name is Walter Hartwell White. I live at 308 Negra Arroyo Lane, Albuquerque, New Mexico, 87104. To all law enforcement entities, this is not an admission of guilt. I am speaking to my family now. Skyler, you are the love of my life; I hope you know that. Walter Junior, you're my big man. There ... are going to be some things that you'll come to learn about me in the next few days. I just want you to know that no matter how it may look, I only had you in my heart. Goodbye.

Walter White, 'Breaking Bad', Breaking Bad (1:1)

Delivered by some of the most compelling characters in American television history, the above monologues also foreground the idiosyncratic stories and perspectives that distinguish the shows to which these characters belong: *The Sopranos*, *Mad Men* and *Breaking Bad*. As acclaimed and groundbreaking TV dramas of the early multiplatform era,[1] these are part of the larger group of American-produced shows – including *Six Feet Under*, *The Wire*, *Oz*, *Boardwalk Empire*, *Dexter*, *True Blood* and *Stranger Things* – whose emergence and success has stimulated the writing of this book. Yet in terms of the 'concept' (or 'big idea') that fuels and locates their stories, these TV dramas could hardly be more different from each other. So what do they have in common, and why does this book place them together?

The first answer is that these are leading examples of the larger group of American-produced TV dramas that can be classified as 'complex serials', the production form at the center of this book. 'Complex serial', a label I first applied to American television in 2009,[2] refers to a particular type of serial drama, whose shared characteristics are introduced in this chapter and whose distinctions within the larger 'meta-genre' of American TV drama are examined in this book.[3] As innovative and influential 'complex serials', the above shows are analyzed here as exemplars of a larger and increasingly pervasive form of drama in American television. Placing this form within television's multiplatform era, as one that has facilitated and accelerated its expansion, this book examines the authorship processes, narrative characteristics, industrial practices and stylistic tendencies of 'complex serial' drama.

The second answer to the above question is that these TV dramas were all produced for American 'non-broadcast' rather than broadcast networks. The first examples, *Oz* (1997–2003) and *The Sopranos* (1999–2007), were commissioned by HBO, the shared formal and aesthetic characteristics of 'complex serials' developing from 2000 onward in the context of their origination by other non-broadcast networks, these coming to combine 'premium' and 'basic' cable with subscription-funded internet networks. While these shows have expanded and attained influence largely within this non-broadcast sector of American television, this trajectory need not infer that 'complex serials' are inherently a non-broadcast form, or that examples of this form cannot be produced for broadcast networks.[4] It seems significant, however, that in American television, this 'complex serial' drama has developed and flourished *only* in the context of the commissioning of original long-format TV drama[5] by non-broadcast networks. This foregrounds the notable fit of 'complex serials' with the market position and imperatives of American non-broadcast networks, along with the perceived deviations of this form, and of the shows that have most successfully defined it, from still pervasive traditions and expectations for American broadcast drama.

Complexity in Television

To call something complex is to highlight its sophistication and nuance, suggesting that it presents a vision of the world that avoids being reductive or artificially simplistic, but that grows richer through sustained engagement and consideration. It suggests that the consumer of complexity needs to engage fully and attentively, and such engagement will yield an experience distinct from more casual or partial attention.

Jason Mittell[6]

Jason Mittell's assertions provide an invaluable sense of what viewers might expect from a 'complex' TV show, including a complex drama. Yet it is not possible to fully separate 'complex' from 'conventional' shows, especially because of the long-standing tendency in television for a new drama to emulate and absorb the most successful features of its predecessors, a process that Todd Gitlin (1994) terms 'recombination'. Hence, whilst complexity is multifaceted, one way to recognize it in TV drama is through the identification of shows that stand out within this meta-genre, not only because they are relatively sophisticated and/or challenging, but also because they strive to differentiate themselves from conventional dramas in additional ways. Complexity in TV drama begins with concept design, gaining impetus in the presence of an original concept and/or a distinctive viewpoint on the show's subject. Mittell's claim that "the consumer of complexity needs to engage fully and attentively" (2013: 46) can help to quantify complexity. Television is often viewed in busy settings in which distractions are inevitable, and many TV genres and forms deploy strategies that can compensate for a distracted mode of viewing. But complex dramas are not among them. Complex dramas are not devised to be viewed casually; instead, they offer their fullest readings and pleasures *only* to those willing to watch and listen closely.

Yet perceptions of 'complexity' cannot avoid subjectivity, and complexity in television is all the more difficult to define or delineate since TV drama is not the only meta-genre considered to have contributed to it. Moreover, audience experience can be very important in informing perceptions of, reactions to and evaluations of complexity in television. In successive publications, Mittell identifies and examines the phenomenon of increasing 'narrative complexity' in American television. He finds evidence of narrative complexity on all platforms of American television, identifying its traits and strategies in both scripted comedies and hour-long dramas, and in 'series' as well as 'serial' shows. Importantly, this kind of complexity has a far wider context than the TV drama form of focus in this book.

The 'complex serial' label is considerably more specific than the range of TV shows and forms to which Mittell's concepts of 'complex TV' (2015) and of 'narrative complexity' (2006) are applicable. This label does not refer, for example, to the large category of 'scripted sitcom' (which has multi-camera, single-camera and animated variants), or to the hybrid form, 'dramedy' (a comedic form of drama, often using a 35-minute episode format). It does not include the large array of enduring 'procedural' drama series, a descriptor that acknowledges, in particular, their setting in hospitals, police stations and law firms or similar institutions, all of which share the capacity to generate a potentially unlimited flow of episode stories.

While many TV dramas deploy a narrative blend of 'series' and 'serial' elements, 'complex serials' not only foreground serial form and narration, but are also *conceived* as serials. One repercussion of this is that their narratives, even though this book profiles long-format examples, have no prescribed length.[7] The grounding of these dramas in serial form, a feature examined in Chapter 4, is important in enabling their perceived deviations from broadcast drama traditions and conventions in terms of the concept that motivates their stories, the kinds of characters they can construct, and the capacities of seriality to subject key characters to unusually probing investigation. Their conception as serials, however, does limit the capacity of complex serials to endure indefinitely. In this respect, the complex serial is very different from the soap opera,[8] American television's oldest serial form and one associated with record-breaking longevity. Most prevalent in the daytime schedules of American broadcast TV, soap operas have remained a modestly budgeted, albeit very high-output form – these two features highlighting their other contrasts with complex serials.

Complex Serials as High-End Drama

Suggesting that higher investment in drama is of rising importance to the competitive strategies of TV networks in the multiplatform era, Denise Mann (2009: 100) contends: "Increasingly, the networks believe that the high production values in most drama today are what is drawing viewers to television". Crucial to the conceptual idiosyncrasies, narrative complexity and aesthetic ambition of complex serials, even though their production costs vary, have been budgets that enable the pursuit and achievement of 'high production values', a term that refers to the more expensive end (or high-end) of the investment spectrum for TV production.

In all its forms, high-end drama commands and is distinguished from 'ordinary' television (Bonner, 2003) by its very high per-episode cost; this currently ranges from US$3–10 million for American-produced examples.[9] High-end drama deploys either 35mm film or ultra-HD digital formats as the shooting medium. Important to it is the strategy of "programme individuation" (Caldwell, 1995: 88), in which selected exterior locations, elaborate sets and cinematography make significant contributions to the distinctive 'look' of a TV drama. While high-end dramas can target and deliver a broad audience, they are often commissioned by networks to target well-educated viewers with higher levels of disposable income.

Higher budgets for TV drama provide their writing and production processes with resources that far exceed those of 'ordinary' television. These include a greater proportion of location scenes, along with production workflows that allow time for meticulous attention to visualization, camerawork and mise-en-scène.[10] Yet high-end budgets are by no means exclusive to complex serials. Instead, such budgets are characteristic of the wider range of TV dramas produced for 'prestige' and other peak-hour timeslots in linear television. If produced for non-linear internet networks, high-end dramas function as 'signature' programming, designed to increase brand awareness, subscribers and revenues.

The Complex Serial Drama Template

Four characteristics of complex serial drama attest to its deviations from long-standing traditions and conventions for hour-long American TV drama, especially from the dominant forms deployed for the long-format primetime dramas produced for American broadcast networks.

First, these shows are grounded in serial form, a contrast with the still evident tendency of broadcast television to develop and deploy long-format dramas, which, while they do involve varying levels of seriality, are often grounded in series form.[11] Although American series dramas have since *Hill Street Blues* regularly incorporated serial storylines, a broadcast TV preference for episodic stories (or those that develop and resolve in the space of a commercial hour) has persisted, partly because, in drama at least, this narrative structure attains higher ratings and greater multi-season longevity than other structures can, and its capacities to attract casual (as well as regular) viewers make it a favorite with advertisers. The persistence of TV drama conceived and produced as series has been directly affected by the advertiser-oriented political economy and linear schedules that have historically dominated American television.

Second, the concepts of complex serials eschew the tried-and-tested institutions (police stations, hospitals and lawyer's offices) of TV drama tradition, in favor of a genuine diversity of settings and milieux, which contribute to their 'individuation' (Caldwell, 1995) and distinctive look. Strongly highlighted in complex serials' elaborate title sequences, these settings and milieux entail unusual attention to mise-en-scène, verisimilitude, cinematography and the use of musical scores to evoke a particular mood. In combination with the conceptual idiosyncrasies of these shows, their aesthetic qualities allow the specificities of place, time and 'mythology' (this term describing the ideological framework that underpins the diegetic world of a TV drama) to be powerfully conveyed. Important in maximizing the aesthetic sophistication of complex serial dramas is their receipt of resources over and above the historic norms for American TV drama, a facet investigated in Chapter 5.

Third, complex serial stories unfold around conflict-riven and usually transgressive primary characters, whose individual struggles usually span the life of the show. While the moral and psychological complexity of these characters has been important to the allure of complex serials, the construction and development of such characters is enabled by the conception of these dramas both in serial form and outside the reach of Federal Communications Commission (FCC) content rules. Although these troubled characters need not be seriously transgressive, the complex serial form is one in which there is potential for them to be more villainous, duplicitous and changeable than has ever been possible for lead characters in other forms of American TV drama. As the primary character in a long-format TV drama, Walter White, for example, could not have made the radical transformation from high-school chemistry teacher to ruthless drug lord if he had been placed in a series drama designed for and destined to confront the content constraints of American broadcast TV. Importantly, however, the narrative emphasis of complex serials on character-driven stories does not preclude the incorporation of a quasi-procedural component into their concepts – with examples in *Six Feet Under*'s funeral home, *Mad Men*'s advertising agency and Dexter Morgan's regular work as a 'blood spatter expert' – through which an additional flow of characters, stories and conflicts is generated.

Fourth, the complex serial incorporates more explicit content than is possible for American broadcast dramas. Broadcast networks remain in the thrall of "least objectionable programming" (Klein, cited in Thompson, 1996: 39). This commissioning philosophy is rooted both in their economic reliance on advertising revenue, as a result of which their programming must be advertiser friendly and ratings driven, and in their obligations to avoid breaching FCC content rules, which place limits upon depictions of violence, nudity and sex, along with the use of profane language. In contrast, explicit content for complex serials is rendered possible by the distance of their non-broadcast networks from FCC regulations. Explicit content is also encouraged by the expectation that non-broadcast networks will take such risks. Accordingly, the complex serial template – regardless of whether its shows are produced for subscription-funded networks (cable or internet) or for 'basic' cable networks (whose incomes combine advertising revenue with 'per subscription' fees received from cable system providers)[12] – can be one in which profane language, nudity, explicit sexuality and graphic violence are both regular occurrences and depictions involving central characters.

The Commissioning and Perceived Risk of Complex Serials

The term 'commissioning' will frequently appear in this book; here it refers to the decision of a given network to invest or co-invest in a new TV drama. In this process, both larger and smaller production companies operate as vital intermediaries, acting for drama writer-producers by providing the first hearing for their pitches, selecting suitable networks for their project, negotiating a deal with the purchasing network, making a sizeable contribution to the investment cost through deficit financing, and facilitating the production of the TV drama by working closely with its creators. Highlighting how the investment costs of original drama are divided between the host network and the production companies, John Higgins (2006: 18) explains that the latter "generally sell their primetime shows to U.S. networks at a loss, hoping to offset part of the deficit with overseas deals" and that the initial purchase by the former "might cover only 75 percent of the production costs". While this traditional sharing of the production costs between networks and production companies continues, important to the evolution of complex serials has been the willingness of both groups to support higher production costs. Aside from HBO-commissioned examples, complex serials tend to receive up to 40 percent investment from their production companies, with remaining finance being covered by their commissioning network. The tendency to share the cost of drama production between networks and production companies fore-grounds the importance of additional sales to other networks and platforms (both domestic and foreign) and of DVD sales, in amortizing these 'front-end' costs via 'back-end' revenues. HBO differs from other networks in this regard, preferring to invest enough to cover the full cost of the TV dramas that it has commissioned (Charles Schreger, author interview, 2013), a strategy that allows it full control over the exhibition, distribution and sales of these dramas from network debut through 'afterlife'.

Demonstrating a pattern of resistance by American broadcast television to the commissioning of complex serials, *The Sopranos* (1999–2006) was first offered to Fox, CBS and ABC (Creeber, 2004: 100), but was rejected by all three. It was then offered to and 'greenlit' by HBO. *Breaking Bad* (2008–13) also struggled to find a willing and suitable host network, notably because its primary character was a high-school chemistry teacher turned methamphetamine 'cook'. But *Breaking Bad* was not even offered to broadcast TV, instead being pitched to a range of cable networks. Underlining just how confronting its concept was perceived to be, *Breaking Bad* was turned down by 'premium' providers HBO and Showtime, as well as by 'basic' cable networks FX and TNT, before it was finally 'greenlit' by AMC (Gilligan, cited in *Emmy Legends* interview, 2011). *Stranger Things* (2016–), the newest of the TV dramas examined in this book, was offered to a larger num-ber of TV networks. However, underlining how little things have changed since the first pitch for *The Sopranos*, the *Stranger Things* idea was reputedly rejected by some "15 to 20" TV networks (Grow, 2016) before finally being offered to Netflix. As a recurring facet of the experience of several other complex serial dramas examined in this book, and a demonstration of just how different they are perceived to be, the 'big idea' for *Stranger Things* was simply not recognized as a potential success by the large number of networks to which it was first offered.

These outcomes suggest that complex serials, at the pivotal concept design stage at least, are frequently perceived as unusually risky properties. There is fur-ther evidence for this in the way that, at some pitch meetings, notably those in which the interest of executives has been piqued, modifications to core compo-nents of the concept presented to them have been suggested. *Breaking Bad* crea-tor, Vince Gilligan, recalls meeting TNT executives who listened, with evident fascination, to his pitch. But, as Gilligan goes on to explain, they could not say yes. Instead, they forthrightly admitted: "If we bought this we'd be fired, we would literally be fired. We cannot put this on TV. It's meth. Meth is reprehensible … Could the guy be a counterfeiter instead?" (Gilligan, cited in *Emmy Legends* inter-view, 2011). When Matt and Ross Duffer pitched their idea for *Stranger Things*, successive networks were evidently concerned by the fact "that the show [would foreground] four kids" but "wasn't TV for children" (Grow, 2016). Matt Duffer recalls their being instructed by some of these networks to either revise the concept to make it a drama that targets children, "or make it about this [detective] Hopper character investigating paranormal activity" (Duffer, cited in Grow, 2016). These examples foreground the tendency of complex serials – even though they deploy one or both of TV drama's foremost generic traditions of 'family melodrama' and 'crime drama' (Newcomb, 2007) – to deviate from established conceptual frameworks for American TV fiction. They suggest that complex serials are ill-suited to the conservative commissioning cultures of American broadcast television (see Gitlin, 1994).

Complex Serial Drama and the Legacy of *Twin Peaks*

Complex serials, this book argues, owe their existence to the ambitions and imperatives of American non-broadcast networks in the early multiplatform era. That said, however, it is truly rare for anything in television to be entirely without precedent. Although different to the complex serial form under analysis here, two shows deployed elements of what would later develop as the complex serial template: the American *Twin Peaks* (ABC, 1990–1991) and the British *Singing Detective* (BBC, 1986), both of which were created for broadcast networks.[13] As a BBC mini-serial with just six episodes, *The Singing Detective* probed the disturbed psychology of a hospitalized character deeply troubled by transgressions he committed as a child. In taking viewers inside the mind of this character, *The Singing Detective* deployed unprecedented narrative and aesthetic complexity. While later chapters will highlight these elements of *The Singing Detective*, *Twin Peaks*, an American-produced drama that was promoted as "the series that [would] change TV" (Collins, 1995: 343), warrants exploration here. In its use of the following six strategies, *Twin Peaks*, an exemplar of the 'quality drama' paradigm identified by Robert Thompson (1996), provides something of a predecessor for the American complex serial form.

First is its conceptual originality. Rather than developing a situation of conflict with the usual capacity to outlast the show's initial core characters, *Twin Peaks* examines a single crime, the rape and murder of Laura Palmer, a murder mystery that unfolds over two seasons of episodes, and is all the more intriguing because its victim is also the town's 'homecoming queen'. Second is its narrative structure. Deviating from the episodic series, as the dominant form deployed for American 'quality drama', *Twin Peaks* used a fully serialized form, perhaps influenced by soap opera, which was one element of this show's 'generic mix' (Mittell, 2004: 155) and a genre to which *Twin Peaks* also paid frequent 'self-reflexive' homage. Its conception as a serial drama allowed *Twin Peaks* to train its narrative focus on the development of a central 'overarching' story,[14] the mystery of 'who killed Laura Palmer', a question posed in the pilot and only fully resolved some 30 episodes and two seasons later. Third is the use of settings and locations. Because its story is geographically located at a distance from the fast-moving, frenetic urban precincts of American procedural drama, the creators of *Twin Peaks* reveled in the freedom to construct a scenic, small-town locale and populate this with idiosyncratic characters, exemplified by the prophetic 'log lady'; loopy psychiatrist Jacoby; naïve but pampering PA, Lucy; and the eccentric detective, Dale Cooper.

Fourth is the extremity of *Twin Peaks*' intertextuality,[15] a feature that begins with the generic mix of soap opera and murder mystery that is the basis of its concept. Intertextuality characterized many other elements of *Twin Peaks*' story and constructs, however. Delighting in self-reflexive references to soap opera, to TV commercials and to iconic movies, film genres and characters, *Twin Peaks* offers an exaggerated demonstration of the postmodern text's tendency toward what Jim Collins (1995: 335) calls "a hyperawareness" of itself. Fifth is the aesthetic approach and stylistic qualities of *Twin Peaks*. *Twin Peaks* was shot on 35mm film, its aesthetic sophistication underscored by its elaborate sets and costumes, deployment of locations, distinctive theme song and musical score, richly detailed mise-en-scène, inventive camerawork and notably slow-paced camera movements and scenes. This kind of achievement requires resources that are over and above the usual range for TV drama, however. Pivotal to it, therefore, was a comparatively high level of investment per *Twin Peaks* episode, as indicated by the then exorbitant cost of US$4 million (Chion, 1995: 100) for its feature-length pilot. Sixth, and supported by all of the above features, the promotion of *Twin Peaks* sought to cultivate what Newman and Levine (2012: 38) describe as 'cultural legitimation'. Directly anticipating the strategies later used by HBO and outlined in Chapter 3, the primary vehicle for such legitimation was the development of authorship discourses around *Twin Peaks*' co-creator, David Lynch.

While it could not transgress the content boundaries of FCC-regulated broadcast television, *Twin Peaks* did deliver on the promises of its promotional hype to "change TV", a movement which, as this book argues, took different trajectories on American broadcast and non-broadcast television, a development examined in Chapter 2.

Alternative Political Economies in American Television

The political economy of American television is most usefully introduced in relation to the 'TVI', 'TVII' and 'TVIII' model, initially coined by Behrens and applied to the changing political economy of American television by Rogers, Epstein and Reeves (2002). Although the above terms will be deployed here as shorthand for the different paradigms involved, alternative names for the three different modes of operation for American television identified by Rogers et al. are 'broadcast television' (TVI), 'broadcast and cable' (TVII) and 'multiplatform television' (TVIII). While this section introduces the characteristics of TVIII, the economic tendencies of the other paradigms are also important to briefly outline. This is because even though the TVI/TVII/TVIII model can be understood in historiographical terms as the trajectory through which the political economy of US television has moved since the early 1960s, all three of the above paradigms remain extant. To date there is no evidence that one paradigm has succeeded the others, even if the first two have needed to adjust to accommodate the arrival and popularity of internet-distributed television (IDTV), one response to which has been the addition of online services to established broadcast and cable networks. It is because of the cross-influence of all three of the main platforms discussed here that the distinctions between TVI/TVII/TVIII paradigms are also a matter of proportion and context rather than being a straightforwardly linear progression.

The characteristics of TVI align it closely with America's 'classic network' era (1960–1980), during which television operated in a broadcast-only context and advertiser-funded economy, the limitations of which included its 'mass audience' orientation, risk-averse commissioning and over-reliance on a smaller volume of TV dramas developed in accordance with a range of well-established formulas. Operating within a Fordist industrial economy, characterized by "the mass production of standardized commodities" and a "consequent mass consumption" (Barker, 1997: 162), television was highly subject to technological scarcity and minimal choice. While such minimal choice rendered TVI the heyday of 'mass marketing', audiences were themselves a commodity, since television aggregated and sold them to advertisers in exchange for revenue. Aided and abetted by technological restrictions on audience uses of television, shows functioned as the appetizing 'bait' that lured viewers to spot commercials.

The transition to TVII began when, from the late 1970s, utility-oriented cable systems used new technologies to increase their carriage capacities and gain national reach, opening the door to the addition of new networks, to a broadcast and cable paradigm for U.S. television, and to unprecedented multi-channel competition. The newer, mostly cable, networks carved out markets by targeting underserved niches, in the process deliberately differentiating themselves from the small number of original broadcast networks (CBS, NBC, ABC and PSB), which continued to target, engage and produce TV shows for larger and broader audiences. In the context of the audience fragmentation that multi-channel competition engendered, TVII also demanded the targeting of audiences for which advertisers were prepared to pay higher rates (see Feuer, 1984a: 26), an approach that appealed to networks because of its ability to compensate them for the loss of audience size. Importantly, advertising remained American television's dominant revenue source, with commercial breaks placed between show segments remaining the favored extraction method. However, TVII's rising interest in audience 'quality' over audience size did stimulate increased risk-taking in drama as, in a busier multi-channel environment, shows gained a more demonstrable value to channel identity and branding.

Added to the TVI and TVII paradigms, but also disrupting the TV networks that defined them and necessitating their adjustment – a process that continues today – the potentials of TVIII began to unfold after 2000. Framed by digitization and thus by what John Ellis (2000) terms 'plenty', TVIII saw 'brand marketing' take precedence over the 'mass' and 'niche marketing' tendencies of TVI and TVII in turn (Rogers et al., 2002). However, because it introduced new TV outlets and modes of delivery along with a new supply of subscription-funded original TV shows, TVIII can be regarded as moreorless equivalent to the multiplatform television environment that is introduced below.

Multiplatform Television and Some Consequences for TV Drama

Restructured by deregulation, conglomeration and globalization in the 1980s and 1990s, the television landscape was transformed after 2000 by the combined impacts of digitization and convergence, consequent multiplatform transmission and continuing inter-network competition. Together, these developments saw American television move from the "multi-channel transition" it entered from 1980 (Lotz, 2007a: 12) into an environment in which broadcast, cable and internet networks all co-exist, a context that this book calls 'multiplatform television'. Whilst it does involve continuities with the earlier paradigms discussed above and remains in an early stage of its development trajectory, multiplatform television has revealed its capacity to work in radically different ways from the economic models that shaped American television's development as 'broadcast television' and then 'broadcast and cable', paradigms that privileged and/or enabled certain forms of TV drama. Although complex serials were emerging prior to the arrival of the multiplatform era, by way of HBO's entry into the commissioning of long-format TV drama (a process examined in Chapter 1), their expansion has coincided with and is indebted to the burgeoning of multiplatform television.

With media conglomeration having anchored TV production and distribution within the horizontally and vertically integrated matrixes of giant, transnational and multimedia corporations, the drama products of multiplatform television, even if the majority are still created to debut on a specific network, could now be accessed through such non-traditional devices as computers, tablets and mobile phones. Accordingly, the multiplatform era currently unfolding is one in which access to TV shows is no longer limited to the linear schedules of the networks whose investment helped create them. Moreover, TV shows are also being originated for internet networks or services that do not use linear schedules. In this multiplatform environment, TV dramas can acquire and accrue a commercial value that goes well beyond either the advertising revenue they might have been created to help generate and/or the reputational benefits for the particular network whose investment helped bring them into being. While many TV dramas still return value to their investors in these traditional ways, they are ideally placed to exploit the potentials of multiplatform television to deliver a potentially lengthy and lucrative 'afterlife' through an unprecedented succession of exhibition and consumption 'windows'.

More profound than the disruption of American broadcast TV by cable networks in the 1980s and 1990s has been the emergence of internet-distributed television (IDTV), a facet that is both unique and integral to multiplatform television. The non-broadcast sector of American television includes an increasing array of IDTV networks and services. Within this IDTV network group, Netflix, Amazon Prime, Hulu Plus and Epix are regularly commissioning original high-end dramas. While some may question the status of such services as 'television', the reliance of their businesses on the streaming of content purchased from TV networks helps to foreground the answer. As Michael Woolf (2015: 32) explains:

> [W]hile Netflix and Amazon, the two leading *non-television* television platforms, attempt to define themselves as alternative to television and even a mortal disruption of it, they pay the traditional television industry more than $3 billion a year in licensing and programming fees.

Foregrounding IDTV's identity as television, moreover, Amanda Lotz (2016: 134) argues: "Contrary to many expectations of 'new media' that circulated in the late 1990s and early twenty-first century, internet-distributed television is not a new medium, but the medium of television distributed through a different technology".

Whereas cable networks, like broadcasters, develop or purchase their programming for a linear schedule, the novelty of IDTV is that shows can be located from a menu and streamed to a range of viewing devices with maximum immediacy and flexibility. Viewers have far more control over TV shows that are delivered through internet portals. This is because, as Lotz (2016: 131) observes, IDTV "has the capacity to send content at a viewer's request in a way that allows viewers uncommon control over [the] pacing and choice of content". As non-linear services for which there are no fixed schedules, IDTV networks provide a menu from which viewers can choose. Although the label 'multiplatform television' acknowledges the expansion of TV to include internet networks and services, IDTV has the potential to offer an alternative experience of television, especially when shows are *originated* for internet networks and portals. Yet with IDTV at an early stage of its development, linear schedules continue to influence the creation of American TV drama. Insofar as a majority of new dramas are being produced for debut on a broadcast or cable network, the influences exerted by these networks and their own linear schedules are simply inherited by IDTV platforms, even if viewers can consume these acquired shows with additional control and flexibility. Yet the increasing consumption of television through IDTV portals, which is occurring in combination with the increasing origination of TV drama by IDTV networks, is fueling the possibilities for change. Complex serial drama, a form whose origination has to date been dominated by non-broadcast networks, stands to benefit from the mere presence of IDTV exhibition options. This is because it offers a form of drama whose serialized and complex narratives are particularly well suited to the "uncommon control over [the] pacing and choice of content" that is characteristic of IDTV (Lotz, 2016: 131).

IDTV services have proliferated since the arrival of software designed to condense and stream screen content with speed and in optimum HD quality (Arango and Carr, 2010). It is because they acquire, aggregate and stream this content directly to viewers that online providers operate 'over the top' (OTT), their businesses taking two main forms. One is advertiser supported, which, as well as describing the online and on-demand services offered by TV networks, is exemplified by YouTube and Vimeo. The other is subscription-funded, with leading examples in Netflix, Amazon Prime and Hulu Plus. Pioneered by Netflix, subscription-funded IDTV networks have attained profile and pervasiveness largely through the acquisition and online delivery of existing television and film content. However, as American cable networks discovered in the 1990s, and Netflix and other IDTV networks are now finding, a reliance on the retransmission of existing content is unsustainable in America's crowded multiplatform TV environment. Increased multiplatform provision has made it more difficult than ever for a new network to develop a distinctive brand unless it offers content that is, for a 'window' of time at least, unavailable elsewhere. It is for this reason that Netflix, Amazon Prime and Hulu Plus, even as they remain reliant on acquired content, are all investing in original material, whose branding and exclusivity they can control.

Closing in on its target for 2017 of 100 million subscribers in total, Netflix is the largest and most established internet-only network, and is now available in most world markets (Shaw, 2017). Only HBO has a larger number of subscribers; these currently around 134 million, a figure that combines HBO's galaxy of domestic and international channels with its 'HBO Now' customers (Liedtke, 2017). While Netflix offers far more acquired than original material, having committed to an outlay of US$6 billion on original productions for 2017 (Spangler, 2016), it is currently in the process of building a larger cache of exclusive programming. While Netflix originals include feature films, documentaries, dramedies and situation-based comedies, its original TV drama can help reveal some of the broader repercussions of internet commissioning on the supply of high-end drama. Following the commissioning strategies of American cable networks, Netflix has preferred original dramas in serial form. Using these to entice a multiplicity of audience groups, its originals have included such diverse examples as *Jessica Jones*, *The Crown*, and *13 Reasons Why*. Importantly, Netflix's two longest-running original dramas, *House of Cards* and *Orange Is the New Black*, introduced in 2013, have both sought to emulate the complex serial template.

The Organization of This Book

This book is structured into five main chapters. While four of these apply different critical perspectives – industrial, authorial, narrative and stylistic – to complex serials, the remaining chapter examines its relationships with 'American Quality Drama'. These five chapters also combine reference to selected TV drama examples with more detailed case studies of exemplar shows. Although these case studies are similar, in terms of the set of details provided for each TV drama, the case studies are also inflected by the critical perspective of the particular chapter for which they have been selected. Chapter 1 investigates the institutional context for the emergence and expansion of complex serial dramas on American cable television, its two case study shows being HBO's *Oz* (1997–2003) and *The Sopranos* (1999–2007). Chapter 2 compares 'American Quality Drama' (AQD), a paradigm that originated and developed on American broadcast TV, with complex serial drama, as one that developed and expanded on American non-broadcast television. This chapter's case study dramas are NBC's *Hill Street Blues* (1981–87) and HBO's *Six Feet Under* (2001–2005). Chapter 3 explores the discourses of authorship that have been applied to complex serial dramas, of which a notable feature has been the valorization of individual creator-showrunners. This chapter offsets the 'auteur' claims often made about complex serials with a detailed exploration of their writing processes, important to which are the contributions of a team of writers. This chapter's case study example is AMC's *Breaking Bad* (2008–2013). Chapter 4 investigates the ways in which complex serials deviate from longstanding narrative tendencies for American hour-long drama, along with the key strategies through which these serials construct and achieve narrative complexity. This chapter's case study show is AMC's *Mad Men* (2007–2015). Chapter 5 examines how the aesthetic traditions and stylistic tendencies of high-end TV drama are deployed in complex serials and incorporates a case study of Netflix's *Stranger Things* (2016–).

Notes

1 While this multiplatform era is bringing many new potentials to television, some of which are still emerging, the term 'multiplatform' recognizes the evident repercussions of digitization and convergence. The key example is emergence of the internet as an additional platform for the medium of television. Internet television operates both independently and as an additional platform for the transmission and exhibition of broadcast- and cable-produced TV shows.

2 I coined this label in the context of a discussion about the categorization of different approaches to the deployment and blending of 'series' and 'serial' elements in contemporary American and British TV drama. See Trisha Dunleavy (2009) *Television Drama: Form, Agency, Innovation*, Basingstoke: Palgrave Macmillan, pp. 152–58.

3 In this book, the term 'meta-genre' denotes the entire category of television drama, as one that comprises all of its distinctive genres (crime, medical, family melodrama, science fiction, thriller, horror), along with its main narrative forms (series, serials, anthology serials, mini-serials and soap operas).

4 There are always exceptions to any rule. The complex serial form has a clear broadcast TV example in *Lost* (ABC, 2004–2010).

5 Long-format drama is privileged in this book and refers to TV drama programming that is devised to endure for more than one season of episodes.

6 Jason Mittell (2013) "The Qualities of Complexity: Vast Versus Dense Seriality in Contemporary Television", Chapter 2 in Jason Jacobs and Steven Peacock (eds.), *Television Aesthetics and Style*, New York and London: Bloomsbury, pp. 45–56.

7 This kind of elasticity is a longstanding facet of serial TV drama. What it means is that 'complex serials' could take shorter form than the multi-season examples of this book's focus. Mini-serials of less than 10 episodes can be complex; FX's anthology serials, *Fargo* (2014, 2015, 2017) and *American Horror Story* (2011–), for example, have complex features. However, as 'anthology serials' these necessarily entail a shorter narrative form than the exemplar serials analysed in this book.

8 Serial dramas produced for American broadcast TV have been dominated by just three main forms: (1) the 'continuing soap opera', a daytime form, exemplified by *The Guiding Light* (CBS, 1952–2009); (2) the primetime 'supersoap', which began with *Dallas* (CBS, 1978–91); and (3) the 'mini-serial', a high-budget form of limited duration, exemplified by the original *Roots* (ABC, 1977).

9 Among the most expensive complex serial that is currently in production is HBO's *Game of Thrones*. Rising with each season of this serial, its Season 6 episodes reputedly cost US$10 million each.

10 'Mise-en-scène', although a larger domain, refers here to performances, dialogue, settings, sets and locations.

11 'Serial' dramas tell continuing stories, whereas 'series' dramas (even though they can incorporate continuing story strands) tell stories that resolve. The distinctions between 'series' and 'serial' drama, which include distinctions of concept design and characterization as well as those involving narrative strategies and structures, are examined in Chapter 4.

12 The revenue differences between American 'premium' and 'basic' cable networks are detailed in Chapter 1.

13 *The Singing Detective*, whose story was written by Dennis Potter, is an exemplar of British 'authored drama'.

14 This term will be examined in more detail in Chapter 4, but refers to the story (usually one) that spans all episodes of a TV drama serial.

15 Offering a succinct introduction to this concept, John Fiske (1987: 108) asserts that "the theory of intertextuality proposes that any one text is necessarily read in relation to others and that a range of textual knowledges is brought to bear upon it". Intertextuality will be examined in aesthetic terms in Chapter 5.

1

THE RISE OF COMPLEX SERIAL DRAMA ON AMERICAN CABLE TV

Introduction

Significant new opportunities for innovation in American TV drama became available as a collision between two related forces unleashed the necessary momentum. One was the expansion and ambition of American cable networks, whose potential to offer quality, alternative programming to a national audience was realized (from the late 1970s) by satellite transmission. The other was the rapidity with which American viewers embraced multi-channel television; this, by the late 1990s, matured to stimulate a gradual expansion in the supply of original programming, which in turn fueled creative experimentation. Cable TV services reached 63.4 percent of American homes in 1994 (Edgerton, 2008: 5) with advances in carriage technology driving an escalation in the number of TV channels being delivered to Nielsen Media's "typical TV household" from 10.2 in 1980 to 43.0 in 1997 (ibid.: 3, 11). This increasing take-up for cable channels was a vital pre-condition for the new opportunities for TV drama alluded to above. Yet, even as the cable sector's penetration reached 'critical mass', broadcast networks continued to dominate the commissioning and, with it, the concept design and form of American high-end drama.

Although the impetus was building by the early 1990s, significant change for American TV drama arrived in the period 1997–2008, seeded by HBO. Even though HBO was just one of a larger group of cable networks regularly commissioning drama in the late 1990s, its subscription-funded position necessitated a different approach. Whereas other cable networks provided a mix of 'off-network' and original shows that could deliver to their age-based, gender-oriented or otherwise specialist audiences, HBO's 'premium' cable footing disposed it to both acquire and, as far as it could afford, to originate programming with a cultural and/or creative distinctiveness geared to resonate with the affluent viewers that were its existing subscribers. Crucial to the success of the trajectory that HBO followed with original long-format drama was its realization that key to the allure and profitability of a premium cable service would be the offer of programming that was genuinely different to that which broadcasters were offering. Pivotal to this achievement was the conceptual, formal and stylistic distinctiveness of the complex serials that comprised HBO's impressive first long-format drama commissions, specifically *Oz* (1997–2003), *The Sopranos* (1999–2007), *Six Feet Under* (2001–05), *The Wire* (2002–2008) and *Deadwood* (2004–2006).

This chapter investigates the institutional context within which complex serials emerged on American cable television. As long-format dramas, the first examples were certainly informed by the conventions of the broadcast TV dramas that preceded them – the nearest of which was arguably *Twin Peaks*, a rare example of fully serialized drama to appear within the larger 'American Quality Drama' paradigm to be examined next chapter. However, as high-end dramas commissioned for ambitious cable networks, drama serials gained new opportunities for experimentation and innovation from their origination *outside* broadcast television. Although a range of cable networks contributed to establishing the complex serial form, this chapter foregrounds HBO as the network on which it originated. Even though these serials gained considerable creative momentum from HBO's 'premium' economy and its appetite for risk-taking, an important question for this chapter is that of how and why 'basic' cable networks such as FX and AMC have also been able to commission them.

The Maturation of the American Cable Sector

Although cable systems, networks and channels had been in place since the 1950s, their function and potentials had changed significantly by the 1980s, due to the effect of four developments which together ensured a different kind of future for American cable television than that previously envisaged (Mullen, 2003). First was the ability of those cable operators who could afford the necessary technology to uplink their signals to satellite and achieve national reach, an opportunity that HBO took up in 1975. Second, as Megan Mullen (ibid.: 128) observes, cable "subscriber numbers grew at a remarkable rate". As at 1970, basic cable systems had penetrated 8 percent of American households (Thompson, 1996: 36); this rose to 21.7 percent of the national market in 1980 and 39.3 percent in 1983 (Edgerton, 2008: 4). Third was deregulation, as a result of which some important restrictions on the operation and programming of cable channels, which had inhibited their commercial development, were removed (Mullen, 2003). Fourth, a change which benefitted from the repercussions of the other three was that earlier expectations that cable services would develop as a complement to broadcast TV gave way to the realization that these would instead compete directly with broadcast networks.

Working in addition to the four developments above would soon be media conglomeration, through which the ownership of "both cable systems and national cable networks" would transfer from smaller local companies to large national media corporations (Mullen, 2003: 133). Beginning in the 1980s and developing into the 2000s, this change was merely one facet of a continuing concentration in global media ownership, as a result of which American TV networks and related media became but smaller elements of an ownership structure led by a small group of world-leading transnational multi-media corporations (Straubhaar, 2007). By 2005, and with mergers and restructurings continuing thereafter, American media ownership was dominated by Time Warner, Disney, News Corporation, Viacom and General Electric, each of which was characterized by horizontally and vertically integrated business structures and interests (Hilmes, 2008).

Beginning in the 1970s, HBO's development trajectory is indicative of the opportunities that became available to cable operators, even if few had the resources to fully exploit them. Although in this decade satellite technology was showing the potential to reshape cable television's future, its prohibitive costs meant that only cable companies with unusual capital could deploy it (Mullen, 2008). Another challenge was that Federal Communications Commission (FCC) regulations, designed to protect broadcast television by inhibiting the commercial potentials of cable networks, needed to be negotiated or challenged (ibid.). In overcoming both of these obstacles, as a result of which it gained additional opportunities as an early, very successful premium cable network, HBO was greatly assisted by the financial support it received from Time Inc. An ongoing relationship that would heighten HBO's ambition and enhance its opportunities, this began in 1971 when Time Inc. provided seed funding for the fledgling subscription service that was conceived as the 'Green Channel' and renamed 'Home Box Office' (Mullen, 2003: 106). HBO gained an important victory in 1975, when, having leased a satellite transponder to telecast a boxing match between Muhammad Ali and Joe Frazier, it became the first cable network to exercise national reach. As Megan Mullen suggests, HBO's coup with the match that was nicknamed 'The Thrilla in Manila' "marked the definitive arrival of cable television's modern era" (2008: 114).

A second significant victory for HBO followed two years later. Preparing the way for HBO to exhibit and invest in feature films was its 1977 challenging of FCC anti-siphoning rules governing the television release of theatrical features. Ensuring that "broadcast network affiliates would have first claim" on the newest and most commercially valuable Hollywood features (Santo, 2008: 21), these regulations could have thwarted HBO's plan to develop a subscription service that centered on the offer of 'home cinema'. However, as HBO saw it, there was a case to be made that in regulating pay TV content to this extent the FCC "exceeded its authority" (Mullen, 2003: 98). Taking the FCC to court on this basis in 1977, HBO won the case and its fortunes took a major upturn. As Mullen (2003: 98) observes, the ruling "allowed cable to replace broadcast

television as Hollywood's first television exhibition window". While this ruling also made viable the creation of other movie-oriented premium cable services, HBO was ready to exploit it immediately and in three main ways. First,
the exhibition of new-release theatrical features was geared to vastly increase
HBO's allure, justifying its charging of higher subscriptions and strengthening
its business model. Second, the creation of a privileged relationship between
Hollywood studios and cable operators by granting the latter first TV play of the
former's products, made "financing and exhibition agreements with Hollywood
studios" (ibid.) considerably more attractive for HBO, as a network with access
to the capital to invest in film production. Third, the incorporation of selected
theatrical features into its schedule would greatly assist HBO to build the kind
of 'upscale' entertainment brand that would distinguish it from the newer basic
cable networks now being established.

These new cable channels catered to smaller, underserved segments of the
audience through a narrower, more focused range of shows than it was possible for broadcast networks to offer in this pre-digital period.[1] The expansion of
cable TV included a slew of entertainment-oriented channels. Underlining the
impacts of the 1977 ruling won by HBO, two of the premium cable additions in
place by 1980, Cinemax and The Movie Channel, were devoted to movies. Basic
cable channels that were either established or rebranded as entertainment-focused
included A&E, USA, Lifetime and TNT, all of which had launched in the 1980s.
These were joined in the 1990s by the entertainment-oriented Comedy Central,
Nick at Nite and the Sci Fi Channel (later SyFy), as well as by movie and arts
channels, AMC and Bravo, which, having started as 'mini-pay' channels, converted
to basic cable status. Although these channels would invest in original shows, as
Mullen (2008: 154) underlines, "the new cable networks lacked broadcast television's programming budgets". Hence their challenge as entertainment-oriented
channels entering an increasingly populated TV environment in which their role
was to cultivate underserved niche audiences (including viewers willing to pay for
additional TV services) was sustaining a supply of suitable shows through which
to differentiate themselves.

The sustainability of the above range of new cable channels was tested and
proven in the period 1995–2005, which saw a more critical rebalancing of broadcast and cable audiences. In 1995, cable services reached a massive 66.8 percent of
American households, to create a total cable subscribership of more than 64 million (Hilmes, 2008: 304). Suggesting that this competition in American television
centered on a tussle for share between 'mass audience-oriented' broadcasters and
'niche-oriented' cable networks, however, was that cable audiences rose largely at
the expense of CBS, ABC and NBC, whose combined primetime share had fallen
to 60 percent in 1995 (ibid.). By 2005, 94.2 percent of American households
were subscribing to "some form of multi-channel video programming distribution (MVPD)", with 69.4 percent of these involving cable services (Banet-Weiser
et al., 2007: 2). By this point, and with the above majority of non-broadcast

viewers together comprising 53 percent in primetime hours, the combined primetime audience share for broadcast networks was just 47 percent (ibid.).

HBO's Emergence and Trajectory as a Provider of Original High-End Shows

HBO's commissioning of fictional programming – which began with feature films and comedies, and later added high-end dramas and 'dramedies' – became increasingly crucial in the context of the explosion in cable TV networks that characterized and stimulated the multi-channel transition in progress from the mid-1980s. Helping to progress HBO's longstanding ambition to provide a genuine alternative to the shows that broadcast networks were offering was the combined impact of three additional but related factors. First was HBO's early inception and continuing tendency as 'first mover' among entertainment-oriented cable networks to anticipate the changing opportunities and move nimbly to turn these to its advantage. This HBO 'attitude' was strongly demonstrated by its successful 1977 overturning of an FCC regulation barring cable networks as 'first window' exhibitors for recent Hollywood movies. Second was that, as the first cable network to target an 'upscale', cinema-going audience, HBO was well-positioned to exploit the opportunities to extend its market penetration. In the years 1977–83, as Gary Edgerton registers (2008: 4), HBO's "subscriber base skyrocketed" from the modest 600,000 it held at the outset of this period to the impressive 13 million it had achieved by the end. Yet, in opting to provide alternative programming for 'upscale' viewers at a time when it seemed "that the most popular and profitable cable networks would be those that reflected what was popular on broadcast television" (Mullen, 2003: 112), HBO took unusual risks.

This foregrounds the importance of the third factor that underwrote HBO's ongoing risk-taking: the continuing support and subsidization it received from its original shareholder Time Inc. (Mullen, 2003: 108). Beginning before it even turned a profit, HBO's production financing from Time Inc. allowed it to complement its developing brand as an exhibitor of 'must-see' Hollywood movies via a move into feature film financing. In 1976, HBO secured a co-financing agreement between Time Inc. and Columbia Pictures, whereby in exchange for the investment from Time Inc., a group of "major feature films" was produced, with HBO gaining "the first television rights" to air them (ibid.). As HBO continued to generate subscriber growth and larger profits through the provision of shows that seemed different from those available on broadcast TV, its nurturing 'parent' Time Inc. responded to the pressures on its own businesses toward increased synergy, economies of scale and market power. It was this set of pressures that fueled the conglomeration of American media between 1985 and 2005. Becoming an indicative example of the trend that enveloped most other American media companies in these decades, Time Inc. merged with Warner Communications in 1989 to form Time Warner Inc., "the largest communications company in the world at that point" (Hilmes, 2008: 286) and a member of the reducing 'top tier' of leading transnational media corporations.

A significant step by HBO toward an ongoing commitment to high-end television production was its airing in 1983 of *The Terry Fox Story*, the first original feature film to be produced for premium cable (Mullen, 2003: 147) and the first of many that would earn the network critical acclaim. In different ways, HBO's movies and comedies were both forms through which it could push against television's content boundaries by allowing the inclusion of confronting, risqué or explicit material. Prior to the 1997 debut of its first complex serial *Oz*, HBO's interest in alternative drama was evident in its commissioning of socially or politically conscious feature films; examples include the Oscar-winning *Down and Out in America* (1986) and acclaimed *The Josephine Baker Story* (1991).

HBO's original programming took a new turn from 1985, when Michael Fuchs was appointed as CEO, under whose leadership another crucial senior appointment, Chris Albrecht to lead HBO's original programming, soon followed. Yet, whereas Fuchs still regarded HBO movies as the main thrust for its high-end commissioning (Motavalli, 2002), it was Jeff Bewkes – a rising HBO executive by 1985 and its CEO from 1995 – who understood the importance of a more diverse commitment to original programming and argued for the necessary finance (ibid.). Underlining Albrecht's influence on this change of direction, Motavalli observes that prior to his arrival at HBO "there were no series of note and few original movies" and that Albrecht "had the relationships that counted ... [and thus the ability to] move the network to the next level in original fare" (ibid.).

Within a few years, Albrecht had started delivering the kind of creative 'edge' that HBO needed in original programming, his first commissions generating a critical buzz and becoming vital building blocks in communicating HBO's point of difference. The starting point for Albrecht, in preparing to expand HBO's original production slate, was knowing what kinds of subscribers it could both entice and retain with this content. On this point, by the late 1990s, Albrecht was especially clear. As Albrecht saw it: "The kind of people we want to attract are people who don't watch a lot of television. These are usually better-educated, slightly older men and women aged 35 to 55, who can probably more easily afford to keep our service" (Meisler, 1998: 48). Important in shaping the kind of shows that would emerge from this increased commissioning was Albrecht's personal disinterest in ratings and prioritization of creative autonomy (Motavalli, 2002). Albrecht began with *Tanner '88*, an 11-part political satire. *Tanner '88*'s election campaign narrative was timed to parallel and satirize the real-life processes of that year's general election and was delivered via multiple viewpoints in a 'mockumentary' style. Achieving the kind of sustained profile that HBO needed, however, because it combined this mixed-genre aesthetic with the ongoing attention that a series could generate, was *The Larry Sanders Show* (1992–1998). TV critics loved its self-reflexive, media 'insider' concept and considered it "perfect for attracting subscribers to a premium service" (Meisler, 1998: 48).

Assisted by these first examples, Albrecht understood that getting HBO to "the next level" of original programming (Motavalli, 2002: 1) required not only an increased investment in and diversity of productions, but also a supply of long-format shows with the capacity for longevity and season renewal. Notwithstanding the cultural cachet that HBO was acquiring from its feature films, documentaries and comedies, a hallmark of the television medium and experience has always been its offer of ongoing 'flagship' shows through which the attention of its core audience can be solicited on a regular, continuing basis.[2] Such shows, as Carl Gardner and John Wyver (1983: 118) observe, "are designed from the start to fit in with fixed points in the schedule … and because the audience is led back to them week after week, they build and attain better ratings than single [shows]". Although HBO first attempted a flagship series with the football comedy *1st & Ten* (1984–91), the continuity and wider appeal of *The Larry Sanders Show* made it considerably more effective in this role.

Albrecht had recently been promoted to president of HBO original programming when, in 1995, he called a meeting in which, supported by Bewkes, he argued for an increased HBO commitment to regular original programming on the basis that HBO's history as an "'occasional use' service, driven substantially by the acquisition of recent theatrical films" (Carter, 2002), was no longer adequate given the intensely competitive environment in which the network now operated (ibid.). Instead, as Albrecht reasoned, HBO needed to become a "regular-use service" (ibid.), pivotal to which would be a far greater commitment to long-format originals. As Albrecht added later, "We see series as a retention device, a reason to buy HBO. After all, if you hear about something good on TV, you can't tune into it unless it's going to be on for a while" (cited in Meisler, 1998: 48). Hence, from 1995, the ambition, strategic thinking and risk-taking that characterized HBO's historic development worked in combination with the push from Bewkes and Albrecht toward a larger volume of original programming. Although HBO had long aimed to build an alternative brand identity by commissioning shows that were sufficiently compelling to entice viewers to subscribe, this objective and distinction became usefully explicit when, in 1996, the network adopted what is now regarded as one of the most successful tag-lines ever used in television: 'It's Not TV. It's HBO'.

In 2002, the year that HBO posted a giant US$725 million profit (Goldsmith, 2002), the network opted to expand its existing cache of original long-format dramas. Contributing to this decision had been the appointment of Chris Albrecht – the executive whose 'no holds barred' attitude to original programming was important in establishing HBO as something of a magnet for American TV drama's leading writer-producers – to the position of CEO. By 2004, and building on its established cachet in feature films and comedies, HBO's reputation and influence escalated on the basis of the complex serials (*Oz, The Sopranos, Six Feet Under, The Wire* and *Deadwood*) that were now among its foremost flagship dramas. Despite the numerical disadvantage of its subscription footing in an American television landscape still dominated by over-the-air channels, HBO managed to attract 'network-sized' audiences for some of these shows. The figure that most resonated with industry watchers and other cable networks was the estimated 12 million live viewers of *The Sopranos'* final episode (Friedman, 2007). This broke records as the first cable show to emerge highest-rating drama overall and the second most viewed of any TV show that week (ibid.). By the end of 2004, Time Warner was the proud parent of the outstandingly successful HBO that Dempsey (2004: 1) termed a "billion dollar baby", an achievement whose significance was that it exceeded the earnings record for any other American TV network to this point (ibid.). This billion-dollar feat was attributed to HBO's ability to harvest higher cable operator license fees than any other network (broadcast or cable), an area from which HBO earned an estimated US$2.2 billion in 2004 (ibid.). Of the larger array of HBO originals involved, the "game-changer", as Edgerton underlines (2013: 7), was *The Sopranos* (1999–2007), whose outstanding popularity helped fuel a 50 percent increase in HBO subscriptions (Edgerton, 2008: 14).

HBO's influence and profitability has continued to increase since 2004, even if its challenge in ensuring continued growth has not only been to find ways to exploit increasing online viewing, without compromising the appeal and profitability of its domestic cable operation, but also to reach new markets by establishing HBO-branded services in non-American countries. In 2010, HBO introduced 'HBO Go', an internet streaming service free to its domestic subscribers. While 'Go' remains vital in providing multi-platform flexibility to existing HBO subscribers, more crucial, as a streaming service that HBO introduced in April 2015 and one that is independent of the necessity for any cable TV subscription, has been 'HBO Now'. With HBO's domestic subscriber numbers stagnating by this point, the objective of 'Now' was to target a growing number of American 'cord-cutter' households, this term referring to those opting out of bundled cable television packages in favor of an increasing array of internet streaming services (Levy, 2017). With current trends showing that the wider cable sector is losing subscriptions in the face of rising 'cord-cutting', 'Now', which has brought more than 2 million new subscribers to HBO since its introduction, offers strong potential for continued growth. Today, while internet TV network Netflix is reaching 100 million international subscribers, HBO's international subscribership is more than 134 million (Liedtke, 2017).

Case Study of *Oz* (1997–2003)

> It was really kismet … It just so happened at that time that HBO was looking for something … I've never had an experience, before or since, where the network and I were so completely in sync about the show we wanted to make. Because a lot of times what'll happen with the networks, and this is true of cable as well as broadcast, is they'll say they want something, but when you give it to them they get a little nervous and they start to back

> away … But with HBO and *Oz* it was just literally that the sun and moon were totally in sync that day when Chris and I got together.
>
> *Tom Fontana*[3]

Albeit rare, Fontana's experience is the most positive kind for a TV drama creator. It was the mid-1990s, HBO had yet to air an original drama, yet Chris Albrecht knew what he wanted, just as Tom Fontana, a talented writer-producer with a track record in innovative TV drama, knew why he had come. Fontana's experience at the helm of drama productions, including the innovative 'American Quality Drama' (AQD) series *St Elsewhere* (1982–1988) and *Homicide: Life on The Street* (1993–99), made him an ideal choice to executive produce HBO's first long-format drama, a role he shared with Barry Levinson, the director-producer with whom Fontana collaborated as executive producer of *Homicide*.

When Fontana received HBO's response to the pilot script for *Oz*, he was surprised by how few 'notes' the network had given him about possible revisions (Fontana, author interview, 2013). HBO's disposition was simply to "make noise" with its dramas (Fontana, cited in Sepinwall, 2012: 28) rather than "hedging its bets" by reverting to the usual risk-averse precautions (Gitlin, 1994: 63). An indicative example of this was one exchange from his conversations with Albrecht about the *Oz* pilot, in which, as Fontana (cited in Sepinwall, 2012: 21) remembers:

> Chris said to me, 'I don't care if the characters are likeable as long as they are interesting'… And he asked me 'What's the one thing you've always wanted to do in the pilot of a broadcast television show that you've never been allowed to do?' And I said, 'Kill the leading man'. And he said, 'I love that! Do that!'

The successful realization of Fontana's idea entailed giving him an unusual level of creative control over the six-season serial that *Oz* became. Even if this belonged 'officially' to HBO, as Fontana recalls, "the unspoken gentlemen's agreement" between himself and Albrecht was that "ultimately they will defer to me" (Fontana, author interview, 2013). HBO self-financed *Oz* (ibid.), and in doing so initiated its tendency of 100 percent investment in its original dramas. This was one contributor to HBO's 'hands-off' approach to *Oz*'s development and production, since with no other investors to be consulted and/or appeased, there were fewer limits on its risk-taking. Pioneered by *Oz*, HBO's investment policy with its dramas also deviated from the maximum of 75 percent production financing that broadcast networks offered for theirs (Higgins, 2006: 18), this practice leaving production studios either to deficit finance the remaining 25 or higher percent, or acquire it from other investors.

As the first TV drama to emerge from the above alternative approaches to commissioning and financing, *Oz* was empowered to break a range of existing broadcast network 'rules' in this genre. One indicator of this was the concept (or central premise) that *Oz* involved, this title being the nickname of the fictional Oswald State Penitentiary inside which its stories unfold. Distinguishing it from the few TV prison dramas previously aired, *Oz* centered on 'Emerald City', a maximum security wing and home to society's most violent criminals. As such, *Oz*'s core characters included a number of murderous 'lifers'. Hence the *Wizard of Oz* allusions in these names ran in ironic contrast with the unusually violent and unforgiving culture that *Oz* constructed, one in which "individuals and groups vie for their share of the prison drug trade, exact revenge for insults both real and imagined, and simply try to stay alive" (Malach, 2008: 53). In devising a show described as "not for the faint of heart" and at times "uncomfortable" to watch (Levin, 2003), Fontana set out not so much to "entertain people" but rather to expose an otherwise invisible dimension of contemporary American society (ibid.), an objective that would later fuel *The Wire* (2002–2008). As such, *Oz*'s criminal characters provided the means to explore contemporary questions of "race, addiction, sexuality, religion [and] elder care" as well as exposing the "dehumanising nature of the prison experience" (Sepinwall, 2012: 26–27).

Another indicator was *Oz*'s deployment of serial form. Albeit unfolding in an institutional setting that seems not too far removed from the police stations and emergency rooms that have dominated broadcast TV's many 'procedurals', *Oz* eschewed the episodic storytelling that has marked procedural dramas. Distinguishing *Oz* from earlier crime serials, including *Twin Peaks* and *Murder One*, is its narrative hybridity. Establishing a narrative model for other complex serials, it blended the kind of progressive, 'overarching story' that characterizes high-end serials with elements of a series-like 'problematic',[4] the story-generating capacities of the latter allowing *Oz* far greater longevity than high-end serials have historically been able to achieve. Its serial form allowed *Oz*'s narrative to emphasize the motivations and troubled psychology of criminal characters over the prison as institution. Accordingly, serial form enabled *Oz*'s distinctive focus on the psychological interrogation of the perpetrators as well as the victims of prison violence, an approach perfectly suited to Fontana's fascination with the complexities of character (Fontana, author interview, 2013).

A third feature, facilitated by the other two, was the foregrounding of seriously flawed, frequently violent characters; this was given additional edge by the survival-struggle to which life in Emerald City is reduced. An indicative example is Tobias Beecher, whose accidental killing of a teenaged girl whilst drunk-driving sees him sent to Emerald City. As a former lawyer who has made a serious, life-changing mistake, Beecher provides a necessary "access point to *Oz* for white middle-class viewers" (Nelson, 2007a: 156). As an Oz inmate who becomes the brutalized, submissive sex slave of neo-Nazi prisoner, Vern Schillinger, Beecher is forced to adapt in order to survive. In a manner that challenged and blurred broadcast drama's clearer lines between good and evil characters, Beecher's tortured existence motivates him to mirror Schillinger's own level of violence. Beecher's revenge is finally exacted through his vicious beating of Schillinger with gym weights, their changed relationship underscored by his 'victory lap' defecation on Schillinger's face (Sepinwall, 2012: 26). Through Beecher, *Oz* initiated the psychological investigation of morally conflicted, transgressive central characters that became characteristic of complex serial dramas. Fontana was equally unafraid to kill core characters, a fate generally reserved in broadcast crime dramas for clearly marked 'criminals-of-the-week'. Disposing of seven major characters by the end of *Oz*'s first season, the carnage began with the burning to death in the pilot episode of Beecher's fellow prisoner and allocated mentor, Dino Ortolani.

As Albrecht later reflected, "[Oz] was the first thing we had seen for premium television that was a true dramatic series … And it was startling how much different it felt from everything else on television" (cited in Sepinwall, 2012: 21). *Oz* and *The Sopranos* both entailed significant risks for HBO, as the flagship vehicles for the reputation it aimed to build in TV drama. What is at risk of being forgotten in the mythology of creative triumph in which *The Sopranos* is now steeped is that significant change in the TV drama paradigm is rarely, if ever, the achievement of one show. Without *Oz*, and the kinds of characterizations it brought to TV drama from its 'insider' perspective on the unusually violent, unforgiving milieu of a male maximum security prison, who can know whether or not HBO would have dared to place a murderous criminal character at the center of *The Sopranos*. Without *Oz*, Netflix may never have dared to commission *Orange Is the New Black*, the female prison serial that has most closely emulated the 'prison insider' concept that *Oz* introduced to American television.

The Expansion of Cable-Originated Drama

The significant shift of American audiences to non-broadcast outlets and shows in the period 1995–2005, as a result of which just 47 percent of American viewers were watching broadcast channels in primetime hours (Banet-Weiser et al., 2007: 2), fueled an intensifying level of competition between cable networks, whose response was a more concerted effort to build a distinctive and sustainable brand identity. Leading entertainment-oriented cable channels had been heavily reliant on flows of ex-broadcast shows, the established popularity of which had rendered them a low-risk approach as the cable sector expanded after 1985. However, as the potentials of television's convergent multiplatform era began to reveal themselves, this reliance on ex-broadcast shows came to seem an increasingly limited strategy (Romano, 2002a). With more TV networks competing for ex-broadcast entertainment programming in particular, the acquisition prices for key properties rose. Ex-broadcast drama became a case in point, bringing additional risks for cable networks in the matching of expensively purchased shows to the requirements of their existing and/or coveted niche audiences (Albiniak, 2010). As *The Sopranos* famously demonstrated, when A&E in 2005 paid a record price of US$2.55 million per episode for it (Edgerton, 2013: 20), high-performing dramas threatened to become almost as expensive to purchase as they were to produce.

The solution for entertainment-oriented cable networks was to commission a limited supply of original shows. As a strategy exemplified in Lifetime's slew of female-oriented comedies – which helped define the 'Television for Women' brand it adopted in 1998, by which point it had reached 1.5 million homes (Meisler, 1998: 45) – basic cable networks were motivated into such costly areas of original programming by the strategic necessity to secure a supply of regular series that could be "tailor-made to the individual specifications" of their audiences (Edgerton: 2013: 9). Although a wider range of cable networks were able to invest in lower-cost dramedies and/or comedies, the higher production values of hour-long drama made it a considerably more challenging and risky investment for any cable network. In view of this risk, and as well as meeting their own ongoing requirements for drama via acquired shows, some found an effective transition into original hour-long drama by taking over the license for a suitable series that was no longer required by its original host network. USA's own successful foray into original drama was achieved via *Silk Stalkings* (1993–99), a series that it opted to renew following its axing by CBS, which had hosted the first two (1991–92) seasons. TNT's vehicle for its move toward original drama was the PTEN-originated *Babylon 5*, which it renewed for a fifth (1998) season, following its initial four-season run (1994–1997). The rebranded SyFy followed this same transition strategy when it took over the license for *Stargate SG-1* (2002–2007), a successful series whose lengthy run was therefore divided between its originating network, Showtime, on which the first five seasons aired from 1997, and SyFy.

It was not until the late 1990s that cable networks, led by HBO, were offering dramas whose "word-of-mouth-generating" success (Lotz, 2007a: 153) would position them to challenge the continuing broadcast dominance of original drama. But the turning point arrived in the early 2000s, by which time, in addition to the flow of successful original dramas on HBO, a small group of other cable networks (Showtime, Lifetime, USA, TNT and FX) were commissioning successful dramas. Encouraged by the different audience objectives represented by this group of networks, two main approaches to this original cable drama could now be observed. One, as exemplified by USA with *Monk* (2002–2012) and TNT with *The Closer* (2005–2012), followed the AQD paradigm that had come to dominate broadcast TV drama output. The other, as exemplified by Showtime, FX and AMC, either veered toward or directly emulated HBO's complex serial form. Premium network Showtime, whose commitment to original drama expanded sharply from 2000, opted to develop shows that could build its subscriber base by targeting underserved African–American, gay and lesbian viewers. Even though Showtime commissioned a wider diversity of dramas, indicative of these specialist objectives for the network were *Soul Food* (2000–04), *Queer as Folk* (2000–05) and *The L Word* (2004–09). Basic cable network FX instead opted to commission dramas that could target "difficult-to-reach upscale male" viewers (Lotz, 2007a: 185).

This audience objective was realized by its successful initial trio of *The Shield* (2002–2008), *Nip/Tuck* (2003–2010) and *Rescue Me* (2004–2011).

While Showtime, FX and AMC would contribute significantly to the development of complex serials in these and later years, FX played a crucial role in the expansion of this form by demonstrating its capacity to succeed in an advertiser-funded context, despite its risqué content. Advertiser responses to *The Shield* (ibid.) suggest that the explicitness and violence so characteristic of complex serials was not necessarily a deterrent for advertisers, because, in the niche-oriented marketplace of cable television, some advertisers saw benefits in being associated with it. By the late 2000s, as Edgerton (2013: 93) emphasizes, "literally dozens" of cable networks had "entered the business of original production". Significantly, the basic cable component of the new supply of non-broadcast TV drama was keyed to be more broadly watched and profitable than that of HBO or Showtime as premium cable networks, due to the much higher market penetration for the former on bundled cable services.

The Expansion of Complex Serials on Cable Television

Having explained how complex serials originated in the first long-format drama commissions of HBO, this chapter section aims to show how, when and through which flagship shows other cable networks deployed this form. Accordingly, the following discussions underline that the origination and development of complex serial drama was the innovation of cable networks alone, and a small group of networks (HBO, FX, AMC and Showtime) at that. Underscoring this assertion is that the narrative and aesthetic characteristics, blend of critical and popular success, and ongoing allure (from debut to 'afterlife') that have been signature features of the complex serials produced to date were all well-established by 2008, several years before additional networks (these combining cable, internet and broadcast operators) commissioned their own examples of the form.

The first basic cable network to deploy HBO's complex serial template was the Fox-owned FX, with *The Shield* (2002–2008). Although established in 1994, basic cable channel FX turned its attention to original drama after its 1997 relaunch as FX: 'Fox Gone Cable'. In 2001, by which point the network's intentions included the commissioning of original dramas, FX was struggling to make headway in a now highly populated, multi-channel environment. FX executives had watched HBO's experiment in original drama unfold with extremely successful results. FX resolved to emulate it, aiming to be the first to try it on basic cable (Goldstein, 2005). Making such ambition possible for a fledgling network like FX was that, as with the investment support that HBO was receiving from Time Warner, FX too had a deep-pocketed parent in News Corporation. Repeating the pattern that HBO had experienced, however, was that FX's ambitious plans in original programming would almost certainly gobble large amounts of capital and several years of effort before any significant profits were returned.

By late 2000, FX was actively seeking, though had not yet found, the idea that would provide the ideal vehicle to support its foray into original drama. It told the industry that it specifically wanted "irreverent, edgy and challenging material" (Reynolds, 2001a: 28). *The Shield* – a serial drama about corrupt policemen, which centered on a four-man 'anti-gang' unit led by Vic Mackey – was not only the best idea FX received but also one well-matched to FX's requirements. As a complex serial whose resonance with "upscale male" viewers (Lotz, 2007a: 185) seemed strongly connected with its explicit and violent content, *The Shield* revealed that not all advertisers were equally nervous about associating themselves with such content. Instead, as Lotz underlines (ibid. :185), it suggested that advertising revenue could be attracted from those advertisers who were willing "to support programming that wilfully offended some viewers".

In 2002, *The Shield* won a Golden Globe award for its first season, and FX finally gained the kind of industry and audience profile that matched its original programming ambitions. In an interview only two months later, Liguori announced that FX would commission three more dramas and four movies per year (Romano, 2002a). FX went on to commission a succession of serial dramas, including some complex serials. FX examples have taken two main forms, one yielding such successful multi-season serials as *Nip/Tuck* (2003–2010), *Sons of Anarchy* (2008–2014) and *Justified* (2010–2015). The other, exemplified by *American Horror Story* (2011–) and *Fargo* (2014–), is an 'anthologized' counterpart to the long-format complex serial, in which, although involving continuities of treatment, theme, aesthetics and other elements, each season tells a different story with unique characters and settings.

The next to commission complex serials was HBO's premium cable rival, Showtime, a subsidiary of CBS Corporation. Established in 1976, Showtime had entered original hour-long drama with its commissioning of *Stargate SG-1* (1997–2002). Whilst the complex serial template did seem to inform some subsequent Showtime originals, including *Dead Like Me* (2003–2004) and *The L Word* (2004–2009), this network's foremost complex serial was *Dexter* (2006–2013). *Dexter*, whose 'overarching story' foregrounds a compulsive albeit vigilante serial killer, is the Showtime example that took the complex serial's capacity to foreground morally conflicted, transgressive central characters to a new level of villainy. Although Showtime has commissioned a succession of high-end serials, including *The Tudors* (2007–2010), *Homeland* (2011–) and *Ray Donovan* (2013–), the allure of its most audacious, widely watched drama, *Dexter*, helped spur a continued rise in subscriptions after 2005. Whereas in 2004, Showtime subscribers numbered around 12 million (Romano, 2004), these numbers expanded to 17.1 million in 2009 (Weprin, 2009), 21.3 million in 2012 (Carter, 2012), and 22.8 million in 2014 (Spangler, 2015). Underlining how even one particularly successful drama can contribute considerably to a network's overall profile and fortunes was the 2012 contention that "Showtime is gaining on HBO" (Carter, 2012), an achievement that referenced the conspicuous popularity of *Dexter*.

Delivering the highest viewing figures for any of Showtime's original dramas to date, *Dexter*'s ratings peaked in 2012 at 6.1 million viewers across all Showtime platforms (Hibberd, 2013).

The second basic cable network to deploy complex serials has been AMC, which began with *Mad Men* (2007–2015). In late 2002, with AMC's penetration reaching 83 million households (Edgerton, 2011a: 7), the network underwent a significant overhaul and brand reorientation as part of a larger strategy by its 'parent' company Rainbow Media, which also brought changes to AMC's sister network, Bravo. A key executive figure in this process was Rainbow Media CEO Joshua Sapan, whose lengthy tenure at Rainbow included development responsibility for AMC and Bravo (Becker, 2008). It was this rebranding that saw 'American Movie Classics' renamed AMC (Edgerton, 2011a: 7). The network's first foray into original high-end drama was the riveting mini-serial *Broken Trail* (2006). Starring Robert Duvall as the cowboy who rescues five Chinese girls from a life of prostitution, *Broken Trail*'s debut drew an astonishing 9.7 million viewers, "the second-largest" audience for any basic cable drama aired to that point (Idov, 2011). The connection between *Broken Trail* and *Mad Men* was that AMC had used *Broken Trail* to "test the waters" (Sepinwall, 2012: 303) for the much larger investment in an original long-format drama.

Whereas *Broken Trail* entailed a one-off US$4 million investment, the first US$3 million that AMC spent on *Mad Men* covered only its pilot episode (ibid.: 315). Even though it was created for a channel supported by advertising, the usual anxieties about its potential for ratings success were surprisingly low profile among AMC's concerns about the performance of its pilot, a moment in the network's development when Rob Sorcher was outgoing AMC president and Charlie Collier was preparing to replace him. The stellar performance of *The Sopranos* had influenced Rainbow CEO Josh Sapan's thinking about the kind of original drama that AMC needed and what results might come from it. Recalling his briefing with Sapan about these issues, Sorcher (cited in ibid.: 303) explained that:

> AMC doesn't need to worry about ratings at that moment of time … What AMC needs is a show, a critically acclaimed and audience-craved show that would make us undroppable to cable operators. Because AMC, as a movie network, was mostly second-tier movies or ones you could get anywhere, unaffiliated with a larger cable empire like Viacom or Turner. They were very worried that the likes of Comcast were creating their own movie channels, and that [AMC could] be dropped completely off of systems. Josh knew that he had to have something that the public wanted really badly.

Mad Men achieved all of AMC's aims for it. As *Mad Men* continued through a particularly successful seven seasons, its critical success was recognized in four successive 'best drama' Emmy Awards between 2008 and 2011, a feat that only two TV dramas have ever achieved (*Hill Street Blues* and *The West Wing*). Yet, in 2008, AMC unleashed *Breaking Bad*, a complex serial that went on to attain an equal, if not more significant blend of 'must-see' allure and critical acclaim, its achievements finally recognized when it won a 'best drama' Emmy in 2013. As important successes for complex serial drama, *Mad Men* and *Breaking Bad* are both case studied in later chapters.

High-End Drama and Television's Multiplatform Environment

The emergence and continued expansion of complex serial drama has been a specific, yet instructive example of the wider and more diverse institutional and cultural repercussions for costly forms of American TV production in a burgeoning multiplatform era. Offering a snapshot of the changed institutional economy that preceded and arguably prepared the way for the emergence of complex serials among other new fictional forms, Robin Nelson (2007a: 55) observes that:

> Instead of securing profits through control by oligarchies over a distribution bottleneck on the back of constraints on bandwidth … profit is to be made through distinctive programme content, with additional income gleaned through dissemination across media platforms in a vertically and horizontally integrated, multidimensional environment.

Nelson's assertions attest to changes affecting most drama-producing countries; however, the "distribution bottleneck" to which he refers was unusually pronounced in American television due to the lengthy dominance of TV drama programming by CBS, ABC and NBC, the repercussions of which will be examined in Chapter 2. In American television, seeded by the deregulation and technological advances that allowed new providers and services to emerge, the bottleneck in TV drama was initially broken by the addition of new broadcast networks, Fox, WB and UPN, and the involvement of an increasing range of cable providers (initially USA, TNT, HBO, Showtime and FX). Yet with the multiplatform era including the introduction and expansion of Internet TV services, some new exhibition and distribution outlets for drama have been created. While complex serials have been a notably non-broadcast phenomenon, this form has been commissioned by a range of American cable networks and is now being deployed in some of the dramas produced for IDTV networks, including Netflix, Amazon Prime and Hulu Plus.

The potential for an alternative political economy to drive TV production has been one facet of the multiplatform environment, which Rogers, Epstein and Reeves (2002) term 'TVIII'. Unique to this, they suggest, has been the ability to use subscription-funded and on-demand services to establish a more direct economic relationship between the originators/owners of content and its consumers/viewers. This exemplifies what Nienhaus terms "first-order commodity relations" and defines as "symbolic objects or flows actually exchanged for money or having prices attached" (cited in Rogers et al., 2002: 46). In television, this 'first-order' relationship remains a minority option, but one, assisted by the streaming capacities of super-fast broadband internet, that is rapidly expanding. The dominant economic model for commercial television has been one in which networks and advertisers function as 'middle-men', working between originators/owners of content and consumers/viewers. For Nienhaus, this approach is consistent with "second-order commodity relations" (cited in Rogers et al., 2002: 46), whereby "symbolic objects or flows" operate to "aggregate individual time for sale to third parties" (ibid.).

While useful to understandings of the political economic distinctions between American broadcast networks, which depend on advertising revenue, and cable networks, for which advertising need not be the only revenue stream, these 'first-order' and 'second-order' differences are less revealing of the institutional agency that is pivotal in permitting or resisting experimentation and/or innovation. Notwithstanding the additional influences that advertisers exert, the possibilities for drama are powerfully determined by TV networks through their commissioning decisions, as well as through their contributions as financiers and distributors of TV shows. In directing and coordinating these activities, the role of TV networks, as the institutions to which John Corner refers below, is one of "brokerage" (1999: 13). As Corner explains (ibid.):

> Institutions act to interconnect funding, product, and use because of the strategic play-off between their investment in specific projects at the levels of station, channel, and programme and their need to gauge audience responses correctly enough to make these projects, and products, viable at a given level of production cost … In a sense, many television institutions, whether funded by advertising or not, act as a junction point between the vectors of supply led demand (what it is in the best interests and profits of the institution to produce, then strongly market to viewers) and those of demand led supply (what specific viewers like and what they don't like, what they will and will not watch, fed back as the recipes for successful production, further development, and profitability).

Corner's vectors of 'supply led demand' and 'demand led supply', as alternative forces working in a push-and-pull fashion to determine which TV productions are commissioned, renewed and/or canceled, have been characteristic of the involvement of American cable networks in original high-end drama. Yet the specific economies of premium and basic cable networks can be seen to exert different pressures on the interplay between these vectors, even if both types of cable network have commissioned complex serials.

As Rogers et al. (2002: 46) emphasize, drama commissioned for subscription-funded networks is not only "free of commercial interruption" but is also "uncontaminated by the demands of advertisers". Instead these networks rely on what Rogers et al. term a "monthly audience appeal" (2002: 47), a response expressed through viewer decisions to either remain in their 'first-order commodity' relationship with the network or 'churn' out. Accordingly, these networks, even if audience size remains important as a determinant of subscription revenues, are less focused on scheduling shows in the attempt to either maximize audience size or demographic quality, being more mindful of the necessity to build or maintain a reputation for value. This is because, as Lotz (2007b: 91) underlines, it is not a matter of "how often or what the individual subscriber views, but rather that each subscriber finds enough value in some aspect of the programming to continue the subscription". While this does not explain how basic cable networks managed to commission complex serials like *The Shield* (FX) and *Breaking Bad* (AMC), it does suggest that it took a subscription-funded context, as one free from the influences of FCC content regulation *as well as* from direct advertiser demands, to enable the all-important first step of permitting the creative experimentation that made this type of TV drama possible.

Carolyn Strauss, who moved to HBO soon after *Oz* had entered production and was integral to the commissioning of *The Sopranos*, suggests that HBO's subscription-funded position, along with the 'devil may care' attitude that characterized its commissioning culture as a fledgling rather than an established network player in TV drama in the late 1990s, underwrote HBO's risk-taking with *Oz* and *The Sopranos*. As Strauss (cited in Sepinwall, 2012: 24) recalls:

> The thing about the *Oz* experience that stuck with me the most is that, compared to how things are now, it was utterly, 'Let's see what happens ... Let's cast this guy, let's do this, let's do that. Let's experiment with form' ... It was very much a 'let's see what happens' attitude rather than a 'we need to know exactly what happens every step of the way'. It was black-box theater, rather than the main stage. I think that gave people a tremendous sense of freedom and experimentation, and just a great sense of, 'You know what? We can try it. It's not going to be the end of the world if something doesn't work'.

Once the initial risk of complex serial drama had been taken by HBO and the reception of the first examples (*Oz*, *The Sopranos*, *Six Feet Under*, *Deadwood* and *The Wire*) revealed such a positive response, the degree of risk in such commissions was considerably reduced, with the potential brand benefits also being clearly displayed. Given the emphasis that scholars have placed on HBO's subscription-funded position and the absence of advertisements in shaping its first drama commissions, it is crucial to consider how the basic cable economy and schedules of FX and AMC have themselves been able to accommodate complex serial dramas.

Although advertiser-funded, basic cable networks differ from commercial broadcasters in two main ways. One is their 'narrowcast' position, this term underlining that viewers opt to purchase them, albeit as part of a larger package of channels that are bundled together by a given cable system provider. The other is that, as cable networks, their economic model comprises two sources of revenue. Basic cable networks, as Mullen explains (2003: 112), "are sustained both by advertising and by a 'per-subscriber' (or 'per-sub') fee – a monthly fee that cable operators pay networks based on [their] total numbers of subscribers". Observing the impact of this dual funding model on the narratives of basic cable dramas, Anthony Smith (2013) cites such examples as TNT's *The Closer* and FX's *The Shield* in arguing that it imbues their original dramas with elements of both subscription-funded cable and advertiser-funded broadcast models. The opportunity for alternative drama to be commissioned for placement in the schedule of a cable channel depends more specifically on both the reduced influence of advertising revenue (as compared with broadcasters who rely on this) and the potential benefits that a stronger brand identity can deliver to a basic cable network's 'per sub' fee.

AMC's experience with *Mad Men* (2007–2015) provides a useful demonstration of the potential impacts of this blend of revenue streams. The unusual allure that *Mad Men* generated not only boosted AMC's overall profile and added distinction to its developing brand, but also increased the value of its commercial spots. *Mad Men's* popularity saw higher advertising rates charged to AMC's advertisers, spurring competition between advertisers and sponsors to purchase commercial spots on the channel, with *Mad Men's* own hour of spots being reputed to "always sell out" (Lafayette, 2010: 20). On the basis of *Mad Men's* unusual appeal, AMC also benefitted from the higher 'per-sub' fees that cable system operators paid to carry the channel (ibid.). Whilst HBO was able to vastly expand its subscriber base via the unusual allure of *The Sopranos*, AMC achieved a basic cable approximation of this outcome. Even though *Mad Men* earned just 1.5 percent of AMC's revenue in 2010, the brand 'aura' that it attained and brought to its network host saw AMC's total advertising revenues increase by 23 percent on its earnings before *Mad Men* (ibid.).

The Creative Conditions of American Cable Television

Although complex serials are also expanding by virtue of the original high-end dramas being produced for IDTV networks, the creative and commissioning culture in which this drama form first developed is crucial to examine here. Complex serials emerged as part of a broader burgeoning of original TV drama on American cable channels. Although complex serials are by no means limited to American productions, the economic and cultural conditions of American cable television were crucial in enabling this form's departures from the conventions of broadcast TV's 'American Quality Drama' (AQD) paradigm, to be examined in Chapter 2.

The cable sector's commissioning of original drama was seeded by an increased market penetration for cable television – key milestones being its presence in

63.4 percent of American homes by 1994 (Edgerton, 2008: 5) and 86 percent by 2005 (Banet-Weiser et al., 2007: 2). An important consequence of these developments was the rising importance of successful original drama to the broader efforts of cable networks to distinguish themselves. From the mid-2000s, the ambition of drama-commissioning cable networks combined with the additional incentives for drama production that accompanied an unfolding multiplatform era. Digital technologies and internet platforms and sites, in concert with the emergence and expansion of online fan communities, added to the existing incentives for cable networks to invest in original drama. In the context of these developments, the potential for a successful drama to generate a global audience and brand 'aura' – an achievement pioneered by HBO and achieved in turn by Showtime, FX and AMC – could transform a little-known cable network into an internationally recognized brand. With these dramas also being created for networks located outside the FCC's content infringement jurisdiction, the 'aura' of leading examples included a degree of notoriety derived from the explicit content that they were able to incorporate.

Network commissioning executives are pivotal agents in the creation and conception of TV drama. This is because, in their responses to the initial pitch, and then to the filmed pilot as a crucial foundation for the finished show, they hold the ability to powerfully shape concept design. The role of the commissioning network, therefore, is one of ideological and creative gatekeeping. In view of the potential of TV networks to exercise their gatekeeping capacities, a striking characteristic of original dramas produced for cable networks has been the sense of autonomy that its writers have professed to experience when working for cable rather than for broadcast networks. One example is David Chase, who likens the freedom he was given with *The Sopranos* to being "let out of jail" and to gaining "a reprieve from the governor" (Martin, 2007: 10). Another is Alan Ball, who realized how different working for HBO promised to be when the only network executive 'note' he received from HBO about his pilot script for *Six Feet Under* was an invitation to make its family more "fucked up" (Ball, author interview, 2013). Another example is David Milch, who was permitted to deploy a lexicon for *Deadwood*, the profanity of which was unprecedented in TV drama (Newcomb, 2008: 96). There is also Matthew Weiner, who, in pursuing critical success for *Mad Men* as opposed to ratings, responded to a direct instruction from Josh Sapan (Sepinwall, 2012: 303), who by this point was CEO of AMC's restructured parent company, AMC Networks.[5] Still unusual in broadcast television, this degree of creative autonomy has been an important contributor to the perceived distinctions of complex serial drama.

This degree of creative autonomy can be perceived as a characteristic of working in cable television, rather than being specific to HBO, AMC or to complex serial dramas. Accordingly, the reasons for it are important to probe here. Having examined drama production in the wider cable sector, Alisa Perren argues that "The business models, production practices, and creative possibilities for cable are substantially different from those of broadcast television" (2011: 133), even if, as she also acknowledges, the writing and production processes for cable television are "strikingly similar" to those of broadcast TV (ibid.: 136). Informed by interviews with scriptwriters and producers whose experience spans both broadcast and cable sectors, the comparisons Perren makes between these creative contexts are useful here because they suggest that some of the distinctions of complex serial drama derive from its origins in cable television. Six main differences, the majority of which are responsible for the above expressions of increased creative freedom, can be observed.

First is the notably limited complement of network executives in cable network contexts to whom a drama writer-producer may need to answer (Perren, 2011). Second is a tendency for cable drama executives to "know the show they bought"; this underlines the imperative for cable networks to closely match the drama creators, showrunners and ideas they select with the audience segments they consider central to their brand identity (Rogers, cited in Perren, 2011: 134). As a difference derived from the higher dependence of broadcast channels on both broad-based audiences and revenues from spot advertising than those of cable channels as niche-oriented services, cable dramas are developed to serve a brand identity notably more distinctive than those of broadcast networks.

Third, cable network showrunners experience a greater level of control over their drama production projects, a consequence of choosing their own creative personnel, having smaller staff, receiving "less creative interference" from the network, as expressed in reduced interaction with network executives and/or active support from them against executive 'higher-ups' (Perren, 2011: 138). Fourth is that the cable environment increases their sense of working in creative partnership with their networks (Rogers, cited in ibid.: 136), a contrast with the kind of embattled or disempowering relationships with network 'suits' emphasized by former broadcast writer-producers Chase and Ball. Fifth is that the reduced episode output for long-format cable drama, this amounting to an average of 13–15 episodes per season (Rogers, cited in ibid.: 136.), makes a difference to the satisfaction that writers feel they can take from their work. Comparing cable season length with that of broadcast drama, John Rogers registers that "You can maintain quality over thirteen or fifteen [episodes]. Once you hit twenty, you're just going to have a few that suck. You are. It's the nature of the beast" (ibid.: 136).

Sixth is that cable drama enjoys greater content liberties because FCC rules, whose restrictions focus on sex, language and violence, do not apply to cable channels. This is not to suggest that basic cable networks (which have far higher market penetration than their premium cable rivals) enjoy the same content liberties as HBO and Showtime. In respect of content freedoms, what really separates premium and basic cable networks is the presence of advertising in the schedules of the latter. Explaining why the F-word cannot be uttered on basic cable channels, Glen Tickle (2015) underlines that:

Cable channels don't have to answer to the FCC, but that doesn't mean they don't have anyone to answer to. Channels make money by selling shows to advertisers, and that's easier if the show is 'family friendly', because more people watch it.

Yet the content freedoms enjoyed by cable networks have ramifications not just for the inclusion of sex, language and violence, but also for the ways in which such content is framed and represented. Attributable to the content liberties of cable television, for example, is their evident extension of the conceptual parameters for cable dramas to involve characterizations that remain largely off-limits to American broadcast networks. In complex serials, these content liberties have allowed dramas to be devised around flawed, anti-heroic characters – as exemplified by 'meth' cook Walter White. One impact of FCC content rules limiting explicit material is that on broadcast channels characters like Walter are narratively marginalized as the 'criminal-of-the-week'. The transition for writers who have written dramas for broadcast TV before experiencing the relative content freedoms of writing for cable networks, as Perren's findings suggest, is one that entails "relearning" the art of writing in adapting what they know to the "noncensorious envrionment" of cable-commissioned drama. An indicative element is the capacity for self-censorship that is integrated into their ideas and scriptwriting practice as drama writers. As *Queer as Folk* showrunner Ron Cowen put it, "In network TV we were so used to Standards and Practices telling us what we couldn't do and censoring us that we would censor ourselves before we wrote" (cited in Perren, 2011: 133–34).

Case Study of *The Sopranos*

Amassing a total of 21 Emmy Awards and five Golden Globes, among the many other television awards it has either won or been nominated for, *The Sopranos*, HBO's second complex serial, was an unusually successful and influential TV drama. Revered by viewers and acclaimed by the TV industry for the quality of its writing, acting and direction, the kind of hyperbolic praise that was lavished on *The Sopranos* is exemplified by Stephen Holden's assertion that it "just may be the greatest work of American popular culture of the last quarter century" (cited in Auster, 2005: 241). Costing an estimated US$3 million dollars per episode (Auster, 2005) and representing a significant investment and risk for HBO when greenlit, *The Sopranos* was shot on film. Its high production values and aesthetic ambition are evident in its cinematography, idiosyncratic locations and richly detailed sets. More expensively produced than *Oz*, *The Sopranos* marked the intensification of HBO's enduring strategy of investing more money per episode than other networks were doing at the time.[6] HBO invested US$ 2–4 million per drama hour (Edgerton, 2008: 8), aiming to bring the production values of its TV dramas closer to those of the feature films it aired, an investment level it was able to sustain by limiting the number of episodes produced per season to 13 or fewer, a notable deviation from broadcast TV's tendency of 22 or more (ibid.).

Testifying to the brazenness of David Chase's concept, the screen precedents for it – from 1930s pioneer *The Public Enemy*, through the epic *Godfather* trilogy, to 1990s features *Reservoir Dogs* and *Goodfellas* – were all feature films. As a 'big idea' with no precedent in TV drama, it was not surprising that this was rejected first by Fox (for whom it was initially developed) and then by CBS and ABC, before finally being accepted by HBO (Creeber, 2004: 100). Underlining the executive timidity to which these outcomes attest, Stephen J. Cannell (cited in Lavery and Thompson, 2002: 20) wrote:

> I think it is a sad commentary on the last two decades of television ... that this man, who was well known to all the networks for almost twenty-five years, could not get his fresh, totally unique ideas past the guardians of our public airwaves ... Instead of *The Sopranos*, we more often got mindless clones of last year's semi-hits, while David made his living running other people's shows, unable to sell his own.

Accordingly, *The Sopranos* exemplifies conceptual innovation in TV drama, a meta-genre in which, on advertiser-funded broadcast channels at least, conventionality and 'recombination' (Gitlin, 1994) have both been important influences on the concept design and commissioning of new shows.[7]

The Sopranos was inspired by its creator's Italian–American ethnicity, his life experience, and his knowledge of and passion for the Mafia movie. As David Chase explained to Peter Biskind (2007):

> Network dramas have not been personal ... I don't know very many writers who have been cops, doctors, judges, presidents, or any of that and yet that's what everybody writes about: institutions. The courthouse, the schoolhouse, the precinct house, the White House. Even though it's a Mob show, *The Sopranos* is based on members of my family. It's about as personal as you can get.

Chase's concept (a topic revisited in Chapter 3) began as a story about the consequences of the troubled relationship between an Italian–American man and his overbearing mother. This initial idea was soon flanked by two other key elements, which would combine to determine the lesser stories, settings and milieux. One was the placing of the troubled central character 'on-the-couch', a means to access and narrate his inner thoughts as well as to critique the processes of psychoanalysis and therapy. The other was the characterization of this man as a mobster, a facet strongly influenced by Chase's love of the Mafia film and its lengthy history since *The Public Enemy* (1931). Like *The Godfather* movies had done, *The Sopranos* intertwines traditional nuclear with equally traditional Mafia 'family' narratives, a conceptual position from which its episodes are free to negotiate and explore the tensions that exist between the mundane domesticity of suburban family life and the routine violence and ritual murder that are conventional themes for the gangster film.

Initiating the complex serial's tendency to foreground a single character, a notable departure from American long-format TV drama's tendency to disperse narrative demands across several characters, usually an 'ensemble' cast, *The Sopranos* privileges the perspectives and struggles of one man, Tony Soprano (James Gandolfini). His embodiment of the show's conceptual tensions is explicit in the show's tag-line, "If one family doesn't kill him … the other family will". Underscored by the low self-esteem that is the legacy of his hypercritical mother, Livia, Tony's struggle to reconcile the conflicting demands of his workplace and domestic families leaves him in a panic-attack-inducing state of anxiety, for which he attends psychotherapy sessions with Dr. Jennifer Melfi and takes Prozac. Unprecedented in television or cinema before *The Sopranos*, the Melfi subplot puts Tony "on the couch", which, as Al Auster (2005: 241-42) observes, "one would hardly expect of a Mafia Don", this also offering "a rare glimpse … of the real dynamics of psychotherapy". However, for a man in Tony's profession, speaking to a psychiatrist seems riskier than his day job. As Edgerton (2013: 76) registers, "Tony correctly assumes that being a mental health patient makes him look weak, while the secrets he discloses in talk therapy pose an implicit threat to La Cosa Nostra's code of silence". Accordingly, as well as providing a direct line into Tony's psychological state, ongoing therapy increases the jeopardy of Tony's efforts to balance the demands of his private/public roles and two 'families'.

Although *The Sopranos* certainly deploys television's rich thematic traditions of domestic melodrama and procedural crime (see Newcomb, 2007), its novelty is the extent to which, in combining the conceptual ingredients above, these themes and traditions intersect in ways that increase the pressure on its conflicted central character. In consequence, and to a degree that before it appeared was unprecedented in American crime drama, *The Sopranos* blurs operational and moral boundaries between ostensible 'business' and 'domestic' spheres of action. Tony's crew, as Nelson (2007a: 29) underlines, includes his "close blood relatives", Uncle Junior and Christopher Moltisanti, and some of his 'waste disposal' business is conducted in awkward proximity to his wife, Carmela, and two children at his home. Conflating these 'family' spheres in a myriad of additional ways, the two groups regularly cross paths as members of the larger Italian-American, North Jersey community. Indicative of the kind of moral conflicts and insecurities that this creates for Tony (and to a lesser extent for his nephew, Christopher) are the successive 'disappearances' of 'family' members, 'Big Pussy' Bonpensiero, Jackie Aprile Junior, Adriana La Cerva, Ralphie Cifaretto and Tony Blundetto. Whilst he must also fudge answers to Carmela's persistent questions as to the fate of some of these characters, for Tony their 'whackings' give rise to increased anxiety (as signaled in his therapy discussions) and psychological disturbance (as reflected in his collapses and surreal dream images). Locking these two families together to produce the central tension that runs through all *Sopranos* episodes, is that despite Tony's strenuous efforts to protect his wife and children from "the less savoury aspects" of his work, these tend to "seep back", as Nelson (2007a: 29) observes, into his domestic life.

Despite its disadvantaged ratings position as a premium cable rather than a broadcast show, *The Sopranos* attained broadcast network-sized audiences during its six-season debut run, fueling significant subscriber growth for HBO. As *The Sopranos* entered its third season in early 2001, HBO reached subscribers in 32 million homes, this amounting to one-third of the potential 100 million homes for broadcast television (Carter, cited in Rogers et al, 2002: 53). Of these, an estimated one-third (11.3 million viewers) watched *The Sopranos'* season debut (McDonald, 2007). When HBO screened its very last *Sopranos* episode in June 2007, some 11.9 million viewers were thought to have tuned in (ibid.). Hailed as an "historic feat", the institutional significance of this 2007 figure was that for the first time ever, a cable show was not only the highest-rating TV drama but was also the second most viewed of any television show that week (McDonald, 2007). Evidence that *The Sopranos'* allure continued into its 'afterlife' was provided by the fierce 2007 bidding war over the show that erupted between A&E, Lifetime, Spike, USA and TNT networks. Won by A&E, the agreed price was US$ 2.55 million per episode, a figure not far below the initial production cost of each *Sopranos* episode and reputed to be the "largest payout" in syndication history (ibid.). Although *Oz* introduced the complex serial form to American cable TV, the success and cultural influence of *The Sopranos* was pivotal to the emulation of this form by other cable networks.

Conclusion

The opportunities for innovation in American TV drama, reopened by the combined impacts of a maturing cable TV sector and the rebalancing of audience share toward this, yielded a new drama form, the complex serial. Its alternative concepts; troubled, often transgressive lead characters; narrative complexity; and stylistic sophistication continue to resonate within the entirety of American TV drama in the still unfolding multiplatform era. Although basic cable networks have the advantage of significantly greater market penetration than their premium cable counterparts, their initial reliance on acquired drama programming left them more vulnerable as inter-network competition for leading 'must-see' TV dramas intensified. However, as a forward-looking and highly ambitious premium network, HBO anticipated these developments, underscored by Chris Albrecht's insightful 2002 analysis as to the necessity for HBO to commission flagship shows so as to become a 'regular-use' service. However, even Albrecht could not have predicted what would happen when HBO commissioned its first original dramas. Between them, *Oz* and *The Sopranos* demonstrated that cable networks could provide inventive, high-end alternatives to broadcast offerings in the expensive, risky area of drama. It now seems very important that when HBO, led by Chris Albrecht, commissioned HBO's first group of dramas, it was unusually open to experimentation. Although HBO's content freedoms were maximized by the subscription network's insulation from both advertiser and FCC influences, these were powerfully augmented, as testimony from Carolyn Strauss underlines, by a certain 'devil may care' attitude derived from HBO's calculation that brand reputation and critical acclaim would be more important to it than popular success in the longer-term.

As earlier paradigm shifts for TV drama (see Thompson, 1996, and Caughie, 2000) have demonstrated, it takes more than one innovative and successful show to provide sufficient impetus to generate significant and lasting change. While *Oz*'s contribution was to take unusual risks through which it forged the complex serial template, *The Sopranos* defined this template more sharply, its resounding repercussions combining unusual critical acclaim (Auster, 2005) with significant economic 'after-effects' (Edgerton, 2013). *The Sopranos* was important not only for securing a significant increase in HBO subscriptions (ibid.: 14) but also because its rewards to HBO included the reputational benefits that made it possible for HBO's drama commissioning to expand and for its risk-taking to continue. Whilst many cable networks have since commissioned original dramas and IDTV networks have followed suit since 2013, testament to the confronting 'edge' and explicitness of the complex serial form, only a few networks initially dared to deploy it. Similarly motivated by the reputational benefits that this form held the capacity to confer, FX, Showtime and AMC moved first, achieving moderate to outstanding success as they did so, as well as delivering to underserved or 'hard-to-reach' audiences. On the basis of *The Shield*, which defied industry expectations by revealing that some advertisers were willing to be associated with drama that "violated [the] norms of acceptable content" (Lotz, 2007a: 185), the door was opened for other basic cable networks to follow FX into complex serial drama.

Notes

1 Attesting to the diversity of channels now on offer, new basic cable examples included news service CNN, public affairs channel C-SPAN, sports network ESPN, Black Entertainment Television Network (BET), children's channel Nickelodeon, MTV, initially a music channel, financial affairs channel FNN and education channel TLC (Edgerton, 2007: 301).

2 As a descriptor for long-format TV shows, 'flagship' refers to their strategic role within an individual linear schedule. A 'flagship' show serves as the vehicle for the particular brand identity through which the channel solicits the attention of its core audience. Because an individual flagship show needs to articulate the channel's identity, many assumptions are inherent in the selection of a particular show for this role. They include the aspirations, values and lifestyle of the audience groups being targeted, along with a presumed age, social status, ethnicity and sexuality.

3 Tom Fontana (2013), TV drama writer and producer, and the creator, showrunner and co-executive producer (with Barry Levinson) of *Oz*, Interview with Trisha Dunleavy, 6 July.

4 The terms 'overarching story' and 'problematic' refer to different ways of conceiving, structuring and organizing a long-format TV drama and are examined in Chapter 4. Whereas 'serial' dramas require the underpinning of an 'overarching story' that entails narrative progression, 'series' drama (in which there are new 'guest characters' in each episode) requires the framework of a 'problematic' or situation of perpetual tension. While this historic tendency is now changing, drama series that are conceived around a problematic have been the dominant approach to the conception of long-format dramas on American broadcast television. Successive examples of AQD (from *Hill Street Blues* to *House MD*) are conceptually based within a problematic.

5 Rainbow Media, the initial parent company for AMC channel, was restructured between 2010 and 2011 to form 'AMC Networks', with Josh Sapan appointed as CEO.

6 While other cable networks have emulated it, HBO's investment strategy for TV drama continues today in *Game of Thrones* (2011–), whose episode costs have also increased with each subsequent season. As the most expensive season so far, episodes for Season 6 averaged US$10 million. Hayley C. Cuccinello (2016) "*Game of Thrones* Season 6 Costs $10 million Per Episode Has Biggest Battle Scene Ever", *Forbes*, 22 April 2016. https://www.forbes.com/sites/hayleycuccinello/2016/04/22/ Retrieved 10 May 2017.

7 'Recombination' (see Gitlin, 1994: 75–79) is a term that describes the strategy of creating a 'new' idea for a long-format TV drama by drawing upon and effectively 'recombining' conceptual elements of previous TV dramas that have demonstrated their audience appeal. As a strategy considered to mitigate the risk of ratings failure for new TV drama, this practice has been widespread in the history of advertiser-funded television, both within and beyond American television.

2

'AMERICAN QUALITY DRAMA' AND THE COMPLEX SERIAL

Introduction

Whereas the previous chapter focused on the institutional context for the inception and expansion of complex serial drama, this chapter examines its relationships with the American TV drama paradigm that Robert Thompson (1996) examined as "quality TV". In recognition of its influence as the generic predecessor for and broadcast counterpart to the complex serial form, the innovations and characteristics of 'quality drama' are important to examine in this book. Accepting the highly subjective nature of a term such as 'quality', which warrants careful contextualization in view of its particular significance for TV drama internationally (see for example Brunsdon, 1990; Nelson, 2007a; Feuer, 2007; Weissmann, 2012), the discussions of 'quality drama' in this chapter do not entail judgments of cultural or aesthetic value. Instead they invoke the mix of economic, cultural and generic connotations that 'quality drama' attained as American television transitioned from the 'mass audience' orientation of its broadcast-only era to the "demographic thinking" (Pearson, 2005: 15) that began to influence TV drama creation during the 1980s.

For the above reasons, the generic characteristics of 'quality drama', or 'American Quality Drama' (AQD), as it is termed in this book, will be at the forefront of this chapter's discussions. AQD refers to the succession of hour-long series and serials whose characteristics were identified by Thompson (ibid.: 12–15) and classified as "quality" drama on the basis of their shared deviations from what Thompson called "regular" drama, which prevailed until the late 1980s. An important difference between AQD and 'regular drama', however, was that they served different commercial objectives for American broadcast television. Consistent with the 'mass audience' emphasis of the broadcast-only era, 'regular drama' (as with other TV programming) was created and produced to maximize audience size. In contrast, AQD, which developed in response to increasing network interest in the commercial value of the audience segments being targeted and delivered, was devised to attract viewers for which advertisers were willing to pay significantly more. As multi-channel television burgeoned – an important impetus for which was that cable penetration reached 23 percent of American homes in 1980 (Banet-Weiser et al., 2007: 2) – AQD functioned more explicitly in American broadcast television as a marker of audience value to advertisers (Feuer, 1984a; Allen, 1987) than as a signifier of cultural or aesthetic merit, even if both these elements have been characteristic of this paradigm (Weissmann, 2012).

AQD originated in police series *Hill Street Blues* (1981–1987) and was soon joined by another 'procedural' example, hospital series *St. Elsewhere* (1982–88). Evolving and increasing in influence in the 1990s, AQD diversified to yield examples as conceptually and stylistically diverse as *Moonlighting*, *Twin Peaks*, *NYPD Blue*, *Boston Legal*, *The West Wing* and *House MD*. Emerging as a narratively and aesthetically innovative alternative to the extant 'regular drama', AQD expanded to attain "super-genre" status by 2000 (Thompson, 2007: xvii), an acknowledgment that it replaced 'regular drama' as the preferred option for long-format primetime drama produced for American television. AQD's expansion was secured by the increasing commercial importance of the 'upscale' viewers it was created to deliver to advertisers. In the absence of non-broadcast providers of original long-format drama for so much of this period, AQD, as it proliferated to dominate American TV drama output by 2000, was unavoidably shaped by the imperatives of advertiser-funded broadcast networks. In addition to assessing the significance of this AQD paradigm and its creative legacies for complex serial drama, this chapter examines two case studies: AQD's point of departure and first success, *Hill Street Blues* (NBC, 1981–1987), and HBO's *Six Feet Under* (HBO, 2001–2005), an early example of complex serial drama.

American TV Drama Design in the Broadcast Era

> Everything emerges at the end of a chain of *ifs*. *If* a producer gets on the inside track; *if* he or she has strong ideas and fights for them intelligently; *if* they appear at least somewhat compatible with the network's conventional wisdom about what a show ought to be at a particular moment; *if* the producer is willing to give ground here and there; *if* he or she is protected by a powerhouse production company that the network is loath to kick around; *if* the network has the right niche for the show; *if* the project catches the eye of the right executive at the right time, and doesn't get lost in the shuffle when the guardian executive changes jobs … then the system that cranks out mind candy occasionally proves hospitable to something else, while at the same time betraying its limits.
>
> *Todd Gitlin*[1]

Describing the culture of American broadcast television in the 1980s, Gitlin's assertions are important for their exploration of the many institutional obstacles conspiring against creativity in advertiser-funded broadcast television, against which its writers, in particular, struggled. Yet this long list of qualifications also celebrates a particular instance of creative triumph against the many odds. The year was 1980, and the show at the center of what the above assertions suggest was an extraordinary confluence of favorable institutional circumstances was NBC's *Hill Street Blues*. A space for risk-taking was briefly opened because NBC, third-ranked for six straight years (Hall, 1984), was becoming desperate to develop a new police drama series, a situation in which the writer-producers selected to devise and create this show gained unusual bargaining power. While the circumstances that underpinned the innovations of *Hill Street Blues* will be examined shortly, the current section investigates the set of broader restrictions on the design of hour-long drama that became pervasive for American broadcast networks between 1960 and 1980, many of which, notwithstanding the creative innovations of the AQD paradigm, remain in influence today.

Institutional restrictions on American TV drama can be sourced to the culture of complacency that resulted from the lengthy 'classic network' era, during which the 'big three' broadcast networks, CBS, ABC and NBC, dominated the American television market in an environment of spectrum scarcity. The 'classic network' system was characterized by a "vertically integrated three-network oligopoly", in which the big three competed mainly with each other and remained "fat and happy" (Hilmes, 2008: 218) on the basis of their combined audience share of up to 90 percent of American viewers. Whilst channel scarcity and oligopoly or monopoly were common facets of television in non-American countries in these decades, that the same results for TV programming were not necessarily replicated in those countries is instructive. Highly characteristic of the U.S., though uncharacteristic of many other national markets in these broadcast-only decades, was that its television was financed almost entirely by advertising revenue. The reliance of American broadcast networks on revenues gleaned from advertising saw TV drama develop in ways that maximized its potential to deliver audiences on the regular, predictable basis that advertisers required. While an American public network, PBS, was added from 1967, as a poorly financed and late arrival compared with the 'big three', it did not garner higher than a 3 percent audience share (ibid.: 224). Because PBS could not finance a non-commercial paradigm for original drama, it was unable to exert any significant counter-influence on American TV drama.

Reducing the diversity of concept, form and approach to TV drama that was possible in countries with well-resourced 'public service broadcasting' services were other facets of the 'classic network' system over which CBS, ABC and NBC presided. First, they controlled the exhibition and distribution of American TV shows. Important to this was their system of 'network-affiliate' relationships, whereby each of these networks was linked with a group of independent TV stations, the latter motivated to remain in this relationship by the daily feed of 'first-run' shows that they could not afford to produce for themselves. Second, the big three controlled American TV production. This meant that regardless of whether shows were being produced by large network-owned studios or small independent companies, the commissioning and scheduling decisions governing them remained largely the province of one of the big three, who collectively owned, or held a controlling stake in, around 91 percent of primetime shows produced for them (Hilmes, 2008: 218). Third, the big three grew accustomed to dividing the national audience between themselves. Unfortunately for TV drama, this generated what now seem extraordinary ratings expectations. From the 1960s until the early 1980s, a new hour-long drama was expected to deliver as much as one-third, or 30–32 percent, of Nielsen's available TV audience (Thompson, 1996: 39). Accordingly, a drama that managed, say, only a 26 percent share was regarded as a ratings 'failure' and liable to be axed (ibid.). Even though these expectations were evidently being adjusted downward by the mid-1980s, the executive anxieties they generated were derived from genuine fears about a potential loss of advertising revenue for the timeslot and network. In 1983, for example, when NBC ranked third "for the ninth season in a row," it was 2.3 points behind ABC and 3.2 points behind ratings leader, CBS, a difference of three points at this time being equivalent to millions of dollars in advertising revenue (Hall, 1984).

The significant pressure on primetime TV dramas to routinely achieve ratings results that would now be unattainable on any regular basis sustained a commissioning culture that was instinctively hostile to experimentation. New drama ideas were marginalized by the predictions it was possible to make on the basis of "previous hits" (Gitlin, 1994: 63). Network programming executives, whose role it was to second-guess ratings potentials during the all-important pitch for a new drama, were encouraged to root out potential failures by rejecting any that threatened to stray too far from tried-and-tested ideas and formulas. In view of the tendency to hold these executives personally responsible for the ratings that their commissions returned, it was not surprising that they gratefully embraced what Gitlin terms a "safety first" approach (ibid.) to the conception of TV dramas. In this culture of timidity, as Gitlin argues:

> The safest, easiest formula is that nothing succeeds like success. Hits are so rare that executives think a blatant imitation stands a good chance of getting bigger numbers than a show that stands on its own. Executives like to say they are constantly looking for something new, but their intuition tells them to … recognize the new as a variant of the old.
>
> *(1994: 63)*

'Safety first' facilitated the dominance of three main approaches to TV drama design (Gitlin, 1994), whose influence, albeit reduced, remains in evidence today.

One is 'imitation', or the 'milking' of an already successful concept and formula (ibid.: 69–75). Another is the 'spin-off', through which, in recognition of the capacity of certain actors or characters to themselves lure viewers, a new show is created as a narrative extension to its predecessor (ibid.: 64–69). The third approach, which continues to be the most prevalent of the three, is 'recombination', which describes the practice of divining a conceptual 'marriage' between earlier successes (ibid.: 75–77). The design and content of American TV drama, already subject to constraints arising from the interruption and commercial objectives of advertising, was further limited by a 'least objectionable programming' (LOP) philosophy (Klein, cited in Thompson, 1996: 39). With LOP flourishing in the context of channel scarcity and limited audience choice, TV drama programming functioned not so much as a means to solicit new viewers, but rather as an avenue for risk-averse broadcasters to retain their crucial 'numbers' through shows that aimed neither to challenge nor offend, nor spur viewers even to switch channels.

The TV dramas generated by this risk-averse and 'recombinant' commissioning culture can themselves testify to its destructive impacts on creativity. Indicatively, the hour-long series, the form that AQD would target and transform from the early 1980s, was in particularly poor shape. As Robert Thompson (1996: 31) explains:

> The form (the weekly series), the venue (commercially supported TV), and even the genres (cop shows, lawyer shows, doctor shows, detective shows) had all been relegated to the cultural trash heap in the minds of most serious people by that time. The three series that ranked in the Nielsen top five for the 1980–81 season were *Dallas*, *The Dukes of Hazzard*, and *The Love Boat* – hardly a moveable feast for the aesthete.

Accordingly, when the first AQD shows appeared it was into a broadcast-dominated environment in which, even if television was universally watched, it was also widely reviled (Thompson, 1996; Martin, 2013). Although the commercial reasons for it are explained here, the above remains a notable indictment on the influences of oligopoly and advertiser-driven commercialism, as well as marking a vivid contrast to the 'golden age' heights that American TV drama was able to achieve in the 1950s. Underpinning this considered 1950s 'golden age' had been a very different set of institutional conditions: the extant 'single sponsorship' funding system; 'live' as opposed to filmed drama; and the cultural influence exerted by anthology-packaged teleplays.

Additional influences on the design, format and output volume of American broadcast TV drama were exerted by the domestic transmission and distribution systems through which the 'big three' (joined by Fox in 1986 and, in 1995, by UPN and WB) provided original TV programming to their affiliates or additional network buyers. The first, whose trade descriptor is 'network affiliate content', refers to the debut run of a new show, on the same day and time in a given time zone, on its originating network and on the stations affiliated to it (Mitchell, 2007). The second, called 'off-network' or 'syndication', is a rebroadcast opportunity in which the emphasis is shows that have shown sufficient ratings promise during their broadcast debut and also amassed enough episodes to become attractive as syndicated shows (ibid.). Although less influential today in view of the additional exhibition 'windows' that the multiplatform era has introduced, the above two systems still shape broadcast TV drama creation to the extent that the networks and stations most invested in these systems continue to rely on broadcast product and/or feeds in genres involving significant production cost.

Whilst enticing to drama producers and drama-commissioning networks because it can be highly lucrative, the syndication market has exerted some additional preferences on what forms and styles of TV drama are favored by the originating networks. Because they can be played in any order and can accommodate irregular patterns of viewing, episodic drama series (or those whose narratives emphasize self-contained weekly stories) are considered to work better in syndication than other drama forms. Conversely, serials (whose stories develop between episodes and seasons) are considered less flexible because they must be played strictly in order and demand the kind of habitual viewing that is more difficult to foster in rebroadcast timeslots (Thompson, 1996: 180). Another consideration for syndication distributors is episode volume, which offers their channel buyers the advantage of schedule continuity. Historically, syndication sales have required a minimum of a hundred episodes, meaning that only long-running shows qualify at all and that up to five seasons of episodes may need to be amassed before a successful TV drama is considered "a good candidate for syndication" (Feuer, 1984a: 11). As well as welcoming TV dramas that can endure for successive seasons, the syndication market has preferred those that are formulaic and conventional as opposed to idiosyncratic or narratively complex.

Working together, these forms of broadcast transmission and/or exhibition for American TV drama have held important repercussions for the considered profitability of some drama formats and styles over others and, ultimately, on the possible range of drama ideas and forms that broadcast television has favored for production. It has been possible for TV drama to develop with greater formal, conceptual and aesthetic diversity in British television, where public funding has provided 'risk capital' to support it. However, the imperative for American broadcast TV drama to maximize its considerable commercial potentials has to date encouraged two related and enduring tendencies in the strategically important area of hour-long drama. One is the preference for episodic over serial storytelling, and the other, a preponderance of 'procedural' concepts and settings. These elements are interlinked in that procedural dramas bring strong potentials for a predominance of resolving 'stories-of-the-week', along with an unusual capacity to generate new seasons and stories, allowing a given show to maintain its audience appeal for a decade or longer. Still generating new episodes even after the proliferation of its original iteration into a multi-series 'franchise', NBC's *Law and Order* (1990–2010), which amassed twenty seasons and around 456 episodes, provides a textbook example of the possibilities.

For as long as they were unrivalled in the costly area of original drama and able to wield a stifling control over the design of dramas that made it through their own filtering processes, CBS, ABC and NBC had nothing to gain and audience share to lose to each other from experimentation with drama in conceptual, narrative and/or aesthetic terms. Hence risk-averse commissioning became a significant element of American broadcast TV culture (Gitlin, 1994) undergirded by the big three's lengthy period of financial and creative control over TV production. Although a rare few new broadcast TV dramas managed to deviate from this pattern – most notoriously CBS's *Dallas* in 1978, NBC's *Hill Street Blues* in 1981 and ABC's *Twin Peaks* in 1990 – few that did so survived beyond their first season.

Hill Street Blues and the 'Quality' Revolution in Broadcast Drama

As acknowledged, AQD originated with NBC's *Hill Street Blues* (1981–87). The space for risk-taking that this series managed to force into being could be sourced first to the 'things can only get better' attitude of NBC, ranked third out of three at the time. More immediately, NBC was in a hurry to develop a new flagship drama (Bochco, cited in Martin, 2013: 27), motivating it to concede ground through the negotiations around the pilot, on the basis of which many creative decisions affecting the subsequent 145 episodes were made. Moreover, NBC CEO Fred Silverman was personally committed to getting "a realistic, gritty, urban police series" (Thompson, 1996: 60).

It was Silverman who dispatched NBC's head of programming, Brandon Tartikoff, to find the necessary talent for the venture. Tartikoff settled on two writer-producers, Steven Bochco and Michael Kozoll, both of whom worked at MTM, an independent production company led by Grant Tinker. Tinker's involvement in *Hill Street Blues*, first as head of MTM until late 1981 and then as CEO of NBC from 1982, was important to the possibility of the significant change for American TV drama that its creative innovations would effectively unleash. This is because, whilst Tinker had worked in a TV industry largely controlled by producers, he was unusually supportive of writers (Martin, 2013), a disposition that emboldened the writers who worked for him. As Tinker himself gained power in the 1981–1982 transition from MTM to NBC, the drama writers closest to him stood to gain greater autonomy and status themselves.

Yet Bochco and Kozoll played it cool in the face of NBC's headhunting effort. Exasperated as well as exhausted by his experiences creating and producing police series, Bochco admitted, "I sure wasn't looking to do another cop show" (cited in Gitlin, 1994: 280). Accordingly, the deal they struck with Tartikoff came with conditions. One was that NBC's "programming people would genuinely leave us alone to do what we wanted" (Bochco, cited in Gitlin, 1994: 281) and the other that, if this new show "was going to accurately capture the police mentality", network executives would have to accept the necessity for it to be "grim, gritty and rude" (ibid.). While NBC assented to both conditions, the process of constant negotiation that ended with the airing of the filmed pilot suggested that it was still an uphill battle for the pair to get exactly what they wanted for *Hill Street Blues*. But his MTM experiences had strengthened Bochco's resolve to exact and retain the necessary autonomy, or he and Kozoll would walk (Gitlin, 1994: 298–99). Fortunately for the drama that *Hill Street Blues* became, NBC was as desperate for the project to proceed as Bochco was determined to hold its executives to their promises.

As the restrictions outlined in the previous section suggest, innovation was an unlikely achievement for a 'police procedural' at this time. Yet the extent of *Hill Street Blues*'s departure from what viewers expected of police shows was overt in the focus group feedback that NBC received on the pilot and passed on, in memo form, to MTM. Excerpts from the memo (cited in Martin, 2013: 29) highlighted the following 'problems' with the *Hill Street Blues* pilot:

> The most prevalent audience reaction indicated that the program was depressing, violent and confusing … Too much was crammed into this story … The main characters were perceived as being not capable and having flawed personalities … Audiences found the ending unsatisfying. There are too many loose ends.

Hindsight renders this memo fascinating in that, as Martin (ibid.) registers, it reads as something of an "unwitting blueprint" for the many AQD examples that followed *Hill Street Blues*. But, as Thompson (1996: 64) acknowledges, "someone was going to have to insist upon breaking the ground rules that kept everything so standardised". *Hill Street Blues*, its battles fought by Bochco and supported by Tinker, was a rare series to be permitted to make the sustained effort that real change would require. MTM's response to NBC's memo, as penned by Tinker, was simply that "The network saw every one of the elements that were to make *Hill Street Blues* an enduring and memorable show as a problem to be overcome" (cited in Thompson, 1996: 65). Although normal process would have seen the pilot revised and reworked until it looked like other broadcast police series (ibid.), Bochco's belligerence and NBC's desperation combined to avert this. NBC executives made the radical decision to bin the focus group results and "take a chance" (Tartikoff, cited in Gitlin, 1994: 297).

An important example of NBC's unusually accommodating stance was its reaction to the pilot's use of the narrative aesthetic whose multiple, rapidly interweaving strands would survive to become a notable AQD convention. In 1980 the accepted number of subplots per hour-long drama episode was not more than three (Gitlin, 1994: 296). Underlining the perceived extremity of *Hill Street*'s attack on the fortress-like conventions of 'regular drama', NBC hired a psychologist to provide a "scientific opinion" about how many stories viewers could cope with in one episode (Gitlin, 1994: 296). Helpfully, the opinion confirmed that viewers would not fall to pieces if an episode's subplots exceeded three. In marked contrast, the opinion concluded that "the 'magic number' was seven, plus or minus two" (ibid.: 296), adding that "as the characters became more familiar", viewer capacity to manage this number of subplots would increase (ibid.). While features like these would gradually become assets rather than liabilities in long-format TV drama, they provide a useful illustration of how supremely difficult it was, circa 1980, for TV drama creators and production company heads, and network executives too, to challenge, let alone successfully overturn, the conservative status quo.

As has also been true of other instances of significant risk-taking and/or departure from convention for TV drama, *Hill Street* is regarded as neither an immediate nor a 'mass audience' success, given its 'disappointing' first season ratings. The notion that this first season performed poorly at all, however, needs to be questioned. As argued above, the expectation then applying, that new dramas return as much as a 32 percent share of the available audience, was overdue for revision by 1981, with more than 23 percent of American homes now receiving cable signals (Banet-Weiser et al., 2007: 2). That *Hill Street*'s first season ratings still averaged a 23 percent share (Feuer, 1984a: 26), just 9 points below the 32 percent target, indicates the strength of its appeal, particularly if these figures are considered against three mitigating factors. First is the extent to which *Hill Street* challenged the prevailing norms for broadcast TV drama in general and police dramas in particular. As indicated by the criticisms arising from its own 'test' audience, NBC was well aware of this but decided to ignore these 'problems' and proceed anyway. Second, *Hill Street* was given some marginal timeslots, one example being the 'graveyard' zone of Saturday night, when, as Thompson (1996: 66) observes, "the very people who might be most interested in a show like *Hill Street* were out having dinner or watching a movie". If the above two factors were not themselves enough to damage *Hill Street*'s ratings, the third was that NBC moved its timeslot no less than five times, this reputedly involving four different nights (Feuer, 1984a: 25). A generous perspective on this third factor is that NBC, in shifting *Hill Street* so many times, was trying to help it 'find its audience'. However, the regular movement of any show around the weekly schedule has its known downside, in that the 'appointment viewing' tendency developing among those following it is unusually disrupted. *Hill Street*'s occupancy of so many different timeslots was an even bigger problem for viewers trying to follow it given that VCR was still relatively new technology in 1981 and many could *only* see it by tuning in at the appointed time.

In view of these challenges for *Hill Street*, it is no less than "a miracle", as industry watchers asserted at the time (Feuer, 1984a: 26), that it survived. The 'miracle' of NBC's renewing of *Hill Street Blues*, despite its being the lowest-rating drama ever invited to return (Thompson, 1996: 66), was the second of two 'miracles' achieved by this innovative and extraordinarily lucky series. The first 'miracle' was, of course, that *Hill Street* even made it through to the end of the long, linked chain of 'ifs' outlined by Gitlin (1994: 273). The achievement of two 'miracles' by the same TV drama suggests that considerations other than ratings were at play. Arguably at some point in 1981, *Hill Street* was simply recognized for what it was: a harbinger of American TV drama's future. *Hill Street* returned in early 1982 and, assisted by the sustained commitment of a Thursday 10pm timeslot, its audience share averaged 34 percent (Feuer, 1984a: 26), allowing *Hill Street* to be declared 'successful' and become a template for other dramas.

Four areas were indicative of the innovations that *Hill Street Blues* brought to American TV drama and pioneered for AQD. First was its concept design, specifically the politically aware ideological positioning that framed *Hill Street's* alternative to the traditional police procedural. Devised to deliver the "realistic, gritty, urban" police drama that NBC said it wanted (Thompson, 1996: 60), *Hill Street* embraced rather than shrank from the 'social realist' obligations that attended this. Its stories understood, as Gitlin (1994: 275) emphasizes, that "race and class tear this society apart, that behaving decently under these conditions is an everyday trial, and that there are no blindingly obvious solutions for the accumulated miseries of the ghetto".

Second, it overhauled conventional characterizations, exchanging the police drama formula's traditional 'detective and sidekick' duo for a multi-racial, gender-balanced ensemble cast. Two examples can be cited. One was *Hill Street's* extending of the moral boundaries for core characters, a turn exemplified by the scene in which, "in a fit of rage", Detective Mick Belker "bit off the nose of a police academy recruit" (Gitlin, 1994: 275). Although critics registered Belker's "animal behaviour" (Buchalter, 1983), such scenes were important to the perceived 'realism' that *Hill Street* brought to American police drama. Another was the progressive female characterizations that *Hill Street* pioneered, a change overdue in 1981, the year that *Charlie's Angels* finally ended on ABC. The foremost vehicle for this was public defender Joyce Davenport, whose lesson to 'regular drama' was that "female characters could combine professional competence and sexuality" (Nelson, 2004: 102). Described by Gitlin (ibid.: 275) as one of the first female core characters to be simultaneously "professional, tough, elegant, intelligent, and sexy", Davenport brought a welcome balance to the construction of TV drama's female characters.

A third innovation for *Hill Street* was its narrative aesthetics and structure. That the 'problems' identified by NBC's focus group were concentrated in the area of narrative, testifies to the radical nature of *Hill Street's* departures from narrative conventions. These included a vastly increased number of stories being told in one episode, with Thompson counting as many as twelve in one example (1996: 70). Stories unfolded in the interweaving pattern adapted from soap opera, although the sheer volume of different story strands and dizzyingly fast pace of intercutting between them was nothing like that of soap opera. This narrative structure, supported by *Hill Street*'s procedural setting through which a mix of workplace and personal stories readily flowed, provided the matrix for its second main narrative innovation: the incorporation of serial strands. Even though police procedural series remain among American television's sites of greatest resistance to serialization, *Hill Street*'s many strands combined resolving with continuing stories.

Hill Street's fourth area of innovation was stylistic. The 'realism' that was central to *Hill Street*'s perceived deviation from its 'regular drama' contemporaries involved many facets, as observed above. However, the 'realism' attributed to this series was vastly boosted by the use of a documentary verité-like aesthetic achieved through its shooting on 35mm film and use of a mobile handheld camera. As a feature strongly evident in the bustling, densely populated station scenes, the expected aesthetic impacts were also exaggerated by the non-traditional placement of cuts when editing. As Nelson underlines (2004: 103), *Hill Street* editors were instructed to "Use [rather than edit out] the bad stuff", to effect a particularly restless, deliberately 'messy' visual style. As Gitlin (1994: 292) explains:

> The fragmentation and juxtaposition of shots and conversations [reproduced] the fragmentation and simultaneity of society. Characters would brush past each other, reach over each other's shoulders, break into each other's conversations, suggesting that its people depend on each other, crisis is everyday, no man or woman is an island.

Adding to the challenges registered by NBC's focus group respondents, this was a style that was keyed to unsettle viewers. Albeit radical in broadcast TV drama of the day, this 'messy' aesthetic was perfectly complemented by the volume of characters crowding morning 'roll-call' and other scenes, the many stories fighting with each other for exposure in each episode and the worked-up cacophony of dialogue and ambient sounds that underscored it all.

Hill Street's innovations were so widely and effectively imitated in broadcast dramas over the next two decades that, as Thompson (1996: 67) registers, "[a]nyone stumbling upon a rerun of *Hill Street Blues* today might be surprised at how tame it looks now". As *Hill Street* completed its first season, MTM was putting the finishing touches on the series it nicknamed "Hill Street in the hospital", *St. Elsewhere* (Feuer, 1984b: 44). Many more shows would follow, including such long-running procedurals as *LA Law*, *ER* and *NYPD Blue*, whose own successes spawned dozens of imitators or recombinants. Important to the degree of influence that *Hill Street* exerted, however, as was realized during its 1982 season, was that its loyalists included "large numbers of the young adults [18–49 year olds] for whom advertisers pay a premium" (Pollen, cited in Feuer, 1984a: 26). Because advertisers were willing to pay US$15 per thousand for these viewers, as compared with US$4 for "the general viewer", *Hill Street* was worth more to NBC "than a Top Ten hit with lesser demographics" (ibid.). Even though the first signs of network recognition of the revenue value of more desirable demographics occurred with quality CBS sitcoms in the early 1970s (Feuer, 1984a; Pearson, 2005), the above realization precipitated the extension of 'demographic thinking' to long-format drama. It was precisely because its innovations held such economic significance that *Hill Street Blues* "catalysed a widespread upgrade of the dramatic television series" (Lavery and Thompson, 2002: 24), becoming a model for the concepts, characters, stories and style of dramas that could attract these high-value viewers.

Revisiting the Characteristics of 'American Quality Drama'

By 1981, testament to the impact of broadcast-only era restrictions on drama form, concept design and style, nearly two decades had passed since 'quality' had been directly linked with American TV drama. The first phase of 'quality drama' flourished in the 1950s (Thompson, 1996: 11) and centered on critically acclaimed live one-offs that combined original teleplays with adaptations of classic theatre and literature. Importantly, fifties television culture and programming was still influenced by the medium's original role as an expensive 'home theatre' for affluent households (Spigel, 1992). Early television's funding through 'single sponsorship', whereby sponsor companies could gain prestige from their investment in a given hour of the TV schedule, provided the institutional stimulus for the 'anthology series' format that housed these one-off dramas (Boddy, 1993; Thompson, 1996).

A second, more enduring phase for 'quality' in hour-long drama began, as suggested, with *Hill Street Blues* (1981–87). However, the label 'quality TV' originated earlier, in an alternative strain of sitcom that CBS helped establish via *All in the Family*, *The Mary Tyler Moore Show* and *M*A*S*H**. Phased into the CBS schedule from 1970 to 1972, these three sitcoms were soon scheduled back-to-back on the same night, creating what Feuer (1984a: 7) considers "the most impressive evening of comedy ever to appear" on television. Importantly, CBS's motivation for replacing its 'hayseed' flagships *The Beverly Hillbillies*, *Petticoat Junction* and *Green Acres* with the above trio was rooted in demographic concerns about the increasing age of CBS's audience. As an adjustment that looked to CBS's future, it was "part of a calculated strategy", Feuer argues (ibid.), "to change the demographics of CBS and to establish the network as the leader in quality comedy with a broad popular appeal that would also capture [an] audience of young consumers, aged 18–34". As some of the first long-format shows to which a 'quality TV' label was attached, these comedies highlight that the developing concept of 'quality TV' had an institutional underpinning in network competition for revenue. Nevertheless, Thompson argues (1996: 30–35) that this second phase of 'quality TV' entailed sufficient risk-taking and creative innovation to constitute another considered 'golden age' for American television, emphasizing the centrality to this of hour-long 'quality' dramas that "defied the traditions of commercial television" (ibid.: 35).

Exploring the nature of AQD and its influence on the cable-commissioned complex serial form introduced by HBO, the following discussions examine Robert Thompson's definition of 'quality drama' (1996: 12–15), revising this in respect of three aims. In view of the large number of shows that now display the characteristics that Thompson associates with AQD, the first is to demonstrate how these characteristics have evolved since the 1990s. Accepting the broader applicability of 'quality TV', a term which scholars have applied to sitcom and other genres, the second is to demonstrate its formal and creative linkages with complex serial drama. Since post-2000 developments in TV drama have enabled new inter-connections between Thompson's original features, the third aim is to make these connections explicit. Accordingly, the original list of twelve features for 'quality drama' examined by Thompson (ibid.) is reconceived here as five textual characteristics, outlined below.

Conceptual Innovation

The focus on conceptual innovation, which is posited here as a first AQD feature, offers a way to gauge the extent of its departure from established norms. The importance of this departure to the definition of AQD is emphasized by Thompson's assertion: "Quality TV is best defined by what it is not. It is not regular TV" (ibid.: 13). But just as HBO's 'It's Not TV' tag-line has stimulated scholarly debate about what is and is not 'TV', it is difficult today to clearly separate 'quality' from 'regular' drama, due to the proliferation of the former and decline of the latter. Registering this consequence when writing in the mid-2000s, Thompson observes that the "very shows against which we used to define quality TV were disappearing" (2007: xviii). If only because of a different mix of American TV dramas in which 'regular' examples remained many and 'quality' few, these distinctions remained meaningful through the 1980s and 1990s. Nonetheless, as a consequence of the expansion and mainstreaming of AQD strategies as conventions for broadcast drama, these terms no longer suffice as ways to signify conventionality or innovation, both of which are relative traits.

The sense of blurred boundaries between the shows and perceptions now attached to these terms reflects the broader transmutability of TV genre itself. A textual perspective on TV genre suggests that it "should be defined", as John Fiske argued (1987: 111), not as any enduring form but "as a shifting provisional set of characteristics which is modified as each new example is produced". Indicating how generic change is endemic in television precisely because of such persistent strategies as 'recombination' and 'imitation', Gitlin (1994: 274) contends: "Breakthroughs in form soon become fossilised as formula. This season's odd characters become next season's stereotypes". The sustainability of a 'quality' and 'regular' drama binary is undermined further by network promotions of new shows, in which there is vested interest in accentuating novelty and disavowing conventionality. As Feuer (2007: 148) registers in relation to *The West Wing*, its boasts of uniqueness and originality were simply unsupported by its "textbook" deployment of what, by this point, were well-honed AQD conceits, formulas and conventions. Instead, this example lends support to Feuer's assertion that "quality drama always claims to be original in relation to the regular TV norms of its era" (ibid.). That the successful conventions of 'quality drama' in the 1980s were main-streamed by the 1990s and emerging as the new 'regular' by the 2000s testifies not to the decline of 'quality' but rather to the tendency of television to replicate its successes and remain ever-responsive to changing generic norms.

Even though Thompson uses terms that were laden with meaning in the 1990s, he did not refer explicitly to conceptual innovation, which is proffered here as an effective marker of textual distinction in TV drama, even if, as with other terms, it too is flawed by subjectivity. Although largely absent from the discourse of TV scholars, the industry term 'concept', equivalent to the 'big idea' or premise of a given TV show, carries more weight than a generic label in pinpointing a given drama's potentials for novelty. Thompson does, however, offer two suggestions as to how this departure might be recognized, and 'concept' is important to both. One is the tendency of AQD to take "a traditional genre and [transform] it" (ibid.: 13), a tactic evident both in the reinvention of the 'murder mystery' by *Twin Peaks* (ABC, 1990–1991) and equally in the subversion of the traditional Hollywood 'Western' effected by *Deadwood* (HBO, 2004–2006). The other is its venturing into "new narrative territory" (ibid.), a feat exemplified by *Homicide: Life on the Street* (NBC, 1993–99), which brought new perspectives to American crime pro-cedural drama by foregrounding the psychological motivations for murder, in doing so eschewing the conventional focus on how, by whom and with what consequences such crimes are committed. Although the above two expressions of a TV drama's point of difference provide useful indications of how this might be recognized, conceptual innovation can override both of them in marking a given drama's departure from what has preceded it. In TV drama, and influenced by its pride of place in the all-important pitch to a prospective network, the concept distils not only the central tensions that will drive, sustain and possibly distinguish the narrative, but also the 'treatment' and/or point of view that is applied to the 'narrative territory' of the show by its creators and writers.

The Pursuit of 'Upscale' Viewers

AQD, as Thompson suggests, has held the capacity to attract a higher proportion than other programming of "blue chip demographics", whose value to advertis-ers centers on their "upscale, well-educated, urban-dwelling" qualities, as well as their youth (ibid.: 14). As observed at the outset of this chapter, one rationale for the use of 'quality' in this paradigm's name has been its orientation toward audi-ences more desirable to advertisers. Accordingly, an important area of continuity between AQD and complex serials is their shared pursuit of 'upscale' viewers. Making this connection across the different economies of broadcast and premium cable TV, Feuer (2007: 147) registers that "[d]elivering a quality audience means delivering whatever demographic advertisers seek, or in the case of premium cable, attracting an audience with enough disposable income to pay extra for TV".

The definition of 'upscale' audience is changing under the influence not only of the tendency of more than 86 percent of American households to receive non-broadcast TV signals and services, but also the allure of additional online options (Banet-Weiser et al., 2007: 2). In this context, advertiser assessments of audience 'quality' are being revised. Two trends can be observed in respect of industry perceptions of today's 'upscale' audience for TV drama. One is that while younger adult demographics (now defined as the 18–34s and 18–49s) continue to command the highest rates paid by advertisers, it is accepted that both of these prized groups want to "watch content anywhere, anytime, on any device", a preference to which networks and advertisers are still adjusting through the "increasing availability and measurability" of online advertising (Lafayette, 2014). The other, is that as the average age of broadcast TV viewers rises and networks revisit earlier assumptions about consumer responsiveness by adult demographics, the notion that the eyeballs of 50-plus viewers are poor value by definition, is less pervasive than it was. While advertisers now specify the 18–49s and 25–54s, as demographics for whom they are willing to pay higher rates (ibid.), psychographic (or consumption-based) indicators are rising in importance, one example of which is NBC's ongoing research into the consumer habits of "Alpha Boomers", aged 55–64 (ibid.). Television's multiplatform era has initiated one other change to the definition of 'upscale' viewers. Bringing the potential for more direct economic relationships between the originators/owners of TV drama and its consumers/viewers, this era has seen the 'upscale' audience attain an economic value that need not even involve advertisers. Instead, this hinges on the ability of certain kinds of TV fiction (of which complex serials are one example) to motivate viewers into the direct purchase of a subscription service or single show, an activity in which 'upscale' viewers, regardless of their demographic or psychographic specificities, are better resourced to participate.

Even if the age of television's 'upscale' audience has evidently risen in recent years, no-one can reliably predict the audience response to a new drama before it is exhibited. Tensioning the texture of network anxieties about expensively produced, though untested TV dramas, therefore, is AQD's capacity for conceptual and stylistic risk-taking. As Thompson emphasizes, "these shows seldom become blockbusters and their survival is often tenuous, at least at the beginning" (ibid.: 14). Accordingly, AQD's institutional context of advertiser-funded broadcast schedules has been unusually keyed to generate what Thompson describes as "a noble struggle" between "creative writer-producers" and "bottom-line-conscious executives" (ibid.: 14). Bearing in mind the commercial context for which high-end American TV drama has always been created, it is instructive that in the case of the two HBO dramas that pioneered the complex serial form – *Oz* and *The Sopranos* – this process of negotiation between creative and executive personnel was conspicuously unlike the "noble struggle" it was for *Hill Street Blues*, with the central concepts and desired aesthetic deviations proceeding largely without compromise. For these examples, the process instead unfolded as a power-balanced negotiation of terms and parameters between the creator-showrunners (Tom Fontana and David Chase) and HBO commissioning executives.

Increased Creative Autonomy for Writers

Thompson makes two observations about AQD in this area: one, "that it tends to be literary and writer-based" (ibid.: 15) and the other, that the writer's name is used in ways comparable to the labeling of 'designer' clothing, to mark "a quality pedigree" (ibid.: 14). These assertions highlight the greater status that AQD brought for writers and writer-producers, a contrast with the 'classic network' era's frequent deference in drama commissioning to the opinions of network 'suits'. The ascendance of writers began in the late 1970s inside MTM, championed by Grant Tinker, who Brett Martin (2013: 25) describes as "that rare, if not unique, creature: a television executive revered by television writers". It gained momentum through the 1980s and 1990s in the context of the demographic triumphs associated with successful AQD examples, consequent falling ratings thresholds for shows to be declared 'successful' (Pearson, 2005: 14) and an industry environment in which 'star' writers and writer-producers became a more valuable commodity as network competition for their talents intensified. In hour-long drama, a category that was redefined by AQD examples in these decades, the ascendance of writers and hyphenates was embodied by such leading writer-producers as Steven Bochco, Tom Fontana, David Milch, Stephen J. Cannell, David E. Kelly and Joss Whedon. Although obstacles to genuine authorship in TV drama would remain, given the necessity for collaboration in the high-volume category of the episodic series, a further step toward increased creative control for writers and producers occurred with the inception of complex serials and HBO's decision to use a maximum of 13 episodes per season as the format for these, a departure from broadcast TV's standard format of 22–26 episodes (Edgerton, 2008: 8). As *Oz*, *The Sopranos*, *The Wire*, *Six Feet Under* and *Deadwood* all demonstrated, it has been more possible for an individual writer-producer to sustain a significant level of influence on a given complex serial drama than it could be in the context of AQD's higher overall and per-season episode volumes.[2]

Serialization and Narrative Complexity

As was demonstrated in focus group reactions to *Hill Street Blues*, one of the foremost differences between AQD and 'regular drama' was in narrative approach. The narrative conventions of 'regular drama', as exemplified by *Columbo*, *Hawaii Five-O* and *Baywatch*, included a small 'regular' cast of characters; a corresponding reliance on episode 'guests' to generate narrative conflict; a striking preference for episodic, linear storytelling; minimal 'arc-of-development' progression for core characters; and a maximum of three storylines per episode with resolutions delivered at the episode's end. Starting with *Hill Street Blues*, AQD eschewed these tendencies in favor of strategies that, albeit 'revolutionary' in 1981, became mainstream in hour-long drama with surprising rapidity. Adapting the multiple interweaving storylines of daytime soap opera to the different concepts, aesthetics and episode structure of hour-long high-end drama, AQD's narrative innovations included: (1) a larger 'ensemble' core cast with additional episode 'guests'; (2) a proliferation of story strands per episode enabled by the enlarged cast of 'regulars'; (3) narrative density engendered by a pattern of interweaving storylines; (4) the capacity, as provided by this pattern, to combine episodic with continuing (or serial) story strands; and (5) the tendency to subject core characters to an 'arc-of-development' facilitated by the presence of serial strands.

More recent developments in AQD narrative testify to its continued evolution in response to the challenges and opportunities of the multiplatform era. First is a movement away from episodic storytelling and toward serialization. Even if 'stories-of-the-week' are a continuing presence in AQD and remain the preferred mode for broadcast TV's many crime procedurals, serial subplots have gained an increased emphasis at the expense of episodic stories, as exemplified in the narrative mix for *Boston Legal* and *Grey's Anatomy*. Although AQD has more often integrated serial strands into series form (as distinct from deploying serial form itself), multi-season serials (the form used by *Desperate Housewives*, *Lost* and *Prison Break*) are more common in broadcast TV drama. Second is conceptual diversity, whereby new AQD shows (following the conceptual forays of *Twin Peaks*, *Moonlighting* and *Northern Exposure*) entail a concept-based 'point of difference', as exemplified by *The X-Files*, *Buffy the Vampire Slayer*, *Firefly*, *Elementary* and *The Blacklist*. Third is an increased range and density of stories, facilitated and encouraged by conceptual diversity and fewer limitations on the extent of serialization in broadcast dramas. Story strands are not only prolific but can 'arc' over different lengths of time, spanning anything from a group of episodes to several seasons. Fourth, as a feature gaining new opportunities from the mix of narrative modes available to the individual episode, is the aesthetic interest in what Jason Mittell (2006; 2015) terms narratively 'complex' storytelling. One facet of this is the regular departure from linearity, involving the combining of flash-forwards with flashbacks, to allow the kind of fluid movement between narrative 'past', 'present' and 'future' that is evident in *Lost*. Another is the use of contradictory lives or perspectives, these possibly defined as 'dream' and 'reality' scenarios. Providing for parallel diegeses and alternative narrative outcomes, this was a marked feature of the final season of *House MD*. Fifth is the increased moral complexity of characters, a feature that, influenced by the extreme transgressions of complex serial leads like Tony Soprano, Dexter Morgan and Walter White, continues to ease out the boundaries for the moral behavior of characters in the more resistant context of broadcast television (Edgerton, 2013: 95).

Indicative of the progression are such morally ambivalent leads as Andy Sipowitz (*NYBD Blue*), Jack Bauer (*24*), Gregory House (*House MD*), and Raymond 'Red' Reddington (*The Blacklist*).

An Interest in Generic Mixing and Self-Reflexivity

'Quality drama', as Thompson acknowledges (1996: 15), has often identified itself as such through the use of 'generic mixing' and 'self-reflexivity'. These strategies are related as different articulations of intertextuality (Fiske, 1987). In television, intertextuality entails references by shows to other screen or literary texts, to their medium and/or their place in popular culture, as well as the acknowledgement through these references, that they too are works of fiction. Applying these traits to American 'quality TV', and thinking of sitcom as well as drama, Jane Feuer (1984b: 44) argues that they "operate both as the normative way of creating new programmes *and* as a way of distinguishing the 'quality' from the everyday product". While the first half of Feuer's assertion references the 'safety first' strategies identified by Gitlin (1994), the second highlights that AQD used them to assert itself as more sophisticated than 'regular drama'.

'Quality TV', Thompson argues, "creates a new genre by mixing old ones" (1996: 15), a strategy later labeled 'generic mixing' by Jason Mittell (2004). Underscoring the conceptual and stylistic risk-taking that has characterized AQD, 'generic mixing' has represented a considerably more radical approach to concept design than its 'regular drama' counterpart, 'recombination' (Gitlin, 1994). As a strategy characteristic of TV programming more broadly than drama (Fiske, 1987), 'generic mixing' begins in concept design and involves the combining of elements drawn from traditionally separate genres, through which the different narrative, aesthetic and other features are cleverly blended to effect novelty. Generic mixing is exemplified by *Twin Peaks'* mixing of murder mystery with soap opera, *Moonlighting's* combining of romantic comedy and detective drama and *The Sopranos'* blending of elements from the gangster film, family melodrama and psychodrama. A feature that is often instigated by AQD's use of generic mixing is 'self-reflexive referencing' (Ott and Walter, 2000), wherein a show acknowledges its textuality through its self-awareness of other texts and/or of its own status in popular culture. Defining MTM's 'house style', Feuer (1984b: 44) argues that self-reflexivity was characteristic of this, observing its influence on *Hill Street Blues* and *St. Elsewhere*, among other MTM productions. In the larger super-genre that AQD expanded to become, self-reflexive references to other TV shows, films and popular culture have been an ongoing tendency, and were a regular feature of such enduring examples as *Boston Legal* and *House MD*.

Although by no means obligatory for AQD, the above expressions of intertextuality are now widespread in primetime TV programming, indicatively in drama, comedy and popular factual categories. Accordingly, while generic mixing and self-reflexivity continue to mark the sophisticated entertainment programming with which AQD aligns itself, they can no longer distinguish it. Fueled by the post-1990 expansion of animated sitcom, whose 'limited animation' aesthetic has been unusually hospitable to self-reflexive depictions (Wells, 2003), the proliferation of these expressions of intertextuality within the above three categories testifies to the wide influence of AQD's interest in intertextuality, encouraged by the effectiveness that its shows have demonstrated in delivering a higher proportion of the audience segments most desirable to advertisers.

'Quality Drama' Versus Complex Serial Drama

The above AQD characteristics warrant detailed analysis in view of their importance as the generic predecessor and closest ongoing counterpart (in American television at least) to complex serials. Yet regardless of these connections, AQD and complex serials are separated in some important ways, not least by their tendency to be created for broadcast and non-broadcast networks respectively. Subsequent chapters will examine the characteristics and distinctions of complex serial drama. In the interim, it is important to foreground the complex serial's textual departures from the AQD traditions and characteristics examined above.

First is that AQD's tendency for conceptual reliance on a central institution (a workplace, location, group of co-workers or close-knit community) is not a necessity for the complex serial. Although most complex serials incorporate a feature of this kind – with examples in *Oz*'s Emerald City wing, *The Sopranos*' so-called 'waste management' enterprise, *Six Feet Under*'s funeral parlor and *Mad Men*'s advertising agency – the central, ongoing narrative importance that institutions retain in AQD is secondary to the emphasis of complex serials on morally conflicted, often transgressive, primary characters.

Second is that, allowing for the creation of central characters who can embody the conceptual tension of the larger show, the narrative backbone of this drama has been serial form, even if AQD has assisted American television's embracing of serial narratives by mixing episodic with continuing story strands.

Third is the complex serial's use of more explicit content and the repercussions of this. Whereas an increased dedication to 'realism' (for which *Hill Street Blues* provided the point of departure) was important in motivating a wider range of character behaviors and attributes in AQD shows, complex serials, assisted by the content liberties of non-broadcast platforms as well by the narrative progression that has long been a tendency of high-end serial drama, are more strongly invested in interrogating the psychology of characters. Among the outcomes of this is the propensity of complex serials to examine the motivations for, along with the consequences of, acts of violence, immorality and other transgressive behaviors.

The fourth departure involves the area of aesthetics and visual style. As the case study of *Hill Street Blues* shows, AQD demonstrated a higher level of aesthetic ambition than 'regular drama', a necessary distinction in view of its 'quality audience' objectives. As a consequence, stylistic sophistication became an overt AQD characteristic, one expression of which has been its self-reflexive references to its own textuality, to popular culture and to other screen texts. In the last thirty years, AQD's aesthetic aspirations have remained high, a tendency exemplified in different ways by *Twin Peaks, Ally McBeal, Buffy the Vampire Slayer, NYPD Blue, Lost* and *24*, and facilitated by TV drama's rising production values. Yet complex serials, encouraged initially by the centrality of feature films to HBO's brand identity, and by the concepts and settings deployed by its most successful examples, have redefined what 'high-end' can mean for TV drama. Overt in the distinctive look and style that its leading examples have cultivated, the aesthetic ambition of complex serial drama is signaled in its tendency to reference cinema canons and history, as exemplified by *The Sopranos, Boardwalk Empire, Breaking Bad, Game of Thrones* and *Stranger Things*. Aesthetic ambition is equally evident in the larger array of settings and locations within which complex serial stories unfold, its notable interest in visual storytelling, along with the tendency of meticulous attention to visual and aural elements of design, cinematography, mise-en-scène and verisimilitude. These aesthetic and stylistic elements are examined in Chapter 5.

Case Study of *Six Feet Under*

As an early and influential complex serial, HBO's *Six Feet Under* (2001–05) can demonstrate the conceptual and aesthetic departures from AQD traditions that is represented by this drama form. The discussions that follow include close analysis of the pilot episode, which, although *Six Feet Under* used a team of writers who worked under Alan Ball as 'showrunner', was scripted by Ball himself. As well as establishing the characters, narrative approach and thematic interests that served all five seasons of this show, the pilot provides an effective showcase for *Six Feet Under*'s innovations. *Six Feet Under*'s significant contribution to the conceptual originality of complex serials can be sourced to its inventive construction of a middle-class Los Angeles family uprooted by the loss of its patriarch, a catastrophic event which puts two brothers in charge of their father's funeral parlor business. Partly because its concept blended an interrogation of society's central institution (the family) with the psychological probing of society's most deeply felt, yet least articulated anxieties (mortality, death and grief), *Six Feet Under* pursued a distinctive visual style that incorporated a range of non-televisual aesthetic traditions. Affirming the novelty of *Six Feet Under*, Akass and McCabe (2008: 71) argue: "Never in the history of American television has a show contemplated the frailty of our lives in quite such a quirky yet deeply introspective way".

Occurring at an early stage of HBO's original TV drama trajectory, the genesis of *Six Feet Under* began when Ball was invited to a meeting with HBO commissioning executive Carolyn Strauss just days after the release of *American Beauty* (1999), whose screenplay Ball had written. Becoming the most acclaimed feature that year, *American Beauty* went on to win all five of the most coveted Academy Awards in 2000, as a result of which Ball "became the most sought-after writer in town" (Weinraub, 2001). After his "toxic" experience as head writer on *Cybill* (Ball, cited in Martin, 2013: 95), Ball had abandoned television to write *American Beauty* and, since he no longer wanted "to be hired to write other people's ideas" (Ball, cited in Weinraub, 2001), the meeting with Strauss was timely. For Ball, who was struck by the "electric" performances and "spectacular" writing he saw in *The Sopranos* (cited in Martin, 2013: 95), HBO offered the opportunity for a different kind of drama to that encouraged by advertiser-funded broadcast television.

While *Six Feet Under* answered HBO's requirement for something "provocative and interesting" (Strauss, cited in Haley, 2002: 6A), Ball's disposition, like that of David Chase, was notably 'anti-TV' when he scripted its pilot (Magid, 2002). His experiences on *Cybill* and *Grace Under Fire* had convinced him that, in broadcast TV, ideas that were challenging and/or interesting were ever-vulnerable to network interference, that nothing is permitted to remain ambiguous and that, ultimately, "any kind of edge is removed" (Ball, cited in Weinraub, 2001). Ball realized that HBO offered unusual opportunities to redress these concerns when the only network 'note' about the pilot script he had submitted to Strauss read, "We love the characters. We love the story. But the whole thing feels a little safe. Can it be more fucked up?" (Ball, cited in Martin, 2013: 99).

Textual influences on the specificities of Ball's family-owned mortuary concept included *The American Way of Death*, Jessica Mitford's non-fictional exposé of the funeral industry; *The Undertaking: Life Studies From the Dismal Trade*, a collection of essays written by undertaker and poet, Thomas Lynch; and Ball's original screenplay for *American Beauty*, which examined a dysfunctional middle-American family. While all three of these sources informed *Six Feet Under*, a fourth crucial influence was Ball's own experiences of death, loss and grief, the first of which followed the death-by-accident of his sister, Mary Ann (Ball, author interview, 2013). As she drove a 13-year-old Alan to his piano lesson, her vehicle was sideswiped by another (ibid.). This experience had important after-effects for Ball and his family, a number of which found a place in *Six Feet Under*'s stories or characters. An important example was the feeling Ball remembered having as a grief-stricken boy in a funeral parlor, gazing down at his dead sister, but somehow alienated by the "bizarre, surreal environment" (ibid.) constituted by the funeral parlor experience itself. Discussing how this experience informed his conception of *Six Feet Under*, Ball (ibid.) remembers:

> Yeah it's your sister. It doesn't look like her. I remember thinking, she would never wear that colour lipstick. And everything is carpeted and over-upholstered and soft and muffled and there's this sad but very subtle music playing and everybody's very sombre. And it's just very strange. And I remember what happened is my mom went, and with the open casket which is such a bizarre thing anyway, and she leaned over and kissed my sister's forehead and she broke down crying and literally a couple of directors came and got her and took her off behind the curtain.

Instilling the sense for Ball that death and grief should be dealt with in "a completely opposite way" (ibid.), the tension between these two positions became important to the perspectives, setting, stories, and look of *Six Feet Under*. One example was his decision to base the show in Los Angeles. This city, which Ball described as "the capital of the denial of death" (Ball, cited in Martin, 2013: 99), brought the "opportunity for sharper satire and deeper poignancy" (Martin, ibid.) in *Six Feet Under*'s critiquing of the ritualization and commodification of funerals. Another was the influence of this tension on the design of the Fisher home's entry and parlor sets. As Martin explains, Ball "instructed the set designer to dress the house as though it were buried under a muted layer of carpeted, upholstered insulation" (2013: 101). A third example, underlined by Alan Poul, who assisted Ball as executive producer, was the camerawork. Martin, citing Poul, underlines that *Six Feet Under*'s "standard-shot angle was just beneath eye level, creating a slightly distorted, detached sensation [and something akin to] 'a corpse-eye view'" (ibid.).

Although, at first glance, the *Six Feet Under* family may appear to be only a small departure from the comfortably resourced, white, nuclear unit that has dominated the family constructs of broadcast TV, the Fishers represent a postmodern, post-patriarchal alternative to this idealized model. The opening minutes of the pilot work to explode the initial sense of familial warmth, security and progress, as suggested by the immaculately presented home, adult son quietly reading the newspaper, a mother cooking pot roast in a spacious, well-fitted kitchen and the mention of an expensive new hearse for the business. In the catalytic event that follows, this semblance of harmony is irretrievably shattered. Nathaniel Fisher, having taken his new hearse to collect Nate from the airport in style, diverts his gaze from the road ahead to reach for a cigarette, whereupon the immaculate vehicle is sideswiped and crushed by a bus.

While Nathaniel Fisher Sr. continues to appear as a ghost in the pilot and later episodes, *Six Feet Under*'s 'living' core characters are the newly widowed Ruth Fisher, whose life of stay-at-home domesticity is radically disrupted by the death of her husband, and David, her younger son who, suddenly elevated to leading as opposed to learning the business, is also a 'buttoned-up' gay man whose personal challenge is to find the courage to come out. The struggles of gay men in American society gain additional opportunities for exploration through David's policeman partner, Keith Charles. The eldest Fisher child is Nathaniel Jr. ('Nate'), whose life plans change after his father's death, in that instead of returning to his job in Seattle, he opts to partner his brother at the helm of Fisher and Sons. Central to Nate's own 'arc-of-development' is Brenda Chenowith, whom he meets on the flight home, their relationship opening Nate to the additional challenges represented by Brenda's dependent, psychotic brother, Billy. Another central character, whose additional importance is as a focal point for the business challenges placed upon Fisher and Sons by its corporate rival, the funeral chain, Kroehner Services International, is Puerto Rican restorative artist Federico ('Rico') Diaz. As a long-term employee who was trained by Fisher Sr., Rico is considered among the 'best in the business', rendering him a potential asset for Kroehner. The youngest Fisher sibling, Claire, begins as an edgier version of the stereotypical teenage rebel, but is followed in subsequent seasons through college, graduation and into a successful career. The 'coming of age' rebellion with which Claire's development arc begins sees her succumbing to her boyfriend's coaxing to try crystal meth just minutes before receiving the tragic news. This tragi-comic convergence of bad behavior and terrible timing leaves Claire high on the effects as she accompanies her mother to uplift her father's body.

The 'overarching story' at the center of *Six Feet Under*'s serial narrative is that of the family and its funeral parlor business, initiated by the death of its patriarch Nathaniel Fisher Sr. However, this first death initiates two ongoing elements of *Six Feet Under*'s narrative, whose stories are serialized for core characters and usually episodic for funeral parlor 'customers'. One is the 'death-of-the-week' with which episodes open, this yielding a new guest character and different means of death for each. The other, which provides *Six Feet Under* with a flow of opportunities to link the perspectives of newly departed guest characters with the problems and concerns of the living core characters, is a 'magic realist'[3] succession of 'talking dead' figures. This gives each body in the Fisher mortuary two narrative functions. It is at once an inanimate object on the slab being artfully restored before being dressed and displayed for those left behind, and an animate ghost who is usefully reflective of its newly dead status, a position from which it attains the omniscient perspective to offer successive insights to core characters. The mere presence of a dead body, let alone the two uses to which these bodies are put, deepens *Six Feet Under*'s capacities for ghostly testimony to inform the actions of core characters and for broader social commentary. As Thomas Lynch, a former undertaker himself, suggests, having "a dead body in the room" encourages "the free range of conversation on what would otherwise be difficult subjects: gay love, love past middle age, young love, life in all its untidiness and grey tone" (cited in Akass and McCabe, 2008: 78). These potentials are exemplified in "A Private Life" (1:12), in which David gains new resolve as to the right of himself and other gay men to live as they choose, after listening to the 'talking dead' testimony of a young man who dies as the result of a homophobic beating. The pressure on David to persevere in the face of these challenges is maintained by the exhortations of this young gay ghost, who continues to appear in later episodes, including the season finale (1:13).

The death of the family patriarch in the pilot episode instigates the first opportunities to demonstrate *Six Feet Under*'s deployment and parodying of TV melodrama, especially 'family melodrama'. Horace Newcomb (2007: 566) underlines that "[t]elevision, with its constant emphasis on family as both 'content' and object (the viewing family), [has] pushed toward melodrama in any number of generic patterns, from comedy to Westerns, medical drama to police procedural". As recognizable in exaggerated plots, integral to which are states of heightened emotion for characters, melodrama is notorious for its "sensational appeals to the emotions" of viewers (Thorburn, 1994: 538). Interrogating the 1980s proliferation of serial melodramas on American television that followed the popular success of *Dallas* (1979–1991), Jane Feuer (1995) finds an explanation for their appeal in the outlet that family melodramas provide to interrogate the ideological contradictions arising from rampant capitalism. Melodramas, Feuer suggests, "offer artistic presentations of genuine problems but locate these problems in the family, the place where they can't be solved" (1994: 554-5). Although *Six Feet Under* eschews the "[a]cting, editing, musical underscoring and the use of the zoom lens" that usually combine to represent the "hysteria" associated with melodrama (ibid.: 556), the Fishers offer a postmodern, post-patriarchal alternative to the "corporate family" construct that was important to *Dallas* and its imitators (Feuer, 1995: 115). Yet melodrama is frequently used for comedic and parodic purposes in *Six Feet Under*, as evident in the more extreme or bizarre behaviors of its core characters. Ruth Fisher's outbursts in the pilot episode, in which her emotional fragility is narratively rationalized by her state of shock following the untimely death of her husband, provides a case in point. As she dresses for Nathaniel Fisher's official 'viewing', Ruth's already aching conscience is deeply pricked when Fisher's ghost quietly affirms, "I know, Ruth. I know everything". A few moments later, in a scene whose emotional hysteria is effectively anticipated by the brief flashback to Nate's travel memory of distressed Sicilian women crying, screaming and angrily hammering on the coffin of their dead, Ruth shatters the muffled decorum of the crowded Fisher parlor with a sobbing admission of her infidelity with Hiram, this attaining a volume certain to be audible beyond the heavy curtain behind which David has ushered her. As both sons move closer to comfort her, their jaws drop in unison as Ruth cries out, "I've done a terrible, terrible thing … I'm a whore!!! I was unfaithful to your father for years … And now he knows. He knows!!!"

Already blending the above references to 'family melodrama' with those to procedural drama (as supplied by its funeral home setting), *Six Feet Under* is additionally novel in respect of its thematic interests in death, the afterlife and human frailty. As themes without a precedent in American TV drama, these provide narrative causation for the third element of *Six Feet Under*'s generic and aesthetic mix: psychodrama. With forerunners in cinema and literature, though few in broadcast TV, psychodrama uses the aesthetics of 'modernism'[4] to externalize a character's internal struggle to deal with circumstances beyond their control. 'Modernist' departures from realism often entail the insertion of dream sequences (see Caughie, 2000: 152-3), which, in view of their purpose – to disrupt narrative flow so as to foster something akin to a Brechtian form of estrangement[5] – are necessarily unannounced. With such sequences also used in *The Sopranos*,[6] television modernism was pioneered in British TV drama through the work of Dennis Potter, exemplified by BBC mini-serials *Pennies from Heaven* (1978) and *The Singing Detective* (1986). 'The Foot' (1:3), an episode titled after the severed foot that Claire steals from the Fisher morgue and places in the locker of an errant boyfriend, pays self-reflexive homage to Potter's proclivity for modernist departures from realism. This occurs, as Feuer (2007: 151–51) explains, when Claire "walks into a realistic scene in the family kitchen and immediately goes into a musical number [in which she is joined by David and Ruth] that might have been a direct quotation from *Pennies from Heaven*".

David Lavery (2005) examines the additional influences of magic realism, "the Hispanic imagination", and "the grotesque" on the visual style and aesthetics of *Six Feet Under*, these derived from art, literature and/or cinema, and without a precedent in American broadcast drama. In 'Parallel Play' (4:3), religious iconography combines with magic realist imagery in a dream for Federico (ibid.: 19), informed by the guilt of his recent 'dalliance' with stripper Sophia, whose breast enhancement Rico has paid for. In this dream, in which his wife, Vanessa, figures as the Virgin Mary, Federico, as Lavery (ibid.) explains, "sees himself sitting on a sofa in a forest tableau, a Christ-like Sophia crucified behind him, wrapped in a loincloth but naked from the waist up, blood streaming from below her soon-to-be-surgically-enhanced breasts". Gaining a wealth of opportunities from the funereal images and symbols comprising *Six Feet Under*'s title sequence, the successive death scenes, the graphic nature of the restorative work that is undertaken on bodies of all shapes, sizes and ages, as well as from the ongoing commentaries from visibly damaged 'talking dead' characters, many more examples of the above types of imagery are incorporated into the visuals and aesthetics of *Six Feet Under*.

In *Six Feet Under*, dream images assist the psychological interrogation and revelation of character. It is through dream images, for example, as cutaway scenes that interrupt an otherwise 'realist' progression of events,[7] that Nate's vulnerability to premature death (arising from the rare brain condition from which he dies in the fifth season) is foreshadowed in the pilot episode. These scenes also suggest that Nate understands, if only at a deep psychological level, that this will be his fate. Out running, ostensibly on the same thoroughfare on which his father was killed, Nate suddenly places himself in the middle of the street and the path of an oncoming bus, which obligingly strikes him down. He falls directly onto the sealed surface, blood pooling beneath his head, even though his eyes are wide with awareness. Following just one minute later, the second scene more overtly articulates the expectation that Nate's 'turn' at death will come. He sees his father, one of a trio of naked ghosts seated around a table in the mortuary basement of the Fisher home, whiling away their 'afterlife' drinking, smoking and playing cards, their activity musically underscored by a breezy 1950s-styled track. Returning what is implicitly Nate's gaze, the ghost of Fisher Sr. looks up as if to register their expectation that Nate will join them, stating "We'll deal *you* in next hand". Situated among many examples of explicit references to cinema, art or literature in *Six Feet Under*, the above scenes function to disrupt the narrative flow, as a means to break the audience suture that is the objective of high-end TV drama's default aesthetic, 'realism'. Although it is not used in any systematic way in *Six Feet Under*, the disruption of narrative flow that is an evident objective for *Six Feet Under* is among the seven features of the modernist 'counter-cinema' schema conceived by Peter Wollen, as one operating in direct opposition to the objectives of mainstream cinema (see Stam, 2000b: 261).

Six Feet Under was HBO's third original long-format drama and a conspicuous success, its first season averaging 5 million viewers per episode as compared with 3.3 million for the debut season of *The Sopranos* (Akass and McCabe, 2008: 71). As this case study shows, *Six Feet Under* is connected with AQD through its blending of 'procedural' with character-driven 'relationship' stories, its conceptual focus on an ensemble 'family' of characters, and its deployment of family melodrama aesthetics and tropes. Yet in the narrative perspectives and strategies it uses, its disdain for commercialism and capitalism, and its deployment of modernist aesthetics that critique the conventions of both 'realism' and melodrama, *Six Feet Under* represents a significant departure from the AQD paradigm, instead providing an early, influential testament to the distinctiveness of complex serial drama.

Conclusion

Examining AQD's creative legacies and its influences on complex serial drama, this chapter has sought to provide a cultural and creative complement to the institutional influences on complex serials examined in the previous chapter. The creative revolution represented by the inception of AQD was well overdue in the early 1980s, during which cable penetration reached a quarter of American homes (Banet-Weiser et al., 2007: 2). Marking *Hill Street Blues* as the vehicle for paradigmatic change in long-format primetime drama, its creative innovations spanned the areas of concept design, narrative strategies, characterization and aesthetics. Allowing these features to inform and stimulate the emergence of the AQD paradigm was *Hill Street*'s ability to deliver a high proportion of the younger-skewing 'upscale' audience for which advertisers were willing to pay three times as much per thousand (Feuer, 1984a: 26). Underlining the demographic connotation of AQD was that NBC executives, who were initially reluctant to allow *Hill Street Blues* to make significant deviations from 'regular' drama norms, adjusted their view of this series once its demographic achievements were apparent. Accordingly, *Hill Street Blues* managed to survive long enough for its significant innovations to be replicated by other dramas. Yet *Hill Street*'s creative struggles, its content battles waged by Steven Bochco, testify to the lingering effects of 'mass audience' thinking into the 1980s. Even though this decade brought increasing competition for the big three, these networks still dominated the origination of TV drama. Indicating that AQD has been inextricably linked with the delivery of what advertisers perceive as a 'quality audience' and pay higher rates to access was that as 'demographic thinking' became an increasing necessity for all broadcast networks rather than an optional strategy for the third-ranked NBC, AQD expanded whilst 'regular drama' declined.

Revisiting and revising Thompson's definition of 'quality drama' (1996: 12–15) in recognition of its dominance of long-format broadcast drama by 2000, coupled with its ongoing importance as the generic counterpart to the complex serial that subsequently developed on cable television, this chapter posits five shared characteristics for AQD, those of conceptual innovation, the pursuit of an 'upscale' audience, increased creative autonomy for writers, serialization and narrative complexity, and an interest in generic mixing and self-reflexivity. These characteristics take account of the large volume of AQD examples that now exist, along with AQD's evolution to date. While the analysis of these characteristics demonstrates the continuities between 'quality drama' and complex serial drama, it also highlights important differences – in characterization, narrative structure and complexity, and aesthetics, as well as in the potentials for conceptual diversity, morally conflicted primary characters, and explicit content – to which non-broadcast platforms have brought new opportunities. These continuities and differences are well demonstrated by *Six Feet Under*, whose complex serial credentials are evident in its pioneering of new conceptual and narrative territory for American TV drama; the explicitness of its content in the Federal Communications Commission (FCC)-regulated areas of sexuality, violence and language; its deployment of psychodrama; the frequency of its 'magic realist' and 'modernist' departures from realism; and the many visual references its episodes make to art cinema and/or to traditions in theatre, literature and art.

AQD has provided a vital precedent for complex serial drama by virtue of the conceptual, aesthetic, narrative, demographic and other foundations that it laid. Yet these forms are separated in some important ways, with consequences for their textuality. One is by their history, whose influences on TV drama combine the advances of digital recording and editing with fundamental changes in media structure, in society and culture more broadly, as well as in the expectations that audiences bring to TV drama. Another is by their conception, commissioning and production for different broadcast and non-broadcast platforms, the latter now combining cable with internet networks. These broadcast and non-broadcast platforms entail different institutional imperatives, creative opportunities and performance indicators for drama, which feed back into its design and creation. A final division between these forms is their emergence in the different eras of 'multi-channel transition' (Lotz, 2007a) and multiplatform television, as distinctive institutional and industrial phases in which different revenue potentials, investment and distribution patterns, and 'value chain' considerations have applied to high-end drama. As this chapter has argued, and its case studies of *Hill Street Blues* and *Six Feet Under* can demonstrate, 'quality drama' and complex serial dramas are distinguishable from each other, insofar as they bear the markers of the different broadcast and non-broadcast political economies in and for which they have been produced, and of the extant creative possibilities for American TV drama in the 'multi-channel transition' and multiplatform eras.

Notes

1 Todd Gitlin (1994) *Inside Prime Time*, Second Edition, New York and London: Routledge, p. 273.
2 The authorship of complex serials is examined in Chapter 3.
3 Citing the ideas of J. A. Cuddon, David Lavery (2005: 28) elaborates upon the characteristics of 'magic realism'. Of these, the most relevant to *Six Feet Under* are its "mingling and juxtaposition of the realistic and the fantastic", along with the "miscellaneous use of dreams, myths and fairy stories, expressionistic and even surrealistic description ... the elements of surprise or abrupt shock, the horrific and the inexplicable". David Lavery, "'It's Not Television, It's Magic Realism': the Mundane, the Grotesque and the Fantastic in *Six Feet Under*", Chapter 1 in Kim Akass and Janet McCabe eds. (2005) *Reading Six Feet Under: TV to Die For*, London and New York: I.B. Tauris, pp. 19–33.
4 The aesthetics of 'modernism' are outlined in Chapter 5.
5 In the 1920s, German dramaturg Bertolt Brecht rejected classical Aristotelian theatre in favor of an 'epic theatre', which aimed to undermine or interrupt the emotional catharsis that classical theatre produced and which he saw as working against active spectatorship. Brecht's key devices in achieving this effect included estrangement/alienation.
6 See, for example, *The Sopranos* episode 'Funhouse' (2:13), in which modernist sequences are inserted to foreground the psychological turmoil of Tony Soprano as he realizes that he will have to 'whack' his long-time friend and colleague, Sal 'Big Pussy' Bonpensiero.
7 The aesthetic tradition of 'realism' is examined closely in Chapter 5.

3

COMPLEX SERIALS AND
QUESTIONS OF AUTHORSHIP

Introduction

This chapter investigates the relationships that complex serial dramas have forged with authorship. The formal and cultural distinctions of complex serials owe much to their conceptual innovation, crucial to which has been the relative creative freedom that is often acknowledged by the originators of these dramas to develop and pursue a particular, and sometimes personal, concept.[1] This process begins with the writing of the pilot, a vital document because it establishes the narrative parameters for the serial, enabling its concept to be communicated to others. What follows are creative processes which, albeit led by a creative individual or duo, involve a larger complement of executive producers, writers, directors, designers and editors, who work collaboratively. Even though the episode volume of complex serials has been somewhat lower (averaging 10–13 episodes per season) than for broadcast drama series (averaging 22–26 episodes), even a 10-episode season of high-end serial drama imposes a challenging and relentless pace for the completion of such key processes as 'breaking story',[2] script-writing, set design, production and post-production, whose investment of time per on-screen minute looks frenzied when compared with the equivalent processes for theatrical feature films (DelValle, 2008). Underscored by the necessity for delegation, specialization and close collaboration in completing these creative tasks to the desired quality, in complex serials it is a practical impossibility for there to be instances of authorship akin to the extent and/or nature of individual creative expression that has been celebrated by 'auteur' theory.

Despite these constraints upon its practice, the idea of individual authorship for complex serial dramas has been strategically mobilized by networks and is frequently invoked by media industry commentators and TV critics. Working in tandem with the allure of the shows themselves, 'auteur' discourses are also produced by viewers. Highlighting the paradox represented by the rising influence of a 'cult of the author' in TV drama at a moment in history when 'auteur' theory has reached a nadir of influence in scholarly work, John Caughie (2007: 410) acknowledges that even as auteur-oriented criticism of screen production has been "slowly vanishing from academic debate", celebration of the individual 'auteur' has been evident "everywhere else – in publicity, in journalistic reviews, in television programmes, in film retrospectives, [as well as] in the marketing" of productions. Initiated by networks and embraced by viewers, 'auteur' discourses have been a notable feature of the promotion, reception and acclaim for the complex serials examined in this book. Accordingly, important questions for this chapter are those of why have 'auteur' discourses arisen in relation to complex serials, what authorship processes are central to the conception and writing of these serials, and how do these processes reconcile individual with collaborative contributions?

Cinema's Auteur Theory and 'Authored' TV Drama

Beginning in the late 1950s, cinema's "cult of the auteur" as Robert Stam (2000a: 83–84) terms it was indebted to the persuasive arguments of Andre Bazin, François Truffaut and Andrew Sarris in *Cahiers du Cinema*. Focusing upon the intrinsically talented theatrical feature film director, arguing that he/she is a creative artist rather than "merely the servant of a pre-existing text" (Stam, 2000a: 83), film auteur theory contends that the director exhibits a "recognisable stylistic and thematic personality" (ibid.: 84) allowing his/her successive works to be analyzed for their continuity. While 'auteur' claims are frequently made in relation to both American and non-American TV dramas, it has been considerably more difficult to apply cinema's auteur theory to the medium of television, particularly to shows whose multi-season lifespan and flagship functions entail a significant ongoing production output that may continue for many years.

In British television, 'auteur' discourses have been applied to short-form dramas with a notably 'art television' sensibility, as exemplified by the idiosyncratic and critically acclaimed collected works of such celebrated TV dramatists as Dennis Potter (see Cook, 1998; Caughie, 2000) and Stephen Poliakoff (see Nelson, 2007a; 2011). For Potter and Poliakoff, as considered television 'auteurs', this has not only involved a 'body of work' that is sourced to them individually through the evidence of a common thematic and stylistic 'signature', but also the successful challenging (as a consequence of their authorial primacy) of established conceptual, generic and narrative conventions. Historically crucial to this achievement for Potter and Poliakoff has been the philosophical support for creative risk-taking that the BBC's public service broadcasting (PSB) remit and non-commercial schedules have permitted. For Potter and Poliakoff alike, PSB ideals and resources have helped to ensure the institutional facilitation of individual authorship through their attainment of what Caughie (2000: 128) describes as "a certain power, a freedom of manoeuvre which allows the truly creative artist to rewrite the rules". Finally, important to the potentials for individual authorship has been the diversity of TV drama form that is possible when shows are produced for non-commercial schedules and in accordance with traditional public service ideals.[3] Since the 1980s, the key format for individually authored British TV dramas has been the mini-serial, a high-end form distinguished by its paucity of episodes and historic confinement to one season. Suggesting that individual authorship is possible for mini-serials because of their limited number of episodes is that such leading BBC examples of it as *Boys From the Blackstuff* (1982), *The Singing Detective* (1986) and *Our Friends in the North* (1996) comprise 5–9 episodes each.

When produced for American networks this mini-serial form has been labeled the 'mini-series'.[4] It has entailed single or dual authorship, and been influential in two different phases of TV's evolution. Yielding a large volume of examples, the first occurred during the peak of the so-called 'classic network' era, with iconic examples in *Rich Man, Poor Man* (ABC, 1976), *Roots* (ABC, 1977) and *Holocaust* (NBC, 1978). The second arrived in the early 2000s, when successive critically acclaimed examples – notably *The Corner* (2000), *Band of Brothers* (2001), *Angels in America* (2003), *Generation Kill* (2008), *The Pacific* (2010) and *Mildred Pierce* (2011) – were produced for HBO. Notwithstanding HBO's own attempts to revive the American mini-serial, it struggled to maintain a regular presence on broadcast television as multi-channel competition intensified from the 1980s. Whilst this same competition fueled the expansion of American Quality Drama (AQD), as discussed in Chapter 2, it also entailed an increased reliance on long-format dramas that promised seasonal continuity.

Outside of the mini-serial, it has been very difficult for American TV dramatists to either assemble or to individually control the 'body of work' considered to constitute an authorial oeuvre. As suggested above, the primary cause is the high volume of episodes and seasonal longevity expected of American TV dramas. Although the output expectations for this drama are changing in the multiplatform era – influenced partly by the critical and popular success of the shorter seasons that are characteristic of complex serials – broadcast drama series and serials continue to be subject to what, when compared with the PSB-infused TV drama paradigms of Britain and Europe, is still an unusually high episode output. Indicative AQD examples include *NYPD Blue* (with 12 seasons and a total of 261 episodes), *CSI* (15 seasons and 337 episodes), *Desperate Housewives* (8 seasons and 180 episodes) and *House MD* (8 seasons and 177 episodes). This linking of limitations on authorship practices to broadcast network expectations for a high and continuing output for successful flagship dramas is not intended to diminish the achievement of the concept creators, showrunners and executive producers of these shows, but rather to underline the practical barriers in drama productions of this scale to the creative primacy of any single author.

Authorship in Long-Format TV Drama

While 'short-format' dramas[5] are most likely to provide opportunities for individual authorship, American television since the 1960s and in the context of increasing commercial pressure has preferred to commission TV drama as long-format programming, whose concepts are conducive to schedule continuity and longevity over multiple seasons. Long-format TV drama production is not only writer-driven and producer-led but also involves the contributions of a group of senior producers usually called executive producers (EPs). It is because of the episode volume and multi-season longevity of long-format TV drama that there has been a notable lack of fit between theatrical feature film and television manifestations of authorship. Informed by the creative conditions for long-format TV drama in particular, Jane Shattuc (2005: 147) contends: "The auteur theory when applied to TV is a highly romanticized worldview and a naïve account of the dictates of commercial production".

Whereas the unique vision and contribution of the director can be a dominant and determining force in the creation of a theatrical feature film, television directors work for executive producers and the pace of long-format drama production requires contributions from several directors, each taking responsibility for a group of episodes. TV drama directors are responsible for the visualization, style and performances of their allocated episodes, but an EP's oversight of the show, either for a specified season or in its entirety, means that his/her responsibilities begin well before production (in concept design, casting, budgeting, script development), continue throughout production (script-writing, design, shooting), and extend through post-production (editing, soundtrack, digital effects). Senior EPs are also responsible to the commissioning network for the delivery of the completed episodes on time and within budget. The reconciliation of creative ambition with the limitations of budget begin when the show's writers gather to 'break' (or conceive the outlines for) a new season of episodes. Foregrounding the linkages between script-writing and production budget, Matt Weiner, creator, showrunner and EP of *Mad Men* explains that:

> I feel like good writers are good producers. When you are writing a script, you're thinking about how big it is, how it's going to work. What really has been the big lesson for me in all of this is thinking about how to save money while you're writing. Thinking about how to give the audience something amazing in a reasonable way.
>
> *(Cited in Green, 2009: 13)*

Weiner's comments underline that script-writing and production, albeit different phases in the creation of a TV drama, ideally entail a continuity of personnel across the key creative activities of writing, producing and directing. In *Breaking*

Bad, for example, the seven staff writers not only worked as EPs for this show, but were also in attendance on set to advise the directors and actors when the episodes they had individually scripted were being shot (Moira Walley-Beckett, cited in Connor interview, 2014).

Another significant difference between theatrical film and TV drama manifestations of authorship arises from the auteur theory's requirement for evidence of a directorial 'signature' across a 'body of work' created by the same individual. The stylistic signature of a film director has a counterpart in the so-called artistic 'vision' and 'voice' that an individual writer-producer can bring to TV drama. However, the auteur theory's requirement for this to be identifiable across a 'body of work' presents a particular challenge in respect of long-format TV drama, whose production is subject to editorial input from network executives, to expectations for shows to serve a particular channel brand, and also (in many cases) to the consumerist ideology and demands of advertisers.

Authorship discourses in American TV drama have been constructed for such writer-producers as Steven Bochco, Stephen J. Cannell, Dick Wolf, David E. Kelley, David Milch, Alan Ball, David Simon and Joss Whedon, whose creative leadership of successive TV drama productions provides a counterpart to the 'body of work' required of celebrated screen auteurs. Even though it has been possible for some of these creators to develop an authorial signature on the basis of a continuity of conceptual, thematic and/or aesthetic features across different productions, for others this has been more difficult due to the historic tendency for TV drama writer-producers to develop their careers as writers and EPs by working on productions helmed by others. Creators and showrunners Tom Fontana (*Oz*), David Chase (*The Sopranos*), Alan Ball (*Six Feet Under*), David Milch (*Deadwood*), Matt Weiner (*Mad Men*), Vince Gilligan (*Breaking Bad*) and Terence Winter (*Boardwalk Empire*) had all written and/or produced long-running TV shows prior to creating and leading the production of complex serials. Although through this work they gained invaluable groundings, the necessity to serve the conceptual 'vision' of another executive producer could also be limiting and frustrating, especially where it also involved confronting the creative constraints of advertiser-funded broadcast TV. There is an overt example in David Chase, whose career was forged in broadcast TV drama, yet who felt compromised by values that jarred with his own ideology and whose pre-HBO experiences led him to conclude: "The function of hour-drama on network TV is to reassure the American people that it's O.K. to go out and buy stuff" (Heffernan, 2004). There is another in Alan Ball, for whom the frustrations of broadcast TV arose from persistent network 'meddling' in the content of scripts (Weinraub, 2001). Both examples testify to talented writer-producers feeling undermined by a lack of creative autonomy and the capacity for self-expression, as well as by problems arising from the consumerist orientation of advertiser-funded broadcast TV schedules.

TV Drama and Authorship in a Producer-Led Medium

Whereas auteur theory's arguments about the creative prominence and 'signature' of individuals have centered on the achievements of film directors, the creative hierarchy of television has been dominated by producers. Characterizing television as a "producer's medium" (Newcomb and Alley, 1983: xii), this explanation from Les Brown (cited in Newcomb and Alley, 1983: 8) highlights the traditional expectation that TV projects are led by producers:

> The producer is the person in charge of a TV production, who establishes the working spirit and dictates the standards to be met. Ideally, as head of the creative team: the producer is both businessman and artist, caring about administration and budgetary details while nurturing the talent and providing the vision for the project.

Despite the many continuities with Brown's historical characterization of the role of TV producers, the ongoing narrative and budgetary challenges of high-end, long-format drama imbue it with some specificities. While the above combination of responsibilities continues to reflect the breadth of responsibility for today's EPs, the creative leadership of TV drama centers on the foremost EP, or 'showrunner'. A more consistent feature of the multiplatform era than it has been historically, the contemporary showrunner attains this role primarily based on the talent they have demonstrated as a creator and writer.

The value of creative leadership by something akin to a showrunner was demonstrated in early AQD productions, the first example of which was the leadership model used by Steven Bochco on *Hill Street Blues* (1981–87), and his own response to the "breakneck pace" of work to produce the first 38 *Hill Street* episodes in just eighteen months (Martin, 2013: 30). Distinctive to the showrunner role as Bochco embodied it was not only the delegation of key creative tasks to other EPs but also sustained, hands-on leadership of the writing. As Brett Martin explains:

> Since he was spending so much time with the writers, Bochco deputized an executive producer whose job it was to oversee shooting on set and all other production issues, leaving him free to concentrate on scripts. And since no director popping in to direct a single episode could be expected to know the full backstory, or what might be important three or four or more episodes down the line, he instituted what came to be known as 'tone meetings'. These are conferences at which the writers, director and production staff all come together to pore over the complexities of each script in fastidious detail.
>
> *(Ibid.)*

Even if the role that Bochco pioneered was not yet called 'showrunner', the creative leadership model it entailed became important not so much because the size and scale of AQD dramas was significantly greater than their 'regular drama' counterparts, but because of the tendency of their episodes to incorporate serial strands. Compounded by the associated challenges of narrative continuity, multi-plot density and the new significance of character 'development arcs', the addition of serial subplots into AQD dramas brought greater complexity to their writing processes, a larger proportion of which would now occur collaboratively in the 'writers' room'.

As serials rather than series,[6] and narratively complex rather than narratively conventional,[7] complex serials have entailed an even higher level of reliance than AQD dramas on collaborative work and 'breaking story' inside the 'writers' room'. Yet helping to fuel the development of 'auteur' discourses around successive complex serials has been the tendency of their showrunners to not only devise the concept (as evidenced by their individual authoring of the 'pilot' script), but to also helm the production (as head writer and foremost EP) from the first to the last episode.

This pattern is exemplified by *The Sopranos*, whose concept first began to form when David Chase was himself in therapy and the people closest to him responded to the stories he told them about his mother. Detailing the thought process from which sprang the conceptual core of *The Sopranos*, Chase (cited in Lawson interview, 2007: 210–11) explains:

> [M]y wife, Denise, had told me since forever, 'You need to write about your mother. Your mother is money in the bank' ... And then someone who worked with me on *Almost Grown* said the same thing. Said something like 'You should do a story about a TV producer with this mother like yours'. And I thought, 'Why would anybody want to see that? A TV producer with a sort of crazy overbearing mother'. I couldn't ... Then something made me think ... that it might be funny to do a story about a guy who was a lot tougher than me. A lot more masculine tough, savage. All those things with a mother like that ... And so I thought it could be interesting if the guy was a mobster ...

The origination of a distinctive drama concept by the same person who, as with Chase, then takes creative leadership of the subsequent production, from beginning to end, has been the predominant model of authorship for complex serials to date. Central to perceptions of authorship in the broadest sense, Robin Nelson (2011: 52) suggests, is evidence of "an integrity sustained by the controlling vision and execution of an individual artist". As the individual who conceived *The Sopranos*, led its writing processes and also helmed the ongoing production as its senior EP and showrunner, David Chase is undeniably its foremost author. However, there is still some distance between Chase's creative leadership of *The Sopranos* and auteur theory's insistence on the presence of a thematic or stylistic 'signature' that can be traced across different productions.

Authorship Discourses and American TV Drama

Authorship discourses in American TV drama first emerged in the 1950s in relation to the creators of such acclaimed single plays as Paddy Chayefsky's *Marty* (1953) and Rod Serling's *Requiem for a Heavyweight* (1956). But as television refocused its schedules on the perceived preferences of a mass audience, this first wave of 'authored' American drama fell victim to increased network control of TV schedules and the decline of live plays packaged into anthologies in favor of filmed drama series (Boddy, 1993). Authorship discourses re-emerged in American television with the inception of the AQD paradigm, assisted by the critical acclaim achieved by successive dramas (Thompson, 1996). However, of all AQD shows that achieved such acclaim, the most overt precedent for the celebration of individual authorship that has also been a feature of complex serials was *Twin Peaks* (1990–91).

Occasioned by the creative contributions of celebrated film director David Lynch, it was promoted as "David Lynch's *Twin Peaks*", "the series that will change TV" and "the most original show on TV" (cited in Collins, 1995: 343–44), all of which played to the avant-garde reputation that Lynch had earned in theatrical feature films. While it was not unusual for AQD shows to have a named writer-producer, different here was that *Twin Peaks* was promoted as 'art television' and 'authored drama', on the basis of the auteur status that Lynch had achieved as a director of cinematic features. *Twin Peaks* was treated as another feature film in Lynch's surrealist oeuvre, as exemplified by *The New Yorker*'s assertion that "within five minutes of the opening of *Twin Peaks* we know we're in David Lynch's world – unmistakable even on a small screen" (Collins, 1995: 344). Moreover, *Twin Peaks* was promoted as Lynch's work, even though its serial narrative was conceived and written as a collaboration between Lynch and Mark Frost (Chion, 1995: 100), important to which were the latter's well-honed TV writing credentials.

Authorship discourses around TV dramas have become more rather than less prevalent in the multiplatform era, as one characterized by an unprecedented abundance of programming, an enlarged range of exhibition/consumption outlets for this, and a vastly increased 'afterlife' for TV dramas, especially for serials. In this context, authorship discourses have provided ways "to distinguish certain kinds of television from others" (Newman and Levine, 2012: 38) and have been a notable feature of the branding, discussion and reception of complex serials. As revealed by *The Sopranos*, complex serials have entailed a process that Robin Nelson (2011) terms 'author(iz)ation', in recognition of the attempt to discursively frame and celebrate individual creative achievement in ways comparable to the auteur theory's claims for cinema. Continuing the pattern started with *Twin Peaks*, such 'author(iz)ation' has sometimes entailed the disavowal of this drama's identity and function as TV programming. Characterized by a tendency in some circles to celebrate it as a non-televisual text, *The Sopranos* provides a case in point, the acclaim of its reviewers and adulation of fans gaining initial impetus from HBO's 'Not TV' marketing campaign. The 'author(iz)ation' of David Chase with *The Sopranos* is not directly comparable to that of Lynch with *Twin Peaks*, particularly given Chase's extensive prior experience in TV drama rather than cinema. Yet the valorization of their shows as 'non-televisual' was common to the promotion and reception of both.

The construction and representation of Chase as sole author of *The Sopranos* initiated the tendency to develop similar discourses around the creator-showrunners of other complex serials. However, such discourses have also been embraced, extended and circulated by audiences. New in TV's multiplatform era is the capacity for authorship discourses to be mobilized across the many internet pages that are devoted to an unfolding TV drama. These combine fan-initiated with institutional websites, discussions and details, and also build momentum as shows develop and endure. Helping to fuel a pattern of audience engagement with authorship discourses for complex serials are the many 'paratexts' (Genette, 1997; Gray, 2010) that circulate around them, including trailers, behind-the-scenes footage and interviews with showrunners, writers and other creative contributors. As Nelson (2011: 43) acknowledges, the 'author(iz)ation' of Chase gained significant velocity from the potentials of the internet to construct fan communities, important to which is the former's capacity to "mobilise, build, and disseminate worldwide [the] valorization of a TV show". Encouraged by media reportage and informed by the successive interviews in which Chase was presented as *The Sopranos*' author, fans exhibited what Nelson describes as "a disposition to celebrate the imagination" of Chase individually (ibid.) as an outlet for their devotion to the show.

Authorship Discourses as a Source of Cultural Distinction in HBO's Drama Strategy

Chris Anderson (2008: 23) argues that HBO's move into original TV drama was augmented by an active marketing campaign whose purpose was to produce "an Aristocracy of Culture" for the network and its dramas. Authorship discourses, as stimulated by network promotions and paratexts, were integral to this achievement. It is significant that HBO's entry to original long-format drama occurred in the period 1996–99 which, albeit a pivotal phase of American TV's 'multichannel transition' (Lotz, 2007a), was a phase in which TV drama was still defined by the offerings of advertiser-funded broadcast networks in the absence of any "word-of-mouth-generating" alternatives (ibid.: 153). Even though several cable networks were making their own forays into drama in these years, HBO's additional challenge (shared only by its subscription-funded rival, Showtime) was that of how to position itself and its dramas in the American market in ways that could increase subscriber numbers and minimize churn. HBO's response to this challenge, Anderson (2008: 35) suggests, "was to translate the reputation for quality earned by its award-winning movies into the realm of [long-format] television, while making this distinction salient for the upper-middle-class viewers who were its most likely subscribers". Accordingly, HBO's move into original TV drama entailed the strategic decision not to replicate the 'upscale' and 18–49 audience appeals of AQD shows, but instead to create a 'high art' form that was imbued for appeal to the "better-educated, slightly older men and women aged 35 to 55" (Meisler, 1998: 48) that were HBO's existing subscribers. Five elements progressed this HBO drama strategy, of which one was the active generation of a brand 'aura' that centered on auteur-like discourses, with the other four being important in enabling these discourses.

First was HBO's welcoming of drama writer-producers whose original ideas appeared sufficiently conducive to establishing a point of difference from broadcast TV dramas. Beginning with Tom Fontana, David Chase, Alan Ball, David Simon/Ed Burns and David Milch, HBO chose passionate writers whose previous work had either associated them with critical acclaim (as with Chase and Ball) and/or demonstrated an idiosyncratic quality or viewpoint (as with Fontana, Milch and Simon/Burns). Common to this first group of complex serial creator-showrunners, however, was experience forged in broadcast television. While their shared frustration with and/or alienation from broadcast TV rendered HBO enticing, the attraction was mutual for HBO's commissioning executives Chris Albrecht and Carolyn Strauss. Their appreciation of HBO's position as the "black-box theater", rather than "the main stage" of American television (Strauss, cited in Sepinwall, 2012: 24), produced a commissioning context in which critical success was integral to the desired outcomes. Hence conceptual and formal innovation in hour-long drama was unusually possible. Both were achieved by HBO's first slew of original TV dramas. These combined the long-format examples of *Oz*, *The Sopranos*, *Six Feet Under*, *The Wire* and *Deadwood* with a succession of mini-serials.

Second was HBO's construction of authorship discourses around these writer-producers. As Anderson (2008: 36) observes:

> HBO promotes the creators of the drama series and encourages reporters to flesh out their biographies so that the public learns to identify the artistic vision of a single creator behind each series, no matter the scale and complexity of the production or the number of people involved in bringing it to the screen.

This foregrounding of individuals served HBO's overall strategy by assisting it to differentiate itself from other cable networks and, more crucially, from broadcasters. Linking named creative work to perceptions of artistry in television, Newman and Levine (2012: 40) observe that the "identification of more aesthetically distinguished programs with the artists credited with imagining and producing them validates some kinds of television, making these instances fit within traditional conceptions of art". In HBO's case this 'author(iz)ing' of drama creators (Nelson, 2011) worked to expand its cultural reputation, subscriber base and revenues. As Albrecht explains: "The product we sell is HBO the network. You can't buy a piece of it. You have to buy it all" (cited in Anderson, 2008: 29). HBO used auteur-like discourses around its original dramas to cultivate a 'high culture' status for its brand. The effect was to entice 'upscale' viewers seeking to align themselves with programming whose 'art television' reputation offered an elitist contrast to universally available 'ordinary' television.

Third was HBO's decision to invest to secure a higher visual/aural quality in its dramas that would appear more consistent with the high-end production values of its original telefilms. It managed this by reducing the volume of episodes per season and increasing the level of expenditure per episode to a level well above what broadcasters and their studios were spending at the time (Edgerton, 2008: 8). Following a pattern of expenditure that began with *The Sopranos*, the episode budget for *Deadwood* (2003–05) averaged around US$4.5 million per episode, a figure that Anderson (2008: 35) estimates to be "twice the average of even the most expensive [broadcast] series" at this point. This comparison is supported by a 2006 industry estimate that US$2-3 million per episode represented the average cost for hour-long primetime drama (Higgins, 2006). As HBO reacted to increased non-broadcast network competition in drama and strategized to extend the 'art television' reputation it earned with shows like *The Sopranos* and *Deadwood*, it was willing to invest even more for dramas it saw as pivotal to this outcome. Arguing the unusual aesthetic ambition and achievement of *Boardwalk Empire* (2010–14), Janet McCabe (2013: 186) registers that its "lavish 80-minute pilot", this "allegedly the most expensive ever made in television history", was considered to have cost as much as US$18 million. Initially a point of difference for HBO originals, more generous budgets facilitate longer shooting schedules, an increased proportion of location scenes, period settings and/or a meticulous attention to the details of design and verisimilitude, all of which have helped to characterize and distinguish complex serial dramas to date.

Fourth, and directly facilitated by the increased production time and aesthetic ambition the third strategy made available, was the aspiration of HBO dramas more consistently toward the extreme high-end of the production spectrum, and, with this, to include scenes that are sometimes described as 'cinematic', a term that recognizes a "film look in television" (Caldwell, 1995: 5). Within TV industries, the 'high-end' tag has provided a way to differentiate high-budget and 'prestige' drama productions from their counterparts in the middle or low-budget areas of the investment spectrum for drama. The least expensive form of TV drama is best exemplified by the daily format of the 'continuing soap opera', whose production time and costs are significantly reduced by the reliance on a multi-camera, studio-shot mode of production, as one involving a 'naturalistic' aesthetic and style of performance. In contrast, the 'high-end' label recognizes the aesthetic qualities and subtleties that are achievable through the use of 35mm film or its nearest HD digital counterparts, the use of cinematographers to develop and achieve the desired 'look' of the show, the deployment of location as well as studio-shot scenes, and a single-camera mode of production. Although the term 'high-end' refers to high production value TV drama more broadly, an additional feature of complex serial drama as HBO pioneered it has been a particular interest in visual storytelling.

Fifth was the branding of cultural distinction for HBO's original dramas, crucial to which was its 1996 adoption of the moniker 'It's Not TV. It's HBO'. This exhumed historic perceptions of television as the cultural inferior of theatrical cinema as well as invoking longstanding aesthetic differences between TV dramas and feature films. *The Sopranos* was not only the first HBO TV drama to deploy this moniker but was also an ideal exemplification of the alternative concept, style and form that might be expected of a drama branded as 'Not TV'. Although HBO's moniker is accurately described as "nothing more than a marketing strategy" (Newcomb, 2007: 561), it gained symbolic weight from its deployment together with the other elements of HBO's strategy outlined here. In this company, the 'Not TV' tag implied that HBO dramas were, as Edgerton (2008: 9) puts it, "a qualitative cut above your usual run-of-the-mill television programming", a perception substantiated by the critical acclaim and iconic status that *The Sopranos* went on to achieve.

Complex Serial Authorship and the Writers' Room

> It is increasingly clear (not just from observing the production process but also from widely available items such as DVD 'behind the scenes' bonus materials) that writers now function as the creative heads in television. I am intrigued why researchers pay little attention to writers but much to producers. Writers usually take on the title of 'producer' as they are promoted through the ranks of the writing staff, yet their primary responsibilities still revolve around their roles in writing and managing the story.
>
> *Felicia D. Henderson*[8]

Henderson's assertions about the importance of "writing and managing the story" to the success of TV drama are especially accurate for complex serials, mitigated by their conceptual idiosyncrasies, serial continuity across successive seasons and their marked narrative complexity (as will be examined next chapter). TV drama writers gained greater prominence and influence in the period 1980–95, as one of 'multi-channel transition' (Lotz, 2007a) in which the AQD paradigm emerged and flourished, fueled by inter-network competition for the most desirable audiences. While writers' rooms were introduced to television in the 1960s as the most efficient way to devise episodes for soap operas and sitcoms, they became a necessary strategy for high-end drama productions as AQD's writer-producers found ways to manage the significant creative challenges of the 22–26 episode seasons still preferred by broadcast networks.

The use of writers' rooms for American TV drama was necessitated, in particular, by AQD's tendency to deploy multiple interweaving storylines and serial subplots. This increased density of storylines was keyed to broaden the demographic appeals of AQD shows (across the 18–49 demographic range), and serial subplots were incorporated as a means to incentivize and reward regular viewing. Accordingly, AQD's narrative strategies represented a significant departure from the A/B/C storyline simplicity and episodic structure of 'regular drama', as explained in Chapter 2.

The move to a more collaborative model for the writing of long-format TV drama started with AQD pioneer, *Hill Street Blues*, initiated by Steven Bochco, its co-creator, senior EP and head writer. As the AQD paradigm expanded within American TV drama, its facets of multi-plot density and serial subplots meant that responsibility for episode scripts could no longer be delegated to freelancers, instead needing to be conceived by a regular group of staff writers who would work for a proportion of their time in the committee-like setting of a writers' room. EP and head writer of *ER* in the 1990s (having earlier created *China Beach*), John Wells, suggested that this approach of 'team-writing' was necessitated by the high volume of writing required to sustain the delivery of 22–26 episodes per season. Introducing 'team-writing' to non-American TV writers and producers at a conference in Spain, Wells (1996: 196) explained that:

> What we try to do in America is work as a group, so that it's not one individual writer who writes the entire show, but 6-8 people who are all, at any moment, able to write the show. We do that by everyone working on the stories from the very beginning of the process, so that if I decide that I'm not able to finish my script because of the time-table of another script that I'm working on, I can hand over a scene or two, or an act or storyline, to another writer in my group, who is able to finish it … It's not unusual therefore, for the stories to be created as a group, for a writer to be assigned one script to write, then a different one to rewrite, while someone else might be rewriting the script that you wrote the teleplay for in the first place.

'Team-writing' has since become highly characteristic of long-format TV drama, both within and beyond American television. However, the narrative strategies that distinguish complex serials (to be examined in Chapter 4) require a particular approach to team-writing. Hence the purposes and dynamics of the 'writers' room' as used for complex serials are central to understanding how their authorship reconciles the contributions of the creator-showrunner with those of the small group of writers who are selected by this showrunner to work together to conceive, write and manage the details of the ongoing story. By examining what happens in the writers' room of a complex serial, this section aims to answer the specific questions posed at the outset of this chapter, as to what approaches lie behind the distinctions of this drama form, and what kind of authorship model these processes reflect.

The establishment of a writers' room is preceded by the pivotal processes of concept creation, successful pitches to both studio and network investors, followed by the writing of a pilot script and a network's 'greenlighting' of a drama's first season. These early processes, albeit still subject to network executive 'notes' on scripts, are led by what is usually one individual, the creator-showrunner.[9] Notwithstanding the individual agency that is crucial to their commissioning, complex serials have involved three main approaches to concept design. One is the devising of an original concept (exemplified by *The Sopranos*, *Deadwood*, *The Wire*, *Mad Men*, *Boardwalk Empire*, *Breaking Bad* and *Stranger Things*). Another is the adaptation for television of an existing source (exemplified by *True Blood*, *Dexter*, *Game of Thrones*, *The Walking Dead* and *The Handmaid's Tale*). The final approach is the format adaptation of a non-American original (exemplified by *Homeland* and *House of Cards*). Despite these differences, common to all three approaches is the tendency for concepts to be devised by the same individual who authors the pilot script and, after securing the network 'greenlight', undertakes the role of showrunner, a crucial element of which is the role of 'head writer', or the person who selects the writers, convenes the writers' room and retains editorial control of the episode scripts. But what is a writers' room and how does it operate?

The authorship of a complex serial entails an overlapping set of processes whose point of departure and most crucial contributor is usually the writers' room. Inside, led by the showrunner-head writer, a handpicked group of around seven writers works out the narrative details of season, episode, characters and individual story beat. The process that lasts the longest is 'breaking story', which is regarded by writers as the most creatively demanding and most crucial to the narrative strategies that distinguish complex serial drama, the process in which story threads are devised, debated, decided upon and developed. Important for its significant contribution to the authorship of complex serials, 'breaking story' is also a particularly vivid example of the dynamics and benefits of collaborative authorship. Beau Willimon, creator/showrunner for *House of Cards* and one-time art student, explains the significance of 'breaking story' using the analogy of painting a masterpiece on canvas. "When you paint", observes Willimon, "you don't paint one little area in fine detail and leave the rest undone. You kind of have to paint within the whole canvas at the same time and the detail is arrived at by layers" (Willimon, *TV Writer Podcast*, 2013). The process of 'breaking story' is described by *Breaking Bad* writer Moira Walley-Beckett (cited in Connor interview, 2014):

> [Writers] sit in a room together for what seems like centuries and riff intensely on the characters, who they are, and what their backgrounds are. [A]fter a period of global discussion about what should happen in say, the

entirety of Season One, then you start to break story more incrementally, meaning discussing what the plot elements are per episode. What's going to happen in episode one, what's going to happen in episode two, etc.

This 'breaking' process determines the composition of a season and then fragments it into workable components so that the necessary narrative details can be developed and agreed upon before script-writing proceeds. Notwithstanding the variation that is brought to it by the head writer, 'breaking' needs to be completed in sufficient detail for the individualized tasks that follow, in which one member of the writing team will work through the decisions made by the team to produce an episode script. The vehicle for this transference of information is a succession of large corkboards, each laden with index cards containing the narrative details that have been 'broken' during writers' room sessions. While one board shows the details of narrative developments for the particular season under construction, additional boards are produced as 'breaking' is completed, one for each episode. Brett Martin's description of the unfinished season board in *Breaking Bad*'s 'room' helps to demonstrate how 'season' and 'episode' details are interlinked:

> On the wall behind Gilligan was a large corkboard. Across the top were pinned thirteen index cards representing the thirteen episodes of the season. In rows beneath them, more neatly printed cards ... contained detailed story points ... Behind [Tom] Schnauz was another corkboard, representing episode 405. As the room worked through the episode, each beat or scene would be written on a card and pinned to the board. The last card was always pinned with a little ceremony that meant the episode was locked down.
>
> *(Martin, 2013: 271–72)*

Beau Willimon's account of how 'breaking story' operated for Netflix's *House of Cards* supports Martin's conviction that, in the case of complex serials, both the overall direction of each season's narrative and the key story beats for each episode are devised inside the writers' room. On *House of Cards*, for which Willimon was creator and showrunner from 2013 to 2016, the writing process began with the production of a large corkboard 'grid' whose index cards detailed the major story threads and characters for the season being devised, this representing two or three weeks of collaborative work for its staff writers. Willimon (*TV Writer Podcast*, 2013) describes the next stage of the 'breaking' process, which is devoted to the individual episodes:

> [T]hen you start diving into episodes, one at a time and you 'beat' those out, story thread by story thread ... And once you feel like you you've got those threads worked out, we then put them up on a board and start playing with

the chronological order, day one, day two, day three, four and five. How do these things line up? What's during the day? What's during the night? How do they happen? And you start to refine what those beats are.

For Vince Gilligan, creator-showrunner of AMC's *Breaking Bad*, 'breaking story' is the "heavy lifting" in TV drama creation (*Emmy Legends* interview, 2011). Even though the 'breaking story' process is followed by the allocation of episodes to individual staff writers who will then script them, this "heavy lifting" metaphor recognizes that the parameters for what each episode will bring to the 'overarching' story and to the current season need to be well-established before script-writing begins. This explains why, in contrast to Gilligan's sense that the 'breaking' process constitutes the "heavy lifting" of complex serial authorship, he characterizes script-writing as a task that is comparatively "carefree because I've got this outline … and I know what happens next" (ibid.).

For *Breaking Bad*, the episodes were 'broken' in 'the room' "in excruciating detail", according to Moira Walley-Beckett (cited in Connor interview, 2014). While Gilligan acknowledges the influence of his *X-Files* training on the model he used for *Breaking Bad*, there are several advantages to the potentials for 'complex seriality' (whose facets and strategies are examined in the next chapter) arising from a collaborative model of authorship. A collaborative approach means that ideas and decisions about the direction of the story are effectively 'pitched' to those seated in the writers' room, before being debated, revised if necessary and accepted by the whole group. Although the extent of authorial collaboration has varied between the different complex serials discussed in this book, more work by the writers together in the room is considered to maximize narrative coherence and reduce time spent revising and rewriting scripts. On this point, Gilligan registers that:

> There's no right way to do this job but I personally hate rewriting. It doesn't mean we don't do it, but I want to lessen it. I want to keep it to a minimum. I don't want one writer … finding [the story] in a draft; I want seven writers finding it in the room as much as possible".
>
> *(Inside the Writers' Room with Breaking Bad, 2014)*

Sam Catlin, who was one of these writers, estimated that as much as "75 percent of the work" of conceiving a *Breaking Bad* episode was completed "with all of us in the room", emphasizing that such close collaboration engenders a sense of ownership of the drama's story and characters by the writers as a group (ibid.). When more detail is 'broken' inside the writers' room it also means, as Gilligan emphasizes: "Anyone in the writers' room for the length of time it took to break that story can go off and write the particular episode. Everyone knows the story, they know it intimately, beat by beat, what's supposed to happen" (*Emmy Legends* interview, 2011). Of final importance to a successful 'breaking story' process for complex serials is the effort to create what TV writers call a 'safe room', meaning one in which writers feel sufficiently comfortable with each other to articulate their ideas. On this point, Gilligan's view is that:

> The 'room' has to be safe [because] everyone understands that positivity allows us all to be free in the room, because you never know where the idea that wins the day is going to come from. It could start off as the craziest idea you've ever heard.
>
> *(ibid.)*

This collaborative approach to story creation, as exemplified by the examples of *Breaking Bad* and *House of Cards*, highlights that, in complex serials, the process of finding and creating the story centers not on the writing of full scripts by individual members of the writing team but on 'breaking story' at the writers' room table. As *Breaking Bad* and *House of Cards* both suggest, the collaborative work completed inside 'the room' extends to creating the specifics of the individual 'story beats' that comprise a given episode, a process that consumes a large proportion of the total time allocated to the writing of a complex serial season. Yet, as the testimony of Gilligan, Willimon and other writers also shows, no two complex serials use the above process in identical ways. Informed and influenced by the preferences and the experience of the head writer, the key variation between different productions is that of how much detail TV drama writers will produce together in 'the room' before writers are allocated specific episodes and asked to produce a full script. The collaborative model represented by the writers' room and its pivotal 'breaking story' contributions to the authorship of the episodes are, in part, a necessary requirement of the 'complex seriality' that narratively distinguishes these dramas. Attributing the importance of collaborative writing directly to the degree of narrative complexity in a TV drama, Gilligan (*Emmy Legends* interview, 2011) underlines: "The shows I've worked on have been very complex, plot wise, very complex. And to that end you've got to know, you can't just sit down and write just a vague inspiration for an episode". More so than for other fiction forms, these characteristics make it particularly advantageous for complex serial episodes to be conceived and mapped out by writers working together, at the same time as making it difficult (if not inefficient or troublesome) for the writers of these episodes to be 'breaking' stories alone.

Case Study of *Breaking Bad*

Like most other complex serials discussed in this book, *Breaking Bad* began as an idea for a new drama that was conceived by one writer-producer before being successfully pitched to studio and network investors, whereupon a pilot script was written. For Vince Gilligan, the idea for *Breaking Bad* germinated from feelings of uncertainty, including fears of failure. A film school graduate, Gilligan had learned his TV drama strategies writing for *The X-Files*. By 2004, when the idea for a new show was triggered by a fanciful conversation with fellow *X-Files* writer Tom Schnauz, he was about to turn 40 and had been without a regular job for two years (Gillian, cited in Brooker interview, 2013). The idea for a drama that centered on a methamphetamine cook arose with Schnauz's mention of a news article he'd read about a recent drug bust. Also unemployed, Schnauz joked that if nothing turned up they could always buy an RV and make a living out of cooking methamphetamine. Within a few days of this conversation, Gilligan had phoned Schnauz to gain his approval to use this conversation as the basis from which to develop a new show (Pierson, 2014a: 3). What followed was the creation of a concept whose point of difference within TV drama was that its central character would be subjected to a rapid and extreme transformation. In contrast to Tony Soprano and Don Draper, whose characters are established in the pilot episode and do not radically change as the narrative progresses, Walter White (Bryan Cranston) moves from law-abiding citizen into ruthless drug lord, a transformation that begins in the pilot and continues throughout *Breaking Bad*'s subsequent five seasons. Boiling his idea down to the simple one-sentence pitch that his film school training had suggested was most advantageous (Brooker interview, 2013), Gilligan's successful pitch to Sony Television executives Zack Van Amberg and Jamie Erlicht promised to turn a 'Mr. Chips' type central character into one more akin to 'Scarface' (ibid.).

It was out of Gilligan's anxieties about how to enlist sympathy for what viewers were expected to perceive as a seriously transgressive character that key elements of the pilot episode took shape. First is the wide shot that opens the episode, in which a pair of trousers falls slowly into the frame to land on a remote desert road, right into the path of a rampaging RV (a 1986 Fleetwood Bounder), which swerves to a sudden stop. Following his exit from the RV, Walter's desert surroundings, odd ensemble and look of sheer panic evoke black comedy. But his first lines – these narrated into the eye of his handycam, as he struggles to cope with the toxicity inside the RV, grabs a pistol from one of the bodies on the floor of the vehicle, and tearfully films a hasty message to family – situate Walter as an ordinary man, unaccustomed to the criminal activity in which he is clearly implicated:

> My name is Walter Hartwell White. I live at 308 Negra Arroyo Lane, Albuquerque, New Mexico, 87104. To all law enforcement entities, this is not an admission of guilt. I am speaking to my family now. Skyler, you are the love of my life; I hope you know that. Walter Junior, you're my big man. There … are going to be some things that you'll come to learn about me in the next few days. I just want you to know that no matter how it may look, I only had you in my heart. Goodbye.

A moment of frantic activity and peak emotional intensity for the episode to follow, this scene positions Walter as the perennial 'fish out of water', in this case, a middle-aged man who unexpectedly finds himself in a criminal milieu. In formal terms, the scene also foregrounds the commitment to non-linear storytelling that is a narrative characteristic of the show as a whole. As the first of *Breaking Bad's* many examples of 'in medias res' storytelling (whereby the action is initiated by an event plucked from somewhere in the middle of a chronological chain of events), this scene is keyed to entreat audience engagement in the dilemma that is Walter White's life.

The scenes that follow, which explain how Walter arrived in such a desperate situation, all take place on his fiftieth birthday, the 'special number' most symbolic of entry to middle age. Inviting audience identification and sympathy with Walter, these scenes offer a point-by-point depiction of the unrelenting struggle that constitutes his life. Following the various images of baby equipment, wall-color samples and Walt's feet pumping a low-budget StairMaster, the camera slows before cutting to an extreme close-up of a wall plaque. A certificate of merit from Los Alamos Research Center, dated 1985, it shows that Walter was once a Nobel prize-winning researcher in crystallography. The effect and intention of these initial scenes is to catalogue the daunting array of domestic and psychological conditions that motivate Walter's decision to 'break bad'. Once a cutting-edge researcher, he has been reduced to teaching chemistry basics to reluctant teenagers, a profession so poorly remunerated in post-neoliberal America that he must work additional daily hours at a carwash (see Pierson, 2014b). Regardless of how many hours he puts in, however, Walter cannot earn enough to meet his family's needs. Yet Skyler is pregnant with a late child and his teenaged son, Walter Junior, has cerebral palsy, so solutions to the financial pressures simply must be found. On top of this, Walter's collapse at the carwash culminates in a visit to the doctor whereupon he learns he has inoperable lung cancer and not long to live. Just when it seems that things cannot get much worse, Walter returns home to a surprise birthday celebration at which the jibes and boasts of Hank Schrader, his hyper-masculine brother-in-law who is an agent with the Drug Enforcement Agency, seem to underline how weak, ineffectual and expendable Walt has become as a man.

Gilligan's efforts to find a network buyer for *Breaking Bad* demonstrate that the idea of the central character becoming a meth cook was considered far too extreme for the majority of networks to which it was offered. Reflecting later on the challenge ahead for Gilligan, Bryan Cranston asserted that "had *Breaking Bad* been introduced as a pilot script in 2000, it wouldn't have seen the light of day. Television wasn't ready for it. It was still populated by all those old-fashioned shows like *ER*, which were dramatic, but safe" (cited in Turner, 2009). Helping ensure a successful outcome for Gilligan was that Sony Television already liked his work, were the first to hear his pitch and immediately gave it their confirmed support (*Emmy Legends* interview, 2011). With Sony on board, the idea was pitched to Showtime, TNT, HBO, FX and AMC in turn (ibid.). The reactions of the different network executives in this line-up confirm that, even in the context of cable rather than broadcast TV – the drama commissioning sector that had greenlit such 'edgy' properties as *Oz*, *The Sopranos*, *The Shield*, *The Wire* and *Dexter* up to this point – *Breaking Bad* was perceived to be an uncommonly risky proposition. TNT's reaction was one of the more positive that Gilligan remembers. Listening intently to his well-rehearsed account of the initial plot, Gilligan sensed they were "loving" it (ibid.). At the end of the pitch, however, as Gilligan recalls, "they looked at each other and said 'Oh God, I wish we could buy this … But if we [do] we will literally be fired" (ibid.). Indicative of the pressure on a TV drama creator to modify his idea rather than risk it being rejected or simply buried, the TNT executives added: "It can't be meth … Could the guy be a counterfeiter instead?" (ibid.).

Having taken the *Breaking Bad* idea "all over town" (Gilligan, cited in *Emmy Legends* interview, 2011), Gilligan and Sony finally found support from FX, which bought it, whereupon Gilligan wrote the full pilot episode. The final steps in *Breaking Bad*'s commissioning process illustrate how difficult it is to secure a 'greenlight' for a drama idea which, from a network perspective, must have seemed promising and daunting in equal measure. Although FX had bought the idea, having read the full script, its executives ultimately decided to 'pass'. But instead of refusing to sell the property and filing it away, as was its prerogative,[10] FX allowed AMC, a little-known but ambitious basic cable network, to purchase the idea and pilot (ibid.). AMC's strong cash-flow position supported the necessary level of investment and its move into original long-format dramas marked its ascent to the top tier of basic cable networks (Lafayette, 2009).

By the time *Breaking Bad* received its hard-won network greenlight, it was 2007. Although AMC was preparing to launch the 1960s' period drama that would significantly raise its profile, *Mad Men*'s first episode had yet to air. But AMC had its reasons for commissioning *Breaking Bad* when other networks were unwilling to take the risk. One factor was simply good timing by Gilligan and Sony. AMC had recently made an institutional commitment to the regular commissioning of original series dramas, and these would be selected to complement its acquired feature films. Having already chosen *Mad Men* as its first long-format drama, *Breaking Bad* appealed to AMC partly because its contemporary setting offered such a striking contrast and complement to *Mad Men*. Whereas *Mad Men*'s story unfolded in 1960s New York, *Breaking Bad*'s was set in contemporary American society. Common to both dramas, however, was a flawed, morally conflicted central character with traits that were keyed for appeal to the male-skewed audience already being delivered by AMC's movies (Pierson, 2014a). The fit between the macho drug world of *Breaking Bad* and AMC's distinctive brand of action-oriented movies was clear when, in preparation for the launch of *Breaking Bad*'s second season, it aired 'March Badness', a month-long festival of movies (Idov, 2011), including such titles as *Dirty Harry* and *Death Wish*, these chosen because of perceived connections between their anti-heroic protagonists and primary characters in *Breaking Bad* (ibid.). Although Gilligan had originally planned to shoot *Breaking Bad* in Riverside County, Los Angeles, the decision to relocate to New Mexico brought additional benefits that contributed to its success. Not only did New Mexico provide tax rebates to screen productions, which reduced *Breaking Bad*'s costs, this setting also encouraged it to cultivate the look of a contemporary Western (Gilligan, cited in Girardot, 2011). In contrast to Los Angeles, whose well-used landscapes are so familiar to film and TV audiences, Albuquerque's deserts, cacti and Sandia Mountains offered "something interesting and unique" (ibid.).

Despite *Breaking Bad*'s evident complementarity with the brand identity established by AMC's movies, its advertisers were initially "squeamish" about being associated with it (Carroll, cited in Consoli, 2011: 12). Yet, as explained in Chapter 1, advertising revenue is only part of a basic cable network's income. Once *Breaking Bad* gained critical recognition, with Bryan Cranston winning a best actor Emmy Award in the show's first year, advertiser jitters subsided (ibid.). Highlighting the positive reaction of AMC's advertisers, Ed Carroll, as COO at AMC Networks, observed that its critical success marked *Breaking Bad* as "a quality show for viewers" making its slot "a quality place to be for advertisers" (cited in Consoli, 2011: 12). Carroll's sense that the kind of 'quality' audience most attractive to advertisers could negate the effect of audience concerns about the 'edgy' content of *Breaking Bad* has since been reinforced by more recent perceptions of an 'upscale' appeal for complex serial dramas. Reflecting on the successes of both *Breaking Bad* and its spin-off prequel *Better Call Saul*, AMC's Scott Collins (cited in Lafayette, 2015: 21) observed that "it's less about the content and more about the viewer that is attracted to that show. *Breaking Bad* had a very affluent audience even though it was [set] in the world of crystal meth-making".

Having explored the conceptual and institutional elements that distinguish *Breaking Bad*, this discussion now turns to focus on the transformation of Walter White, as the most significant conceptual distinction and creative risk of the show overall. The extreme nature of this transformation, one without obvious precedent in long-format TV drama, took the very real risk of rendering Walter unlikeable and *Breaking Bad* unwatchable. As Gilligan saw it, the strategy was to enlist initial audience sympathy for Walt before gradually chipping away at this response so as to "get viewers questioning their allegiances" (cited in Brooker interview, 2013). While there are several key examples, the key turning point in the trajectory that sees Walter reveal his villainy, and viewers come under pressure to reconsider whether he still deserves their continued sympathy, occurs at the end of the second season in 'Phoenix' (2:12).

Making a visit to Jesse's house in 'Phoenix', Walter finds Jesse and his girlfriend Jane Margolis asleep, both comatose from heroin. Raising the stakes on how he reacts to what he finds is Jane's earlier threat to expose him unless he agrees to hand over the money he has been holding for Jesse. In Gilligan's view, there was sufficient motive for murder, hence he envisaged that Walt would administer a second dose of heroin and kill Jane deliberately. However, at the episode outline stage of the 'breaking' process, the scene initially envisaged became contentious, provoking a rare intervention from production executives and further debate by the writing team. As Gilligan recalled, this "was the one moment that both Sony and AMC called me up and said, 'This one makes us nervous'" (cited in Brooker interview, 2013). Testifying to AMC's non-interventionist approach, Gilligan added: "We'd done a lot before that moment that would have made a lot of networks nervous, so it's a credit to them that this [scene] was the one we had a big phone discussion about" (ibid.). AMC and Sony's concerns centered on how unsympathetic Walter might seem to viewers if he killed his partner's girlfriend to protect himself. Even though Walt's involvement in Jane's death is important in marking a new stage in his transformation, the writers worried that Walt's killing of Jane might be too much for viewers. Gilligan admitted to being "voted down" (ibid.) about what action Walter would take, and the scene was revised in the writers' room. Rather than acting to kill Jane or to intervene by turning her on her side, Walt's face conveys a moral battle with himself to refrain from doing anything. In consequence, Jane chokes to death while Jesse sleeps beside her, just as she would have done had Walter not been in the room.

Having opted not to save Jane, Walter unwittingly initiates a much larger crisis, the crash of a passenger airplane over Albuquerque, a catastrophe ostensibly involving the deaths of hundreds of people. The evident cause is the incorrect set of landing coordinates that were given to the plane's pilot by Jane's grieving father, Donald Margolis, the air traffic controller on duty at the time. A foremost example of *Breaking Bad*'s broader interest in narrative complexity, the linkage between Walt's inaction with Jane and the plane crash is anticipated by the 'cold open' scenes that introduce four of this season's thirteen episodes.[11] Additionally, each of the selected episodes bears a title – 'Seven Thirty-Seven' (2:1), 'Down' (2:4), 'Over' (2:10) and 'ABQ' (2:13) – to form a trail of clues. Compelling and disorientating in equal measure because they are placed outside of their narrative context, the four cold opens make up a montage of extreme close-ups in which debris from the plummeting airplane penetrates the surface of the White swimming pool. Appearing well out of context and difficult to comprehend on first viewing (underscored by the dominance of extreme close-ups and dearth of wide shots), these cold opens are distanced from the rest of Season 2's narrative through the use of monochrome. Focusing audience attention on the teddy bear, however, whose burned, disfigured body is a poignant signifier of the death of innocents, is that this object, afloat in a monochrome pool, appears in hot pink. The confluence of tragic occurrences that closes Season 2 underlines that Walter, even though he justifies his own actions in terms of the protection and preservation of his family, is already having a horrendous impact on the families of others.

Walter's transformation functions as *Breaking Bad*'s 'overarching' story, this term indicating not only that it progresses in every episode, but also that, as the central narrative, it subordinates all other subplots to its own requirements. Like *The Sopranos* and *Mad Men*, *Breaking Bad* folds together the functions of its overarching story and central character, but as highlighted above, that is where the similarity ends. The ongoing transformation of Walter in the direction of a 'Scarface'-like figure, a process during which viewers are encouraged to "[question] their allegiances" (Gilligan, cited in Brooker interview, 2013), required *Breaking Bad* writers to work in a notably collaborative manner to ensure that narrative developments could account for and explain Walter's actions. The objective, as underlined by Gilligan, was to retain the identification of viewers even as he loses their sympathy. 'Buried' (5:10) offers a reflexive acknowledgement of this particular challenge for the writers. The episode's context is the crisis that is unleashed for Walter and Skyler after Hank Schrader realizes that his brother-in-law is the drug lord 'Heisenberg'. Involving Walter and Saul Goodman, the conversation addresses the question of what should happen to Hank:

Saul: Have you given any thought to um, sending him on a trip to Belize?

Walt: Belize?

Saul: Yeah. Belize. Where Mike [Ermintrout] went to. Off on a trip to uh … Belize.

Walt: Saul, you'd better not be saying what I think you're saying …

Saul: It's just conjecture …

Walt: Hank is *family*!!! Don't you understand that?

Saul: Okay! But it's an option that's worked very well for you in the recent past …

Walt: Jesus, what is *wrong* with you?

Saul: My mistake. Family, off limits, of course!! I'm just throwing thoughts out there. This is a *safe room*, isn't it?

Through its articulation of the moral boundaries that stand to prevent the consignment of Hank, this conversation gives Walt the opportunity to declare, to the audience in particular, that, despite all he has done to this point, he is still worthy of their trust. Walter's faux outrage in this scene (which the camera captures in big close-up) recalls his emphatic denial to Jesse as to any involvement in the poisoning of Brock ('Face Off', 4:13). Because of this, the exchange contains a hint that, even as he declares his brother-in-law to be off-limits, the idea that Hank might take a trip to somewhere like 'Belize' has already crossed Walt's mind. Referring to the pitching of ideas in the 'safe room' created by *Breaking Bad*'s writers, this conversation reflexively mimics the kinds of debates that were occurring inside it. The testimony of *Breaking Bad*'s writers foregrounds the recurring questions of "Where is Walt's head at?" and "What will Walt do next?" (*Inside The Writers' Room with Breaking Bad*, 2014), questions that were also asked about Jesse and Skyler, whose individual transformations are instigated by Walt's actions. Revealing the priorities of Gilligan and his writers, these questions were crucial to "letting the characters tell us what the story should be, as opposed to making any rushed or arbitrary decision" (Walley-Beckett, cited in Connor interview, 2014). This strategy of "letting the characters tell us what the story should be" demonstrates that although *Breaking Bad*'s writers knew the endpoint toward which they were working with Walt's transformation, neither they nor their head writer and show-runner, Vince Gilligan, had advance knowledge as to when and how the changes would occur. Their fruitful collaboration, the details of which are typical of the authorship model so characteristic of complex serials, was pivotal to determining how Walter White would get to his destination (Heisenberg) and the extent to which he would bring viewers with him as he traveled there.

Conclusion

This chapter has examined the authorship of complex serial drama, with par-ticular interest in the demands upon TV writing and creativity that arise from its function as long-format television. Although it might be argued that TV drama authorship continues after episode scripts have been completed (with adjustments to the content of episodes remaining possible through to post-production), this chapter's focus has been on the conception and writing of complex serials, as their most significant authorship phases. The chapter's investigation of authorship processes yields contextual details that conflict with the auteur-like discourses that have formed around the creators and showrunners of leading complex seri-als, with clear examples in *Mad Men* and *Breaking Bad*. The process by which an individual creator/showrunner is constructed and represented as something akin to an 'auteur', as exemplified by David Chase and *The Sopranos*, is labeled one of 'author(iz)ation' by Robin Nelson (2011), a process to which networks, media paratexts and viewers all contribute. But because it functions to mark complex serials as culturally superior to 'ordinary' television, 'author(iz)ation' serves first and foremost the interests of the TV networks who commission such dramas to increase or maintain their own cultural status. The unqualified recognition and valorization of an individual creator/showrunner as author takes insufficient account of the processes of complex serial authorship, and the industrial realities of TV production, moreover. Reducing the visibility of writers, whose creative investment in complex serials is both individual and collaborative, 'author(iz)ation' diminishes *their* authorial achievement. Nelson's (2011) analysis of *The Sopranos* is particularly revealing in this regard. It suggests that the 'author(iz)ation' of David Chase persisted despite public knowledge that he did not write all the episodes and despite the fact that some senior producers who worked with him (including Matthew Weiner, Terence Winter and James Manos Jr.) subsequently led other notable complex serial productions.

These findings about complex serial authorship testify to the ongoing lack of fit between the auteur theory and the conditions of TV drama creation. However, the discussions of this chapter also suggest it is problematic to simply apply one model of authorship universally across the formally diverse meta-genre of TV drama. Whilst it cannot resolve these problems, this chapter's investigation of authorship has identified elements of the model used for complex serials that are vital in facilitating narrative complexity in the challenging context of a long-format serial. Central to this complexity and continuity is an ongoing push-and-pull interplay between individual and collaborative contributions. Although this kind of interplay is more broadly characteristic of TV drama authorship, in complex serials it entails a greater reliance on 'breaking story' in the writers' room, whose processes are vital to the complex storytelling characteristics of this form. Underscored by cable television's tendency for "less creative interference" from network executives (Perren, 2011: 138) in its writing, the complex serial authorship model also entails more creative autonomy than is usually possible for TV dramas produced for American broadcast television. As demonstrated by the case study of *Breaking Bad*, increased autonomy for writers means that debates about such pivotal story beats as those of whether or not Walter White should kill Jane Margolis (2:12) are more likely to be resolved in the writers' room than they are to hinge on network approval. Maximizing the opportunities for risk-taking by writers is the priority, to which Gilligan alludes, of creating a 'safe room' in which writers feel 'free' and supported. Useful to the above interplay between individual and collaborative authorship is that complex serial writers are handpicked by creator-showrunners, and hired not just on the basis of their perceived suitability to write for a particular show, but also for their capacity to maintain a 'safe room'.

As one dimension of this 'push and pull' interplay, complex serial authorship is unusually dependent upon the initiative of what is most often a single creator, usually an experienced writer-producer, who earns this position as the originator of the show's concept. Having successfully pitched this concept, obtained the finance and network commitment to realize it, and then written the pilot episode, the creator can legitimately claim authorial primacy over the project, a position established before any additional personnel are hired. As the creator moves on to assume the roles of head writer and showrunner, what started as authorial primacy extends to creative leadership and oversight of the entire production, including editorial control over the scripts and frontline liaison with network executives. In view of such significant contributions, which in complex serials usually span the life of the show, this creator-showrunner figure provides a close approximation of the traditional author or artist, allowing the ensuing production to achieve the attributes of 'authored drama' (Caughie, 2000). It is the complexity and high-stakes nature of this set of contributions that makes it difficult to simply dismiss the relevance of traditional notions of individual creativity and authorship to complex serial drama.

The other dimension of the complex serial's interplay between individual and collaborative authorship centers on the contributions of other personnel in senior creative roles: writers, EPs, directors, cinematographers and designers. Of these, most pivotal to the authorship model for complex serials are the staff writers. Since complex serial writers devise the details of the unfolding narrative during 'breaking', write the individual scripts and are likely to make additional input as producers and EPs, they make vital contributions to a show's authorship. However, the extent of their authorial influence varies from one complex serial to another. One variation arises from how much a given showrunner opts to revise scripts and thus exert editorial influence over the content of episodes. Another is whether writers are able to be present on the set as 'their' episodes are being shot, which is particularly beneficial to the directors and actors involved. A third variation is the proportion of writing time that is devoted to 'breaking story' collaboratively, as compared with the writing of full scripts by writers working alone. As demonstrated by *Breaking Bad*, a greater investment of the available writing time into 'breaking story' brings a range of benefits, including the engendering of a sense of collective ownership of the ongoing story, a capacity to reduce the time needed for revising scripts and greater flexibility with the allocation of scripts to writers.

Notes

1 The term 'concept' appears often in this book, especially in this chapter. A term used widely in TV production industries, it refers to the premise or idea at the core of a particular show. Although every long-format TV show is grounded within a concept, important to those developed for long-format drama is the potential to generate new episodes and sufficient narrative intrigue for the show to endure for several seasons.

2 'Breaking story', a term that refers to the processes for the initial conception of story strands and character arcs, will be examined in-depth in a later section of this chapter.

3 In contrast with shows that are created for TV networks, which are either wholly or part-funded by advertising, national public service broadcasting (PSB) networks have been able to facilitate alternative forms of programming, one example of which is a category that I term 'public service drama' (Dunleavy, 2016: 203). Pivotal to the opportunities that these dramas attain for experimentation with concept, form and aesthetics has been the combination of a PSB philosophy, public finance as 'risk capital' and schedules whose non-commercial footing removes direct commercial influences on show design. This distancing from advertiser influences is crucial for maximizing the possibilities for conceptual, formal and stylistic diversity, as well as for risk-taking and experimentation. There are longstanding examples in the United Kingdom's BBC (see Caughie, 2000) and Denmark's DR networks (see Redvall, 2013).

4 Despite its historic usage, the term 'mini-series' is a misnomer, because these TV dramas use serial rather episodic series form. Hence this book will use the term 'mini-serial' for American and non-American examples.

5 The category of 'short-format' TV drama has traditionally comprised the three main forms: feature films (traditionally termed 'made-for-TV movies' or 'telefeatures'), one-off productions of shorter length (these often commissioned and packaged into anthologies) and mini-serials.

6 The key distinctions between series and serial forms of TV drama are examined in detail in Chapter 4.

7 The attributes of narratively complex TV drama are examined in Chapter 4.

8 John T. Caldwell (2009) "Both Sides of the Fence: the Writers' Room", an interview with TV writer, Felicia D. Henderson, Chapter 16, in Vicki Mayer, Miranda J. Banks and John T. Caldwell eds. *Production Studies: Cultural Studies of Media Industries*, New York and London: Routledge, pp. 225–26.

9 There are some exceptions to this tendency for a single creator-showrunner. Complex serials involving two or more people sharing this role include HBO's *The Wire* and *Game of Thrones*, along with Netflix's *Stranger Things*.

10 The option of hoarding a drama idea by the network that has bought it, though is not willing to proceed with commissioning it themselves, can be tempting for a network as a form of insurance against the possibility that the rejected idea might become a hit for another network.

11 Historically, such scenes have either been termed 'the hook' or 'teaser'. However, as this discussion confirms, opening scenes have different potential functions in a complex serial episode as compared with the conventional 'hook' for a crime procedural drama episode. For more about the function and distinctiveness of 'cold opens' in *Breaking Bad*, see Rossend Sánchez-Baró (2014) "Uncertain Beginnings: *Breaking Bad*'s Episodic Openings", Chapter 8 in David P. Pierson (ed.), *Breaking Bad: Critical Essays on the Contexts, Politics, Style, and Reception of the Television Series*, Lanham and Plymouth: Lexington Books, pp. 139–53.

4

COMPLEX SERIALS AND NARRATIVE INNOVATION

Introduction

Noticing the media industry's historic deployment of serial fiction as a way to encourage the consumption of new media services, Roger Hagedorn (1995: 41) argues that, "when media industries decide to target a new sector of the population in order to expand their market share, they have consistently turned to serials as a solution". In American television, examples of this strategy can be found in the 1950s, when broadcast networks and their commercial sponsors used daytime soap operas to target housewives, and from the late 1970s, when these networks commissioned high-budget mini-serials to provide an 'event television' boost to the allure of their schedules. A more recent instance of the pattern outlined by Hagedorn is evident in the deployment of high-end serials by American non-broadcast networks (cable and internet) as a means to increase the profile and allure of their brands in an emerging multiplatform era.

Prior to the expansion of original serials on cable television, the high-end serials commissioned for American television were dominated by two main forms. One was the 'supersoap', a high-end form of soap opera,[1] a form exemplified by CBS's *Dallas* (1978–1991), Fox's *Melrose Place* (1992–1999) and ABC's *Desperate Housewives* (2004–2012). The other was the 'mini-serial', a form with a limited number of episodes, exemplified by ABC's *Rich Man, Poor Man* (1977) and HBO's *Band of Brothers* (2001). Beyond these, and with the exception of such inventive dramas as *Twin Peaks* (1990–1991) and *Lost* (2004–2010), high-end serials have been more of rarity on American television than they have internationally, which helps to foreground the risk-taking and innovation of the complex serial form that HBO pioneered and other non-broadcast networks have since emulated.

The label 'complex serial' refers not to drama serials broadly, but to a specific type of serial whose design for longevity is a major departure from the historic tendency of high-end serials (outside of 'supersoaps') to develop and conclude within a limited number of episodes. Three related characteristics, which complex serials deploy in tandem, underline their break with longstanding narrative traditions in American TV drama. First, this form deploys seriality rather than episodicity (whose contrasting narrative modes will be examined in this chapter), its basis in serial form establishing a narrative matrix in which it is possible to maximize complex storytelling. Second, again enabled by serial form, the concepts for these dramas eschew the institutions (police stations, hospitals and lawyer's offices) of American long-format drama tradition. As this chapter explains, complex serials are conceived in terms of a central 'overarching' story rather than a story-generating 'problematic', an approach that allows their narratives to investigate morally conflicted primary characters as opposed to investigating situations in which conflict is a regular occurrence. With both these features underpinning the approach that this chapter calls 'complex seriality', these dramas gain additional potentials for narrative complexity from a third characteristic. Designed to progress the brand ambitions of non-broadcast networks and to exploit the new potentials of multi-platform delivery and consumption, complex serials are conceived to foster a notably intense form of audience engagement, this contributing to their capacity for a lucrative 'afterlife'.

This chapter pursues two main questions. First, how do 'complex serials' deploy and deviate from longstanding narrative strategies in American hour-long series and serial drama? Second, what are the narrative distinctions of complex serial dramas and how do they achieve complexity? The chapter culminates in a case study of *Mad Men*, whose critical acclaim and successful deployment of narrative complexity over some 92 episodes places it among the most influential American complex serials yet produced.

American Cable Television and the Strategic Value of Serial Drama

Underlining the continuing validity of Hagedorn's assertions at the outset of this chapter, American cable networks have sought to reach new audience markets by commissioning original drama in serial form. American cable networks have provided a regular platform for three main types of serial drama. One is the complex serial (exemplified by HBO's *The Wire*, AMC's *Breaking Bad* and Showtime's *Dexter*), whose stories unfold over multiple seasons, allowing them to accrue complexity over time. Another is the mini-serial (exemplified by HBO's *The Corner* and *Band of Brothers*), a form with the capacity to deploy complexity, but limited in this by its short duration. Third is the anthologized serial (exemplified by FX's *American Horror Story* and *Fargo*), whose seasons are conceptually and thematically linked, but have the capacity to deploy unique settings and characters.

Of all these serial forms, the most acclaimed and influential, underscored by a longevity through which they attain a higher, more sustained audience profile, have been complex serials. In investing in these shows, cable networks have sought to stimulate a more intense level of audience commitment that can extend their market share (as HBO experienced with *Game of Thrones*), make their services more enticing for existing subscribers (as Showtime found with *Dexter*) or make their channels more attractive to cable system providers (the objective for which AMC 'greenlit' *Mad Men*). These considerations attest to the economic benefits of complex serials for both basic and premium cable networks. Cable television's ability to make this drama profitable derives from the "first-order commodity" relationship (Nienhaus, cited in Rogers et al., 2002: 46), which, as optional services, its networks must cultivate both with their existing audiences and with cable system providers. For subscription-funded networks (both cable and internet) this relationship is explicit in the viewer's payment of a monthly subscription to access their shows. For basic cable networks, whose income combines advertising revenue with monthly 'per-subscription' fees charged to cable system operators for carrying its channels (Mullen, 2003), there is an accountability to viewers in the offer of shows with the capacity to increase the channel's attractiveness to the larger operators in particular, a way for cable networks to maximize their 'per-sub' fee incomes.

Series Versus Serial Forms in Contemporary American TV Drama

Both in American television and internationally, the term 'series' is widely used and routinely misused, whereby all long-format TV programming is likely to be termed 'series', regardless of the particular narrative form it deploys. Although serial and series dramas have served different institutional functions and these continue to shape the commissioning decisions of American networks, the once clear boundaries between these narrative forms was reduced following American Quality Drama (AQD)'s incorporation of serial subplots into otherwise episodic programming, a strategy that began with *Hill Street Blues* and continued in *Boston Legal*. While AQD has preferred series form, its paradigm has included a smaller proportion of fully serialized shows, exemplified by *Twin Peaks*. Sustained from the 1980s onward, AQD's integration of serial subplots and arcs into series dramas effected the mainstreaming of what Horace Newcomb (cited in Sconce, 2004: 98) terms "cumulative" narrative, in which story arcs engender narrative understandings that accrue in the context of loyal viewing. However, differences between series and serial drama forms, which are initiated in concept design, remain in evidence despite contemporary TV drama's tendency, especially in the last three decades, toward increased serialization. Hence the task of this chapter section is to investigate and clarify the remaining distinctions between 'series' and 'serial' narrative forms and modes.

Overt within the range of characteristics that have been used to describe the drama series has been its capacity to tell stories that can be termed 'episodic' in that these are introduced, developed and resolved in the space of a commercial hour. However, this does not preclude the existence, as a complement to this episodic storytelling, of serial threads that arc over several episodes or an entire season. Testifying to the broadening of AQD's influence across hour-long examples of American TV drama (Thompson, 2007), the ideal concept for long-format broadcast TV drama is one that allows for this kind of flexibility. Identifying the narrative engine that fuels and sustains series drama, John Ellis (1982: 154) observes its conception around a 'problematic', or as I suggested in 2009, "a situation with the potential for perpetual conflict" (Dunleavy, 2009: 54). In long-running Fox series *House MD* (2004–12), this problematic is constructed as the diagnostic lab of an emergency hospital wing, a milieu in which the 'patch and dispatch' focus of conventional medical dramas is replaced by an interest in the detection and resolution of obscure medical conditions. While *House MD* obtains a point of difference within medical drama from the incorporation within this problematic of a single title character – the irascible, pain-killer addicted, yet genius doctor, Gregory House – in facilitating a continuing flow of new medical mysteries-of-the-week, its problematic still maximized the show's longevity by providing a stable, recurring episode formula. *House MD* episodes open with the collapse and hospitalization of an acute patient, whereupon Greg House and his team spend the rest of the episode pursuing an accurate diagnosis against time pressures and mounting odds for the patient. In terms of broad popularity and the potential to deliver a consistent viewing experience from week to week and season to season, the drama series problematic has two main functions.

First, it endows the series with a narrative openness that overrides and usefully complements the temporary closure offered at the end of individual episodes and seasons. However, while serial narratives always progress as they unfold, the series problematic anchors the situation in stasis, this providing a "steady state" to which each new episode of the series returns (Ellis, 1982: 156). Whilst different core characters will inevitably move in and out of a long-running series, a successful problematic need not change very much between the first and last episode. *ER*, for example, follows the professional and personal lives of staff working in the emergency room of a large public hospital (the fictional 'Chicago County General'), this problematic helping to sustain the series for 15 seasons and 331 episodes. Perhaps because it foregrounded a single character, by contrast with the ensemble cast deployed by *ER*, *House MD* was unlikely to match *ER*'s longevity, yet it still amassed eight seasons and 177 episodes. In these ways, the problematic gives the drama series the capacity to endure over time for, as Ellis (ibid.: 156) underlines, "[t]here is no final closure to the series' own recurring problematic". Even though a problematic can also be conceived around a community of characters, or a humorous situation (as in sitcom), American broadcast television has retained a preference for the kind of institution in which dramatic conflict takes the form of extreme life and death situations. Hence the prevalence of procedural milieux – especially police stations, hospitals and law firms – as settings for some of the longest-running drama series that American television has produced.

Second, its problematic allows a given drama series to strike a balance between repetition and novelty that is evident at the level of the individual episode, which is important in broadening its potential appeal. Repetition in the drama series is provided by its 'core' characters (who generally appear in each episode), by the settings and conflicts (which are much the same in successive episodes), and through the use of a recurring episode formula. Novelty in the series is offered by its guest characters, who differ in each episode, and by the set of events that those characters (and their interactions with core characters) bring to the episode. With guest characters providing the specificities, novelty in series is ensured by these self-contained stories, which tend to consume the majority of episode time, usually relegating the story arcs (whose function is to provide continuity and reward regular viewers) to a lesser role. Elements of repetition in *House MD*, for example, arise from the continuities of character and situation. Even though episodes are similarly structured, benefitting from the continuities of character and situation, novelty is nonetheless offered by the life and death potentials of the new medical cases that are usually resolved within the space of the episode.

Distinguishing drama serials from drama series has been the former's tendency to tell a complete story from beginning to end. Pursuant to this, their episodes are interrelated and interdependent, must be viewed in strict order, and the interpretation of new events in the narrative present is always informed by events of the past. A serial story unfolds in a sequential fashion, with each episode contributing new developments and often ending in some kind of cliffhanger to incite audience speculation about what might happen next. Unlike the continuing soap opera (a modestly budgeted form that deploys multiple interweaving storylines and consistently evades narrative closure), the high-end serial constructs a hierarchy of plots whose importance is generally overridden by one main story, the 'overarching' story, which spans all the episodes. This prioritization of one main story – as exemplified by the ongoing battle for control of the Iron Throne in HBO's *Game of Thrones* – underlines that the narrative engine that drives a high-end serial is quite different to the static problematic that sustains a drama series.

The high-end serial's 'overarching' story entails unavoidable change and an inevitable end. An important characteristic of drama serial episodes and one that continues to distinguish them from series drama is that – although they do include secondary subplots, which begin and conclude at different points to the main story – they are not required to resolve *any* of their stories at each episode's end. Because their form is narratively powered by an overarching story carried by one or more cast members, serial characters are less interchangeable than is possible in series and their personalities or idiosyncrasies can be more fully fleshed out by writers. Pursuant to this, high-end serials entail more differentiation between central characters (whose ongoing presence is vital to resolving the overarching story) and peripheral characters (whose narrative role is to progress the overarching story or smaller story arcs).

Along with the prominence of the serial's overarching story comes the necessity for a continuity of cast and characters that does not apply as firmly to drama series. It means that lead characters may appear in all or most of the serial's episodes, and at least some of the core characters who were present when the story opened will contribute to the way it ends. In the serial's narrative context of progression and change, core characters are under considerably more pressure than their drama series counterparts to remember their history and be affected by what happens to them. Hence the psychological state of primary characters tends to be narratively investigated, allowing writers to create more complicated characters than are possible in series. Pursuant to this investigation, high-end serials refer to the past, present and possibly the future of their characters by way of flashbacks or, more rarely, flash-forwards. It is because of the serial's focus on the narration of a specific overarching story that progresses with every new episode that it remains highly resistant to casual patterns of viewing and aims instead to cultivate a more intense level of audience loyalty and engagement.

The above distinctions provide crucial underpinnings for the arguments of this chapter because so much of contemporary American TV drama – especially that created for broadcast networks – has been influenced either by episodic storytelling or by the blending of episodic and serial modes in the context of series form. With the introduction and expansion of AQD, the latter approach developed and expanded. Yet, with original dramas devised to serve the objectives of their debut platform as well as their host network, broadcast and non-broadcast TV dramas have used this blending differently. While there will always be TV dramas that deviate from the conventions of their institutional contexts – as demonstrated by the episodic tendencies of HBO's *The Newsroom* and the 'complex seriality' of ABC's *Lost* – a recurring tendency in American hour-long drama of the last two decades has been for broadcast dramas to ground their concepts in series form (so as to maximize narrative accessibility, audience size and seasonal longevity) and for non-broadcast dramas to ground their concepts in serial form (so as to boost the audience allure of an optional TV service and minimize 'churn'). As one preferred by American broadcast networks, the first of these blending strategies can be termed 'serialized series', in recognition of dramas (such as *House MD*, *The Mentalist*, *Bones* and *Grey's Anatomy*) that incorporate serial threads and arcs into the framework of a series problematic. As the preferred approach of American non-broadcast networks, the second can be termed 'series-serial', in recognition of dramas (such as *Six Feet Under*, *Mad Men* and *Dexter*) whose progressive overarching story marks them as serials but whose concepts incorporate a series-like problematic to provide a flow of additional stories and 'guest' characters. Pioneered by *Oz* and further developed by subsequent HBO dramas *The Sopranos* and *Six Feet Under*, this 'series-serial' addition to the narrative matrix of complex serials is one of the six facets of what this chapter terms 'complex seriality'.

From Narrative Complexity to 'Complex Seriality'

The increased narrative complexity of American TV fiction, both drama and sitcom, has been investigated by Jason Mittell (2006; 2015). "To call something complex", as he observes (2013: 46), "is to highlight its sophistication and nuance, suggesting that it presents a vision of the world that avoids being reductive or artificially simplistic, but that grows richer through sustained engagement and consideration". Such complexity can be found, for example, in narrative strategies that involve experimentation with form and modality, the deployment of non-linear storytelling, self-conscious play with narrative perspective, and the use of what Mittell calls "operational reflexivity" (2006: 35), whereby a show uses spectacle to invite audience appreciation of its aesthetic or narrative construction.

Although complexity has been an increasing characteristic of contemporary TV fiction, the above characteristics of complexity have long been available to dramas produced as high-end 'closed' serials (or mini-serials) as distinct from modestly budgeted 'open' serials (or continuing soap operas). Historically, miniserials have functioned as 'event television', gaining opportunities for conceptual diversity and creative ambition from their more lavish production budgets and limited on-screen duration than most other TV drama. Opportunities for more complex modes of storytelling, albeit few, have long been available to 'authored' mini-serials created for broadcast channels and timeslots in which a public service remit and non-commercial schedule make it possible for networks to sanction creative experimentation.

In the 1980s and 1990s, British public networks the BBC and Channel Four both provided such opportunities. Forming part of the resulting output is what John Caughie (2000: 4) terms "serious drama" in recognition of the 'seriousness' with which it has been regarded and received in public culture. Reflecting on the distinctiveness that has marked this 'serious drama', John Caughie (2000: 128) attributes it to the inventiveness of writers and to the creative freedom they have gained from a public service philosophy, important to which has been an official permission "to 'push the boat out' and take audiences where they [have] not been before". Elaborating on his concept of 'serious drama', Caughie (ibid.) adds that:

> The most honoured writers in 'serious' television drama (the most 'serious' writers) are those who invent new forms of expression, bringing cultural prestige to television by preventing it from being routine, by preserving the rough edges of the non-classical, by being 'original' rather than 'conventional'.

These achievements, along with the closed serial's potentials for narrative complexity, are exemplified by *The Singing Detective* (BBC, 1986), a six-episode drama written by Dennis Potter and produced by Kenith Trodd. It tells the story of an ageing writer, Philip Marlow, whose crippling psoriasis necessitates his extended stay in hospital and confines him to bed. It is this disease – which has clenched his fists, immobilized him and disposed him to high temperatures and feverish hallucinations – that fuels his need to 'escape' into a multi-faceted story in which memory and fantasy vie with the above contemporary story for prominence. At the creative cutting edge for TV drama of its era and characterized by complexity in both the story it tells and the modernist aesthetics through which this unfolds, *The Singing Detective* features a mix of competing story strands (imagined and actual) narrated from the viewpoint of a single character, the psoriatic Marlow, whose condition is linked to his guilt about the serious transgressions he committed as a child.

While *The Singing Detective* demonstrates the degree of complexity that is possible for mini-serials, despite their very limited number of episodes, an important characteristic of the complex serial form is that its narrative canvas is considerably larger, requiring the devising of concepts and strategies that can sustain stories which may unfold over some 40–90 episodes. It is in the context of this enlarged canvas that some specific elements of complexity come to the fore as ways to stimulate and sustain the kind of intense audience engagement that non-broadcast networks are seeking through the offer of this drama. This chapter coins the term 'complex seriality' as shorthand for the approach to complexity that formally unites such notable examples of American TV drama as HBO's *The Sopranos*, *Deadwood*, *Six Feet Under*, *The Wire*, *Boardwalk Empire* and *Game of Thrones*; AMC's *Mad Men* and *Breaking Bad*; Showtime's *Dexter*; Netflix's *Orange Is the New Black*, *House of Cards* and *Stranger Things*; and Hulu's *The Handmaid's Tale*.[2] These shows not only highlight the preference of ambitious non-broadcast American networks for original high-end drama as serial rather than more enduring series programming, but also testify to the unusual tolerance of their commissioning networks for risk-taking with drama concepts, characterizations and stories.

'Complex seriality' entails the deployment of six narrative strategies which are interdependent. One is conceptual originality, specifically the exploration of subjects or topics without direct precedent in TV fiction, a feature that is enhanced by the pursuit of a particular point of view on these. Another is the potential to incorporate into the concept design a series-like problematic, this operating as an additional 'series-serial' narrative component that complements the overarching story and helps to prolong it. A third is an unusual integration between the dilemma of the central character/s and the overarching story that the serial tells. Fourth is the deployment of morally conflicted lead characters, whose potential for criminal transgressions are a departure from the longstanding tendency of broadcast dramas to create lead characters who, albeit flawed, are not so deviant that they risk audience rejection. Fifth is the embedding of additional scenes, usually flashbacks but more rarely flash-forwards, which deepen narrative intrigue, add detail to the understanding of characters and inform character motivations and behavior in the narrative present. Sixth is the extent to which conflicted and/or transgressive lead characters are subjected to in-depth psychological investigation, facilitated by the overarching story's foregrounding of their problems and progress. While the second of these strategies (the series-serial component) is explained in the previous section, the upcoming discussions and case study of *Mad Men* will examine the other five.

Conceptual Originality and the Adoption of a Point of View

The first facet of complex seriality is conceptual originality, a distinction assisted by the adoption of a particular point of view on the overarching story being told. While complex serials are sometimes adapted from literature (including *True Blood, Dexter, Game of Thrones* and *The Handmaid's Tale*), it is indicative of their capacity for conceptual originality that more examples (including *The Sopranos, The Wire, Deadwood, Mad Men, Breaking Bad, Boardwalk Empire* and *Stranger Things*) have been conceived for television.

In an interview for *Variety* in 2003, following his first year as HBO's CEO, Chris Albrecht (cited in Johnson, 2003) registers the importance to HBO of creating original drama whose conceptual difference is derived from the particular perspective it offers. As Albrecht explains:

> We always knew we had to be different … not different just from an adult content point of view, but different in terms of the essence of the show. What filmmakers or truly talented people usually have is a point of view about something … Broadcast networks in particular tend to flatten out points of view, because these points of view are opinion and opinions might offend certain people. [Broadcasters] don't want to do that because they are in the business of not offending anybody.

By this point HBO was preparing to launch *Deadwood*, a show that Albrecht describes as the kind that "you haven't seen before", a drama "with a point of view" and really "about something" (ibid.). HBO's fleet of complex serial flagships now included *Oz, The Sopranos, Six Feet Under* and *The Wire*, all of which are indicative of HBO's commitment to drama with a point of view. In *Oz* this entails the investigation of male prison life from the 'inside', a contrast with procedural crime drama's consistent interest in the detection of crime and identification of criminals. As Chapter 2 demonstrates, *Six Feet Under* uses its funeral parlor setting not just to investigate death and grief (a new topic for TV drama) but also to critique the commodification of these things in contemporary American society.

Underscored by the tag-line "It's Not TV. It's HBO" that marketed these shows, Albrecht and other HBO commissioning executives understood that the provision of drama whose "point of view about something" was an important way to entice educated, affluent viewers to pay extra to access it. While it began as an element of HBO's own drama strategy, Albrecht's notion of drama with a 'point of view' was embraced by other cable networks, developing as one of the markers of complex seriality in the resulting drama. Again, Caughie's (2000) notion of 'serious drama' as that which prioritizes 'originality' over 'conventionality', and derives the creative license to do so from the institutional objectives it is created to serve, can inform this notion of drama with a point of view. 'Serious drama', as Caughie suggests, attains distinctiveness and cultural influence partly through its effort to challenge or provoke audiences, important to which is the adoption of a particular point of view (or narrative perspective) on the stories it tells.

The cultural impact of drama that takes a distinctive point of view can be seen in HBO's *The Wire*, a five-season serial co-created by David Simon and Ed Burns. Preceded in TV drama by HBO mini-serial, *The Corner* (2000),[3] *The Wire* drew on the career experience of Simon, a former journalist for *The Baltimore Sun*, and Burns, a former Baltimore police department detective whose specialist foci were its homicide and narcotics divisions. *The Wire* is a revealing exemplar of the potentials of complex seriality, insofar as, while it can certainly be classified as a 'crime drama', it rejects well-established approaches to concept design, characterization and narrative structure in this category so as to accentuate a particular argument about contemporary, post-neoliberal America.

While it may look like a police drama at first glance and a proportion of its action does involve policing work, *The Wire* tells a politically charged story about the city of Baltimore, investigating a society whose lived experience is the very antithesis of the long-mythologized 'American dream' in which hard work is imagined as the key to social advancement. Beginning with Season 1's focus on the drug war as a 'game' whose central players are the police and drug organizations, each subsequent season introduces an additional domain in the lives of Baltimore's impoverished and vulnerable: the docks in Season 2; local government in Season 3; the high school in Season 4; and the media in Season 5. Testifying to the conceptual and narrative complexity of *The Wire*, the investigation of each of these domains is interwoven with other story strands. Of these strands the most consistent is the drug war. As the domain of focus for Season 1, the drug 'game' is also a continuing narrative strand that spans all *Wire* episodes, even though the perspectives upon it do change in line with the different foci of the docks, local government, school system and media, as domains foregrounded in subsequent seasons. In these ways, what begins as a drama that overturns the perennial 'police drama' formula by dividing its attention and sympathies between drug dealers and police, becomes a multi-faceted, epic story about the systemic failure of Baltimore and its central institutions to make any meaningful difference to the lives of the vulnerable citizens they serve. In this larger narrative context, *The Wire*'s title alludes to the dividing line between what David Simon sees as two contrasting versions of contemporary America. As Simon describes them, one is the "functional, post-industrial economy that is minting new millionaires every day and creating a viable environment for a portion of the country" (cited in Ethridge, 2008: 154). The other America, whose characteristics are well-illustrated by *The Wire*'s different institutions, domains and perspectives, comprises the individuals and groups who are "consigned to a permanent underclass" and thus to a life of exclusion from the many possibilities of 'functional' America (ibid.).

Accordingly, *The Wire*'s focus is on the kinds of neglected people and sectors of American society that are rarely seen on television, let alone closely examined. This feature distances *The Wire* further from conventional crime drama in which the narrative perspective lies firmly with the professionals who maintain law and order, and there is little investigation of or sympathy for the criminals who disrupt it. At odds with the police drama's pursuit of resolution and incarceration as a psychologically reassuring, though unrealistic, outcome, *The Wire* is fueled by an ideological commitment to exposing how Baltimore's problems and the plights of its poor are rooted in the injustices and failure of the city's key institutions. Hence, even though *The Wire* shares with the police drama an interest in the procedures of police work, this is where the narrative similarities end. Even though policemen are among its most regular and enduring characters, *The Wire* is relatively disinterested in the challenges of police work and is intensely focused on its array of criminal and/or disadvantaged civilian characters. In striking contrast with American TV's large cache of conventional crime dramas whose 'crimes-of-the-week' are efficiently resolved, *The Wire* examines ongoing problems as the product of systemic failures rather than errant individuals. Highlighting how violence and murder have filled the power vacuum created by ineffectual institutions and large scale unemployment, few of these characters – the drug bosses and corner dealers, addicts and their neglected children, unemployed steel-workers and stevedores – survive through to the serial's end.

The Wire stands out within complex serial drama on the basis of its prioritizing of public and social problems over the development and retention of familiar characters. Its conceptual frame is distinguished by three main elements. First, whereas most other complex serials devise their concepts around primary characters, *The Wire*'s central 'character', even though its successive individual characters are meticulously drawn, developed and investigated, is not an individual but a traumatized society. Second, its flawed institutions are represented as inherently more powerful and determining than the individuals who move through them, hence the problems depicted cannot be resolved despite the efforts of successive police and civilian characters. Third, whereas other complex serials use a narrative structure whose domains inform and fuel the character-driven central narrative, *The Wire*'s approach to its own central 'character', the beleaguered Baltimore, is to analyze and probe it from different perspectives, each involving an institution and/ or domain with the capacity to profile a different experience of post-neoliberal America. As the above arguments suggest, *The Wire*'s deviations from the conventions of crime or police drama are conceptual and considerable, so much so that the same kind of drama would never have been 'greenlit' for American broadcast TV. Yet *The Wire* gained its opportunity from HBO's subscription-funded schedule and the support of its then CEO, Chris Albrecht. In acknowledgment of the point of view that was pivotal to *The Wire*'s cultural significance as reputedly "the most serious and ambitious fictional narrative of the twenty-first century so far" (Michaels, cited in Vint, 2013: 1), David Simon registers: "It wasn't supposed to exist. It could have – if we'd done everything wrong – been a cop show" ("The Game is Real", 2007).

The Foregrounding of Morally Conflicted and Transgressive Characters

Another facet of complex seriality is the narrative foregrounding of morally conflicted primary characters whose potential for transgressive behavior is without precedent in American TV drama. Flawed lead characters have a lengthy history on television. But while it is not uncommon for lead characters to be flawed, in conventional dramas these characters are neither villainous nor irredeemable. Flawed lead characters have been prevalent in conventional crime dramas, frequently constructed as 'mavericks' who regularly break the rules in their pursuit of justice. In broadcast-era British TV, for example, the violent behavior of the two leads in police series *The Sweeney* was considered to have "blurred the sharp distinctions that are normally drawn between good and evil characters in crime melodrama" (Millington, cited in Creeber, 2004: 91). That Federal Communications Commission (FCC) rules and internal network censorship constrained the behavior of core characters in American broadcast crime dramas is indicated by the regular battles that Steven Bochco fought with NBC's 'standards' department in pursuit of the "grim, gritty, and rude" depictions (Gitlin, 1994: 281) that he wanted for *Hill Street Blues*. Bochco's efforts to depict more authentic police characters despite the protestations of NBC gatekeepers continued in *NYPD Blue*, a long-running and critically acclaimed series whose lead character was Andy Sipowicz (Dennis Franz). Even though the alcoholic and violent Sipowicz is considered to be a prototype for some of the more transgressive complex serial characters, the difference between Sipowicz and the errant characters frequently at the forefront of complex serials is that Sipowicz is troubled by his own behavior, strives to modify it and ultimately succeeds. As Mark Singer (2005) explains:

> When viewers meet Sipowicz in the first episode of the series, he's a self-subverting racist drunk who does everything but literally shoot himself in the foot. Instead, a Mafioso with whom he's obsessed shoots him, giving him a near-death experience that leads to sobriety. Over the next several years, Sipowicz endures wrenching personal tribulations and occasionally falls off the wagon, but repeatedly rights himself and strives, despite his instinctive bigotries, to do good ...

The flawed lead characters of *NYPD Blue* and other AQD dramas – particularly since they were welcomed by viewers – undoubtedly helped to enable a gradual transition away from characters whose behaviors rarely breached broadcast

TV's morally conservative 'least objectionable programming' philosophy toward the possibility of morally flawed and/or villainous lead characters. There is evidence of broadcast TV's willingness to construct such characters in *24*'s proficient counter-terrorist, Jack Bauer, and *House MD*'s titular character, the cantankerous, addicted and frequently cruel, Gregory House. Yet, as Gary Edgerton (2013: 95) observes, these characters only appeared *after* the demonstrated popularity of HBO character Tony Soprano. NBC's commissioning of *Hannibal* (2013–2015) provides more recent evidence of transgressive lead characters on American broadcast TV. Yet the disappointing ratings *Hannibal* returned and the show's axing after three seasons suggests the continuing reluctance of broadcast networks to commission long-format dramas with villainous lead characters.

Despite the above indicators of television's increasing interest in transgressive lead characters, dramas originated by cable networks have pushed out more boundaries than all other American TV drama in the foregrounding of such characters; this assertion is evidenced by the willingness of cable networks to allow such villainous lead characters as mafia boss Tony Soprano, serial killer Dexter Morgan and meth cook Walter White. Pinpointing the institutional imperatives that place limits on drama design for broadcast networks whilst simultaneously reducing them for cable networks, Amanda Lotz (2014: 61) registers that:

> Where the strategy of the *broad*caster is to erect a big tent that welcomes heterogeneous audiences with content unlikely to easily offend, niche entities such as cable channels succeed by developing programming that strongly interpellates narrower sections of viewers with content that connects deeply with their beliefs or interests.

Their position as niche providers allows cable networks to commission a type of serial drama that has been conducive to the use of morally flawed and potentially villainous lead characters for two main reasons.

First, as observed in earlier chapters, the cable environment is differentiated from that of broadcast TV by its greater content freedom. However, the onus is on cable networks to exploit this freedom as far as they dare as a way to demonstrate *how* they are different from broadcast networks. Although their distance from FCC content rules is not itself responsible for the kinds of drama that cable networks originate, this greater freedom, as recognized by drama writers, does widen the possibilities for concept design, characterization and the use of explicit content. Moreover, as Tim Goodman (2005) underlines, "chance-taking" with drama "is a must" for cable networks. Notwithstanding HBO's pioneering of an effective template for the complex serial form, an important example of this chance-taking was FX's *The Shield* (2002–2008), the first complex serial produced for a basic cable network. Although HBO serials had already shown that villainous primary characters could attract and even fascinate viewers, HBO had not needed to consider the response of advertisers to villainous lead characters, which made

The Shield an 'all or nothing' experiment for the re-branded FX. Fortunately, its risk-taking was successful. While the first episodes of *The Shield* did prompt some FX advertisers to recoil and withdraw, there were others whose clients proved "willing to tolerate" *The Shield*'s edgy characters and stories (Romano, 2002a: 16), a realization that opened the door to the use of seriously flawed lead characters in dramas created for other advertiser-funded cable networks.

Second, complex serials can probe many qualities of their lead characters, which derives from their tendency to devise concepts that foreground one main character, as in *The Sopranos*, *The Shield*, *Mad Men*, *Dexter*, *Boardwalk Empire*, and *Breaking Bad*. This is a point of contrast with American broadcast dramas which, even if they do emphasize one character, are usually obliged to regularly disperse their stories and arcs across an ensemble cast. In the context of their character-centered concepts, as distinct from concepts devised around precincts, workplaces or character communities, complex serials have the scope to subject several different features of these characters, both appealing and despicable, to ongoing investigation. As Lotz (2014: 63) underlines, these non-broadcast dramas not only "probe the circumstances and conditions that have led [such characters] to transgress" but also "depict them struggling with their responses to circumstances not entirely of their making". As exemplified by the desperate state of Walter White which leads to his 'breaking bad' in the pilot, the parallel investigation of transgression and struggle helps viewers to reconcile the opposing dimensions of these characters.

Investigating the appeal of flawed characters in the wider context of contemporary TV drama, broadcast as well as cable, Jason Mittell (2015: 143) observes the increasing incidence of morally flawed characters, arguing that the expanded spectrum for such characters extends from "misanthropic, selfish, but ultimately redeemable heroes" (like *Rescue Me*'s Tommy Gavin), through "arrogantly superior, destructively flawed, but moral figures" (like Gregory House), to "outright amoral villains" (like Tony Soprano). Yet Mittell's analysis also suggests that the most extreme examples of lead character villainy, in American drama at least, are to be found in cable rather than in broadcast examples. Comparing the two sectors in respect of their tolerance for transgressive and/or villainous lead characters, Lotz (2014: 53) argues that "a difference in the characters, nearly to the one, [can] be correlated with whether a broadcast network or a cable channel originated the series". This is not to imply that broadcast drama is incapable of hosting villainous lead characters; NBC's three seasons of *Hannibal* stand to counter that. There is also the non-American example of *The Fall* (BBC and RTÉ, 2013–2016), a complex serial created as a British/Irish co-production to function as 'public service drama', whose foremost character is serial murderer, Phil Spector.

The demonstrated popularity of such notoriously villainous characters as Tony Soprano, *The Shield*'s Vic Mackey, Dexter Morgan and Walter White – especially since this outcome runs contrary to the longstanding expectations of broadcast TV executives that viewers will find such characters unpalatable – raises the question of why it is that characters whose villainy may extend through immoral and/or criminal behavior to include murder have held such appeal? Grappling with this question in regard to *Breaking Bad*, Richard Woodward (2011) highlights the allure of characters who regularly confront "murky ethical dilemmas", in doing so challenging viewers to "rationalize their heinous behavior". Two strategies, which are deployed similarly in different complex serials, are vital to the ability of this process to enlist audience identification and sympathy with transgressive lead characters.

One is the narrative centrality of morally conflicted, troubled individuals in shows conceived around them (see Lotz, 2014: 55). What such a focus on the lead character produces, as Lotz observes, is an unusual ability "to divide narrative time between stories of the protagonist['s] work and home lives and provide considerable exploration of their motivations, dilemmas and underlying neuroses" (ibid.). Again *The Sopranos* provides an early and influential example. As 'boss' of the North Jersey Mafia 'family', consistent with established 'Mafia law' and the dictates of *omerta* (the Mafia code of silence), Tony Soprano is obliged to authorize and sometimes administer the 'whacking' of anyone who offends this code. While Tony is indirectly responsible for many murders over the show's six seasons, HBO expected viewers to react most strongly to those he committed personally, in full view of the camera. Tony's first on-camera murder occurred in 'College' (1:4), when, taking time out during a college tour with his daughter, Meadow, he strangles informant and 'rat', Fabian Petrulio. Another example, this one motivated by the accidental death of Tony's racehorse Pie-O-My, is Tony's beating and strangling of Ralph Cifaretto in 'Whoever Did This' (4:9). Important to the continuing allure of Tony as lead character, despite such horrendous on-camera murders, is that his professional life is given almost the same narrative weight as his domestic life (with Carmela, Meadow and Anthony Junior). A third element is the investigation of Tony's psychological state (as narrated through Tony's dreams and his 'on the couch' sessions with Dr. Melfi). Together, these narrative elements pair the violence and criminality of a contemporary Italian-American mob culture with the recognizably 'ordinary' problems of sustaining a marriage and career, raising a family and dealing with stress.

The other is the strategy of 'relative morality' (Mittell, 2015: 143), which entails the regular juxtaposition of a morally flawed or villainous lead character with other characters "more explicitly villainous and unsympathetic" as a means to foreground the lead character's "more redeeming qualities" (ibid.). Although neither exclusive to TV dramas nor indeed to the medium of television, relative morality gains opportunity in complex serials in the context of a narrative focus on morally conflicted primary characters and the enhanced depth of character investigation that is possible in serial form. Speculating about the audience effects of relative morality, Richard Woodward (2011) contends that:

> Asking a TV audience to side with the lesser evil has lately become a standard strategy for producers of dramatic series on cable. When greater evil is

obviously afoot in the world, manifest in forces more violent, deceitful, and hypocritical than your central character's, thievery, assault, adultery, bootlegging, drug running and murder can be excused. *The Sopranos, The Wire, The Shield, Deadwood, Weeds, Dexter, Mad Men, Boardwalk Empire,* and *Sons of Anarchy* have all created sympathy for and, in some cases, glorified liars, killers, and sociopaths by pitting them against worse liars, killers, and sociopaths.

As a strategy that Woodward identifies in cable rather than broadcast dramas, relative morality is strikingly demonstrated in Showtime's *Dexter,* whose eight seasons make it the most enduring example discussed in this book. As a serial whose titular character carries a 'dark passenger' whose blood lust must regularly be satisfied, *Dexter,* Mittell suggests, "accomplishes what would seem to be an impossible task – making a serial killer into a sympathetic hero whom we enjoy spending time with each week" (2015: 147). Important to the achievement of relative morality in *Dexter* is the probing investigation of a new 'big bad' character in each season whose unmitigated, repeated killing of innocents marks them as clearly worse than Dexter, a vigilante whose victims are selected for elimination in line with 'Harry's Code'. Dexter's interactions with the 'Trinity Killer' in Season 4 offer an indicative example. By this point in the serial, Dexter has moved in with Rita and her children, and the couple have a son of their own. Struggling to reconcile his identity as a serial killer with the demands of family life, Dexter looks to Arthur Mitchell (aka 'the Trinity Killer'). Like Dexter, 'Trinity' is a serial murderer with a family. However, that is where the similarity ends, including the fact that Trinity's family are aware of his killing (in contrast with Dexter's), which encourages Trinity's abuse of them as a means to enforce their silence. In comparison to Dexter, Trinity's unmitigated approach, catalogue of innocent, vulnerable murder victims and terrorizing of his wife and children combine to characterize him as by far the "greater evil" in Woodward's terms. It is through the juxtaposition of Dexter and Arthur, as husbands, fathers, serial killers and citizens, that relative morality positions the former as 'vigilante hero' and the latter as extreme villain whose urgent elimination will save a succession of innocent lives.

Adding Complexity to the Narrative's 'Syuzhet' Through the Embedding of Additional Scenes

Another facet of complex seriality is the deployment of additional scenes which, temporally distanced from the main story, function to inform character motivation, add depth to the understanding of character or, more rarely, foreshadow events in the narrative future. As scenes that usually interrupt rather than progress the overarching story, they provide details that support the understanding and/ or investigation of key characters. While these scenes are usually flashbacks, more rarely they take the form of flash-forwards. These scenes not only deepen narrative intrigue by providing additional, often unique information about characters but also imbue these serials with an additional complexity due to their fragmented delivery and dispersal across the larger multi-season narrative. Important to understanding the contribution of such scenes to narrative complexity are longstanding distinctions between the 'fabula', which refers to the chronological order of events that constitute a given narrative, and the 'syuzhet', or the order in which these events are narrated to viewers (Gripsrud, 2002). Highlighting the potential for a complex relationship between syuzhet and fabula as interdependent narrative dimensions, Jostein Gripsrud explains that the syuzhet is the "text [that viewers] encounter and read" as opposed to the fabula's "underlying 'actual' series of events" (ibid.: 199). Accordingly, as Gripsrud posits, "the syuzhet is the way in which [viewers] are informed of the fabula" (ibid.). While the conventional linearity of TV serials tends to foreground the fabula as the primary structural device, these additional scenes add significance and complexity to the syuzhet. These elements of the deployment of such scenes underline their specific function, which is to contribute (in combination with other facets of complex seriality) to the moral and psychological investigation of key characters in ways that deepen audience engagement with their conflicts, decisions and/or behaviors.

The effectiveness of the above strategy is evidenced in *Breaking Bad* through the narration of the ongoing thread about Walter's connections with Elliott and Gretchen Schwarz and their company, Gray Matter Technologies, as one which spans all of the episodes. This strand centers on Walter's origination of the chemical formula responsible for the considerable commercial success of Gray Matter Technologies, the company he co-founded with Elliot and sold to him. Scattered through *Breaking Bad*'s five-season text are insights about Walter's interest in Gray Matter which, only when considered together, can explain why Walt, having made enough money to support his family whatever happens to him, feels he cannot stop cooking methamphetamine. A key motivation for Walter's persistence as Heisenberg, this thread reveals, is the conviction that he has lost a vast fortune to Elliott, his former friend, and Gretchen, his onetime girlfriend. This story's 'kernel' (or pivotal) scenes are offered in 'And the Bag's in the River' (1:3) when a younger Walt discovers the formula and shares it with Gretchen; in 'Gray Matter' (1:5) when Gretchen, under pressure from Skyler, offers to pay for Walt's cancer treatment; in 'Peekaboo' (2:6) when Walt tells Gretchen that she and Elliot are wealthy on the basis of his own research discovery; and in 'Buyout' (5:6) when Walt tells Jessie that the company he sold for US$5,000 is now worth over US$2 million. As one of several 'loose ends' tied in the final episode 'Felina' (5:13), this thread resolves when Walt enters the Schwarz home, frightens Elliott and Gretchen (with assistance from laser pointers wielded by Skinny Pete and Badger), whereupon the terrified pair agree to take secret custody of Walt's illicit earnings and drip-feed the money to his family after his death. Underlining the watch-and-listen-closely expectation of complex serial viewers, this pivotal thread is narrated neither at the show's outset nor in a single episode (where a conventional serial might have located it), but through a succession of brief 'kernel' scenes appearing at different points of the show. Viewers must remember and link together these different kernels to fully understand the Gray Matter thread.

Although complex serials can locate these extra scenes at any point of a given episode, *Breaking Bad* sometimes constructs them as 'cold opens', or scenes placed at the outset of an episode and designed to powerfully solicit audience attention. Two features of *Breaking Bad*'s use of the cold open are particularly distinctive. One is that these sometimes involve 'in medias res', a term that means 'in the middle of things' (Gripsrud, 2002: 197). In screen texts, 'in medias res' is used to enlist audience engagement in a story, before returning to the beginning of the event chain to provide context. *Breaking Bad*'s inventive deployment of 'in medias res' is exemplified by the first scene of the pilot episode, in which an agitated Walter enters the frame wearing 'tightey-whitey' underwear and a gasmask, as examined in Chapter 3. Becoming clear as the pilot episode approaches its climactic point is that this scene – because it follows Walt's fiftieth birthday decision to 'break bad' and precedes the climactic events with which the episode ends – was plucked from its chronological home within *Breaking Bad*'s fabula to ensure a compelling opening for the serial.

Another use of cold opens is to anticipate the future. Describing its cold opens as *Breaking Bad*'s "most distinctive signature", David Lavery (2012) underlines that they "demand we be seated and in place the second a *Breaking Bad* episode begins" and "leave us riveted, not even thinking about changing the channel". In *Breaking Bad*'s second season, four inter-connected cold open scenes, each offering a different fragment or perspective on the same event, are deployed as a sequence of flash-forwards. Their purpose is to anticipate the airplane accident with which the season ends. From the 13 episodes that comprise this season, four episodes, aptly titled 'Seven Thirty-Seven' (2:1), 'Down' (2:4), 'Over' (2:10) and 'ABQ' (2:13), are the recipients of cold opens that foreshadow this disaster, as observed in the previous chapter. The four scenes are connected through what is called the 'Rashomon effect' (named after the Akira Kurosawa-directed 1950 feature in which a singular event is narrated from different perspectives). These four cold open scenes are united by a succession of extreme close-ups of poolside objects, the action taking a dramatic turn in each of these shots with the sudden entry (from above) first of a synthetic eyeball (which is seen to bob steadily down the length of the pool toward the drain and eventually disappear) and then (an object positioned within the frame to suggest a longing one-eyed gaze in the direction of the moving eyeball) of a hot pink children's teddy bear. As these strategies show, *Breaking Bad* deploys the cold open in ways that contribute to its narrative complexity through temporal manipulation. In *Breaking Bad*, cold opens only sometimes refer directly to the specific episode in which they are placed, preferring instead to reference developments from the narrative past or to foreshadow developments in the narrative future. Used in these ways, it is possible for *Breaking Bad*'s cold opens to disorientate viewers whilst simultaneously acting to emphatically solicit their more intense engagement through the deepening of narrative intrigue.

The fragmented and non-linear deployment of the kinds of additional scenes outlined above intensifies the narrative demands that complex serials make of their viewers. Viewers are invited to remember and apply details revealed, possibly at widely disparate points of the show's entirety, to gain the fullest understanding that the text makes available to them. Because it implies that viewers themselves should develop a comprehensive narrative memory, this strategy is rather more complex than the now widely used mode that Horace Newcomb terms "cumulative" narrative (cited in Sconce, 2004: 98). Introduced by AQD shows in the 1980s, this 'cumulative' mode developed as a way to reward audience loyalty through the offer of additional details (often involving the personal lives of core characters) not fully accessible to irregular viewers. In contrast to this 'cumulative' mode, the narrative history and memory of complex serials is built beat by beat and important to every episode. Viewers of complex serials are expected not merely to watch all episodes, and watch them in order, but also to watch and listen *closely* so as to remember new revelations and apply them to future episodes.

Case Study of *Mad Men*

Mad Men, AMC's first attempt at a long-format flagship drama, is an exemplar of the strategies and repercussions of complex seriality. *Mad Men* is also significant for its demonstration of the complex serial's capacity to emulate the critical acclaim and profitability of *The Sopranos* in the environment of basic cable. This case study investigates *Mad Men* in relation to the remaining two of the six facets of complex seriality identified in this chapter. One is the integration within the drama's concept of central character and overarching story, and the other is an unusual capacity for the ongoing psychological investigation of primary characters.

Exploring one distinction in the group of cable dramas that she calls "male-centered serials", Amanda Lotz (2014: 55) observes that the "centeredness" of an individual male character in these dramas is so prominent that these dramas are "essentially about" this character, a feature that "enables a particular type of narrative" in which it is possible to explore "the entirety" of his life in both "personal and professional spheres". If we focus more narrowly on complex serials, however, what we see is not so much a drama form that tells the story of one character, but rather one whose concept design entails an unusually close integration between a show's overarching story and the defining conflict for the character/s at the forefront of this story. *Mad Men*, for example, even though it is about the work of advertising executives, was conceived around just one conflicted character. When asked about how he arrived at the concept for *Mad Men*, Matthew Weiner (cited in Handy, 2009) emphasizes how this began with the creation of a conflicted character:

> I start with me, like any writer. I start with what I'm feeling, what I identify with … [L]ike Don, I'm trying to hold on to what I have. He invented

himself. He is always going to be presenting something to the outside world that's not who he really is. You don't have to be from his background to understand that. In fact, all you have to do, really, is to have any success at all and you immediately feel like a fraud, most of us, right?

A point of difference between complex serials on the one hand and conventional serials and series on the other, such close integration of character and story indicates that complex seriality begins with the conception of one or more *conflicted characters* rather than the conception of *situations of conflict* (such as police stations, hospitals, law firms) that characters are subsequently created to inhabit. This level of integration of character and story is distinctive within TV fiction because it means that the primary character in a complex serial can (though is not necessarily obliged to) *embody* the kind of overarching story that frames the show from the first to the last episode.

At the center of *Mad Men* is the enigmatic yet morally flawed Don Draper, who has suppressed his real identity (as Dick Whitman) and reinvented himself for a chance at success. Although it is partly because his own reinvention was so radical that he's so successful at finding ways to reinvent consumer products, Don Draper is a troubled, anxious man who lives in constant fear that his secret identity will be exposed. While confident and successful at work, Don is contrastingly uneasy at home, a sphere in which it is far more difficult to maintain his secret and the consequences of exposure are (as is evident when Betty discovers his photo box) especially serious. The story of Don Draper, *Mad Men*'s overarching story, unfolds by placing him in the context of a Madison Avenue advertising agency, initially Sterling Cooper (SC) and finally Sterling Cooper and Partners (SCAP). Although its story extends into the 1970s, *Mad Men*'s narrative focus is the 1960s, the first decade in which there is finally a TV set in the majority of American homes. With their work intensified by the pervasive cultural influence of television in an 'era of scarcity' for this medium (Ellis, 2000), *Mad Men*'s advertising executives aim to re-envisage consumer items so as to transform them from the non-essential objects they are into must-have commodities. In the pilot episode, for example, SC seeks a way to market Lucky Strike cigarettes, despite new evidence that smoking is a health hazard. Don's response to this, as Lilly Goren observes (2015: 43), is to ascribe a new value to the now discredited cigarette, which he achieves by convincing Lucky Strike executives "that what they are selling is not a cigarette" but rather "happiness".

Having successfully reinvented himself, Dick Whitman/Don Draper is the personification of what a successful advertising campaign can achieve. Noticing how closely the faux Don Draper and the capacity for reinvention that is so pivotal to effective advertising are integrated in *Mad Men*, David Marc (2011: 232) posits that "Dick Whitman-as-Don Draper is a life as an advertising campaign: a child spawned in the lost America of love [who] drapes himself in the trappings of a gentleman to sell himself to the world". Such close integration between overarching story and central character means that Don Draper is not just a character, but one of two core elements comprising *Mad Men*'s overarching story. He embodies *Mad Men*'s interest in the difference between what is on the surface (how things appear to be) and what lies underneath (how things really are) that is central to this show's concept and is also interrogated through its advertising agency milieu. Accordingly, the ongoing investigation of Don Draper works hand-in-hand with *Mad Men*'s critique of advertising and its contributions to the formation of consumer desires.

A final facet of complex seriality is the psychological investigation of central characters, a feature that gains impetus from the narrative prominence of what is often one character, from the transgressive tendencies of primary characters in complex serials, and from the integration between central character and overarching story discussed above. Emphatically in serials in which one character fulfils all these roles, as is the case in *Mad Men, The Sopranos, Breaking Bad* and *Dexter*, there is a necessity for audiences to understand a character's motivations by getting 'inside their heads' to reveal their psychological state – their 'inner life' as Denis Potter termed it (cited in Cook, 1998: 30).

In complex serials, key strategies for psychological investigation include the use of dream sequences, subjective camerawork or hostile landscapes as vehicles for 'psychological realism'; of extra-diegetic voiceovers to allow a character's thoughts and omniscient insights to be shared with the audience; and of embedded, non-linear flashbacks. Of these three strategies, flashbacks are particularly important in *Mad Men*. In complex serials, however, flashbacks are not necessarily used to nuance the understanding of characters, which is how they tend to operate in conventional drama, a function that in those dramas renders them more of a reward for loyal viewers, as distinct from being information that is essential to understanding the larger narrative.[4] Instead, as used in complex serials, flashbacks contain details that are *integral* to the psychological investigation and revelation of character, which makes them vital to understanding the overarching story that these serials tell.[5] In view of this more crucial function, complex serials use flashbacks as narrative kernels (pivotal events) rather than as 'satellites' (lesser events). In complex serials, these flashbacks also tend to be delivered out of chronological order and are deliberately fragmented and dispersed throughout their multi-season narratives, these tactics underlining that their purpose is psychological revelation rather than narrative progression. Testifying to the demands that complexity makes of viewers is that the 'inner life' of complex serial characters is only available to viewers who register and remember all the contributing narrative kernels. Complex serial flashbacks also contribute to narrative complexity at the level of the episode by endowing developments in the narrative present with a larger context and thus a deeper meaning.

Although other characters are subject to investigation, *Mad Men* gives narrative emphasis to the psychological probing of Dick Whitman/Don Draper, an investigation that bookends the serial itself. In the pilot episode, 'Smoke Gets in Your Eyes' (1:1), Don denies the existence of romantic love, telling Rachel Mencken:

"What you call love was invented by guys like me to sell nylons". But it's not until the end of 'Person to Person' (7:14), the final *Mad Men* episode, that it is possible to fully understand why Don is so convinced that "love doesn't exist". What happens between these two points is that the 'inner life' of this foremost *Mad Men* character, the confident, charismatic 'Don Draper' on the surface and the rejected, frightened Dick Whitman deeper down, is gradually revealed. In *Mad Men* two ongoing strands effect this psychological investigation. One, unfolding as the linear narrative, is the story of Don Draper, a man valued for his creative genius but undermined by his alcoholism, infidelity and guilt. In this strand, Don Draper interacts with two important figures from his past, Adam Whitman and Anna Draper. The other, a strand that is narrated in flashbacks, profiles Dick Whitman, former soldier, furrier, car salesman and unloved 'whore's child'. Two examples demonstrate how these interlinked strands reveal Don's psychological 'inner life'.

The first occurs in 'The Gypsy and the Hobo' (3:11), when Betty discovers the box of photos through which she learns that 'Don Draper' is an assumed identity. Having met her next husband, Henry, by this point, Betty's discovery is the catalyst for her decision to divorce Don. As Don tells Betty some of the details as to how Dick Whitman became Don Draper, viewers have encountered these and more details in earlier kernel scenes, with an important example in 'Five G' (1:5) in which Adam Whitman pays a visit to his half-brother. Key flashback kernels are offered in 'Babylon' (1:6) which introduces Uncle Mack, the brothel and Abigail Whitman, who gives birth to Adam, Don's half-brother; in 'The Hobo Code' (1:8) where desperate poverty and alcoholism are seen to cause the death of Archie Whitman; in 'Nixon Vs. Kennedy' (1:12) where flashback scenes reveal Dick Whitman's actions on a Korean battlefield, which saw him return as Lt. Don Draper; in 'The Gold Violin' (2:7) in which used-car salesman Don is suddenly confronted by Anna Draper; and in 'The Mountain King' (2:12) which establishes the genuine relationship that Don develops with Anna. Accordingly, the account that Don gives Betty in 'The Gypsy and the Hobo' serves two purposes. Not only does it extend what viewers already know to include Betty, precipitating her decision to divorce Don, but it also coheres a historical narrative for Don/ Dick by recounting information that was offered earlier, though only in disparate episodes and disconnected kernels. As Don's confessional conversation with Betty reaches its most painful revelations – his explanation of what happened to Adam and why – his confident persona recedes to reveal the suppressed identity within:

B: What happened to them?

D: They're all dead.

B: Even Adam? The little boy in all the pictures, I assume he's your brother.

D: He was my half-brother and he died. He killed himself. He came to me because he wanted help and I turned him away. He didn't even want help, he just … just wanted to be part of my life. But I couldn't risk all this. He hung himself.

If only for this moment, the weight of guilt Don has been carrying since 'Five G' (1:5) is vividly evident, and viewers see and hear the suppressed Dick Whitman. As this scene shows, this suppressed identity is a striking contrast with the confident, decisive and persuasive Don Draper. Although equally articulate, Dick Whitman is hesitant, ashamed and terrified, an adult version of the rejected child whose difficult early life is gradually revealed as *Mad Men* continues.

The second example is from 'In Care Of' (6:13), the episode in which a pitch to Hershey's executives occasions a public meltdown for Don Draper, a narrative counterpart to the private one with Betty in Season 3. The disastrous Hershey's pitch is the climactic point for a series of mistakes by Don in this season, as a result of which his anxiety and drinking both increase, his resilience is reduced and his childhood consumption returns. The trigger for this downward spiral is the abrupt end of Don's affair with neighbour, Sylvia Rosen, in 'Man with a Plan' (6:7). Although Don is genuinely in love with Sylvia, she is terrified by his obsessive urge to control her, which culminates in his locking her in a hotel room. It is not until the next episode, 'The Crash' (6:8), that Don's destructive urge to control women, whatever the emotional cost, is finally contextualised via a flashback to his boyhood as Dick Whitman. Weak with consumption, the teenaged Dick is raped by Aimee, one of Uncle Mack's prostitutes. Still devastated by the loss of Sylvia in 'Favors' (6:11), Don attempts to entice Sylvia back by securing a way for her son, Mitchell, to avoid the draft. But things unravel still further for Don, when Sally enters the Rosen apartment and discovers her father, trousers down, "comforting Mrs Rosen" as he later explains it to her.

Sally's subsequent withdrawal from her father precedes her drunken exploits at boarding school, which, as Matt Zoller Seitz points out (2015: 347), unnerve Don into imagining that she's inherited the Whitman family curse. It's the terror of this that sees Don make the rash decision to give up drinking in the hours leading up to the Hershey's pitch scene (6:13), a meeting during which, as close-ups of his trembling fingers emphasize, he is suffering alcohol withdrawal. As a scene emblematic of *Mad Men's* fascination with what Handy (2009) terms "the deceptive allure of surface" and the "deeper mysteries of identity", Don opens the all-important pitch with his customary salesman's confidence, asserting that Hershey's "relationship with America is so overwhelmingly positive that everyone in this room has their own story to tell". He begins with the kind of idealized childhood experience that he thinks will ingratiate him with the Hershey's team in which its chocolate bar – a reward from a loving father for his son's lawn-mowing – evokes the bond between father and son. But the response of one Hershey's executive, "Weren't you a lucky little boy", proves too much in view of the neglect and abuse that blighted his youth as Dick Whitman. Compelled to smash through the mythology he has built around himself professionally, Don relates the memory of Hershey's he stored up as Dick Whitman, an unloved brothel-raised child. He recounts his friendship with a prostitute who bought him the occasional Hershey's bar to reward him for the money he stole from the pockets of her clients "while they screwed".

Although *Mad Men* investigates other core characters throughout its seven seasons, the most confronting are the two strands in which the 'inner life' of Don Draper is excavated, unearthed and dragged reluctantly to the narrative surface. While this process begins in the first season, in the form of a yawning contradiction between two seemingly irreconcilable identities for the character played by Jon Hamm, it concludes with something akin to their integration in the ultimate episode (7:14). Important to this integration, a narrative turn that is most closely anticipated by the Hershey's pitch scene, which occurs an entire season earlier (6:13), is that Don Draper does not want to erase Dick Whitman any longer. Suggesting that the personas of Dick Whitman and Don Draper actually converge in this last episode, Seitz (ibid.: 421) highlights three clues to this reading. First is Don's deliberate surrender, in the lead-up to this last *Mad Men* episode, of "all outward signifiers" of his New York persona (ibid.: 420). Second is his reaching out to his protégé and colleague, Peggy Olsen, to whom he makes the shocking confession, "I broke my vows, I scandalized my child, I took another man's name and made nothing of it". Third are behaviors which, even if they are seen to be mitigated by the introspection of a spiritual healing course in a remote location, are uncharacteristic of the Don Draper that viewers have come to know. One is his public sobbing during his phone call to Peggy and the other is his embracing of a complete stranger (Leonard from the spiritual healing seminar). Accordingly, this episode's title, 'Person to Person', references something deeper than the long-distance calls that Don makes in this episode. 'Person to Person', a title whose double meaning follows the pattern of others in *Mad Men*, points to the psychological reconciliation that appears to occur between Don Draper and Dick Whitman (ibid.: 421).

Conclusion

Through its focus on narrative structures and strategies, this chapter shows that TV dramas as conceptually different as *The Sopranos*, *The Wire*, *Mad Men*, *Dexter* and *Breaking Bad*, among other examples, are united by their shared deployment of complex seriality. Even though the complex serial can be said to have historic precedents in the mini-serial form, with a notable precursor in British example *The Singing Detective* (BBC, 1986), unique to the newer form is its longevity through multiple seasons and thus the unprecedented scale of the narrative canvas involved. Whilst complex serials aspire to neither the episode volume nor the longevity of conventional drama series, two of this chapter's examples – *Mad Men* (which reached seven seasons and 92 episodes) and *Dexter* (which amassed eight seasons and 96 episodes) – demonstrate that the distinctions of this form include a capacity for continuity and longevity that is simply unprecedented in high-end serials, with the one exception of the 'supersoap', a variant of soap opera.

Complex seriality provides a framework through which to examine the narrative approaches that unite complex serials and distinguish them within TV drama.

The chapter's exploration of complex seriality suggests that the innovations of this high-end serial form are not to be found in any unified approach to episode architecture, nor in any distinctive deployment of narrative beats and arcs as formal elements of narrative. What does distinguish these dramas, both from the episodic series of broadcast TV tradition and from other high-end serials, is their use of the six interdependent strategies of complex seriality identified and examined in this chapter. Complex seriality foregrounds an approach to the conception of drama in which characters are created not to serve situations of conflict but as individual sites of conflict, exemplified in this chapter by Walter White, Dexter Morgan and Don Draper. Exploiting the conceptual diversity that has long been available to high-end serials, complex seriality encourages a degree of conceptual innovation and originality which, although prized by drama writers, has been difficult to achieve on American broadcast television for the reasons outlined in this book. The six features of complex seriality that are identified and examined in this chapter, will be revisited in this book's final (Conclusion) chapter.

This chapter has used *Mad Men* as a case study; a show that is not only the first high-end TV drama to be set in the advertising industry but which also takes this industry back to its formative years in the era of TV scarcity (Ellis, 2000), a position that allows this show's objects of critique to include advertising. Complex seriality entails the exploration of a particular perspective on the central problem or milieu under investigation. Accordingly, *Mad Men* revisits and re-envisions 1960s America, the colder eye of its revisionist gaze and self-reflexive commentary deconstructing and re-evaluating popular nostalgia for this era. While it is not necessary for their lead characters to be villainous, complex seriality provides a platform for the transgressive lead characters that commercial broadcast TV dramas are obliged to consign to the narrative margins, constrained by their servicing of broad-based audiences, as well as by an institutional economy in which large audiences remain vital to profitability. Transgressive, even villainous, characters have gained the opportunity to be placed at the forefront of complex serials, not just from the niche-audience orientation and appetite for risk-taking that were available first to American cable networks and are now available to internet networks, but also from complex seriality's capacity to undertake the ongoing psychological interrogation that allows these characters to be fully developed and understood.

Notes

1 The 'supersoap' has been prevalent in American primetime television since the inception and success of *Dallas*, as the first example. Its distinctions from the 'continuing soap opera' (a form discussed in Chapter 5) include its high production values, its production in seasons of episodes (and thus its narrative and schedule discontinuity, a contrast with other soap opera), its offer of just one new episode per week, and its role as primetime, not daytime programming.

2 Since many more examples of complex serial dramas, both American and non-American, have been produced or are currently in production, this list and range of titles is intended to be indicative only.

3 *The Corner* was adapted from a 1997 nonfiction book authored by David Simon and Ed Burns. Simon partnered with David Mills for the mini-serial version of *The Corner*.

4 The work of Roland Barthes helps to explain how particular events are aligned to move a story forward in ways that can regulate ebbs and flows in its intensity. Crucial here, however, is Barthes' (1977: 93) observing of a hierarchy of events in stories, the division he perceived between "classes" of events of either pivotal or lesser importance to narrative progression. See Roland Barthes (1977) *Image/Music/Text*, translated by Stephen Heath, New York: Hill and Wang.

5 Agreeing with Barthes' division and fleshing out the narrative contribution of each group of events, Chatman (1978: 53–54) gives them the names of 'kernels' (for pivotal developments that advance and shape the main story) and 'satellites' (for lesser events, which fill in and regulate the gaps between pivotal developments). Underlining the consequential significance of the kernels, Chatman (ibid.) describes them as "narrative moments that give rise to cruxes in the direction taken by events" or, more precisely, as "branching points which force a movement into one of two (or more) possible paths", and emphasizes that kernels "cannot be deleted without destroying the narrative logic". See Seymour Chatman (1978) *Story and Discourse: Narrative Structure in Fiction and Film*, London and New York: Methuen.

5

AESTHETICS AND STYLE IN COMPLEX SERIAL DRAMA

Introduction

This chapter investigates the stylistic tendencies of complex serial drama, a critical perspective located within the field of 'television aesthetics'.[1] While aesthetics are crucial to the examination of style, the chapter does not deal with the evaluative analysis that aesthetic criticism is considered to include. Instead, it investigates the aesthetic traditions and stylistic approaches deployed in the *production* of complex serials. As the chapter's discussions appreciate, the aesthetics and style of complex serials are not distinctive to this form. Rather, the aesthetic traditions and stylistic approaches they deploy are indicative of the capacities of high-end TV drama more broadly. Yet complex serials have attained unusual creative opportunities and resources on the basis of their role as 'prestige' original fare devised to draw viewers to optional TV services for which, even if only a minimal charge, they must pay. In view of this 'prestige' role and the attendant investment and expectations, complex serials reside outside Frances Bonner's definition of 'ordinary' television (2003: 29–63). Along with the elements of conceptual originality and narrative complexity examined in earlier chapters, the aesthetic and stylistic tendencies of complex serials provide an important manifestation of their status as 'exceptional' television.

The chapter begins by examining some of the controversy that has come to surround the term 'cinematic', as one that frequently appears in scholarly, industrial and journalistic appraisals of high-end TV drama, including complex serials. This is followed by explorations of the impacts of convergence, beginning with its repercussions for the delivery and viewing of high-end screen fiction and proceeding to an investigation of how convergence is forging closer aesthetic and stylistic connections between feature film and high-end TV drama at the level of production.[2] Several chapter sections are devoted to the exploration of aesthetic traditions in TV drama, in which 'naturalism', 'realism' and 'postmodernism' are emphasized as the contexts for so-called 'zero-degree', 'first-degree' and 'second-degree' styles. While the first of these terms highlights some longstanding constraints upon TV drama style, the other two foreground the production modes and approaches that enhance stylistic complexity. The chapter culminates in a case study of Netflix original *Stranger Things* (2016–).

The Idea of 'Cinematic Television'

Although it has been applied to a wider range of TV dramas, and has often been misused, the term 'cinematic' has been a feature of industry, audience and scholarly discourses on complex drama serials. Yet perceived problems with the application of the term 'cinematic' to television begin with its lack of specificity, not only in describing the diverse approaches to visual style that are characteristic of television, but equally in pinpointing precisely which stylistic qualities of theatrical feature films invite their own evaluation as 'cinematic'. Key connotations of the term 'cinematic' are outlined by Deborah Jaramillo (2013: 67):

> 'Cinematic' connotes artistry mixed with a sense of grandeur. A cinematic movie is one that requires a theatrical viewing in order to extract every ounce of visual and aural depth from it. The term is reserved for films that reveal the exploitation of filmmaking technologies in the service of skill and creative vision. It is an inherently positive, even boastful word that many people rally around and ascribe to the best of the best on TV.

Appropriated from discourses on theatrical feature film in particular, the term 'cinematic' can be contentious when applied to television, in three main respects. First, if used to appraise the stylistic qualities of TV shows, it can be accused of failing to evaluate them within the context of their medium (see Jaramillo, 2013). Second, if television can be considered 'cinematic', then how do we explain why this descriptor is applicable to high-end drama but not to other TV fiction forms, to soap operas, for instance (see Mills, 2013)? Third, if high-end dramas can be appraised as 'cinematic' but soaps cannot, does this reflect an implicit assumption that some forms of TV are culturally 'superior' to others? The following discussion seeks to explain why, despite these problems, the idea of 'cinematic television' has persisted in discourses about high-end TV drama.

While television's aesthetic relationship with the 'cinematic' remains a topic for further debate, this debate is itself complicated by the unusual diversity of styles available to television, a medium that, historically and internationally, has never been entirely separate from 'cinema' in categories such as the feature film and documentary, as these forms' production history has spanned both mediums. High-end TV drama and theatrical feature film have also been industrially connected through the shared use of 16mm or 35mm film, a practice that continues to cultivate linkages between them in terms of aesthetic possibilities and creative approaches. BBC docudrama *Cathy Come Home* (1966), ABC serial *Twin Peaks* (1990–91) and HBO mini-serial *Band of Brothers* (2001) can demonstrate not only the stylistic diversity of filmed television, but also some specific ways in which film's cinematography, mise-en-scène and editing[3] have influenced the evolution of TV drama.

Some of the problems that scholars have identified with the idea of 'cinematic television' arise from the foregrounding of high-end TV drama, rather than a wider range of TV forms, as examples of it (Mills, 2013; Jaramillo, 2013). As perceived by these scholars, the implication of finding 'cinematic' elements only in high-end TV drama is not just that "some television texts [are deemed] better than others" (Mills, 2013: 64), but also that television is being stylistically appraised in relation to cinema, an activity that may on the face of it seem grounded in the assumption that "[cinema] has a clearly understood [stylistic] essence" (Jaramillo, 2013: 67) while television does not. These criticisms raise useful questions about why the term 'cinematic', although regularly invoked for 'prestige' TV dramas, is never applied to soap operas. While this question has rarely been directly posed, an answer can be found in the different 'modes of production' involved.[4]

High-end TV drama's aesthetic and stylistic differences from low-cost forms of TV fiction has been a longstanding and important one in TV drama scholarship.[5] The different modes of production used to create high-end TV dramas and modestly budgeted soap operas entail contrasting approaches to the *production* of style, differences which have at times encouraged stylistic comparisons between high-end TV drama and feature film and discouraged those between high-end TV drama and stripped soap opera. Although soaps and high-end dramas are both key forms of TV fiction, they are subject to vastly different expectations as to production pace and the volume of episodes created week-by-week. Whereas high-end TV dramas are single-camera productions whose default aesthetic is 'realism' (or 'first-degree' style), soap operas rely on the aesthetic of 'naturalism' (or 'zero-degree' style). Later sections of this chapter will detail the consequences of these different aesthetic traditions and modes of production for the stylistic diversity of TV drama.

In the last decades of the twentieth century, thus well before the arrival of new potentials for convergence between feature film and high-end TV drama at the level of production, the term 'cinematic' was used to imply "a film look in television" (Caldwell, 1995: 12). Although increasingly possible from the 1980s, a "film look" in TV drama had until then been unaffordable and/or impractical due to the combined effect of technological constraints on TV production and the medium's appetite for a high volume of new episodes. However, enabled by advances in screen production technologies and rendered strategically useful as 'mass' targeting gave way to "demographic thinking" (Pearson, 2005: 15), the 1980s brought a shift to the use of 35mm film for primetime drama series, telefeatures and mini-serials. As Caldwell observes: "Not only did shows shot on film dominate television in the late 1980s, the quality of film stocks allowed for a kind of visual sophistication impossible during the zero-degree telefilm years of the 1960s and 1970s" (1995: 84). Importantly, it was this shift from 'zero-degree' to 'first-degree' style, rather than the increasing use of 35mm film on which to shoot it, that made it possible for high-end TV drama to pursue a 'film look' (ibid.).

TV drama does not attain film-like stylistic qualities on the basis of its shooting medium alone, and aesthetic differentiation between TV drama and feature film (whether it is made for TV or produced for theatrical release) has remained significant in the context of network demands for a high and continuing episode output for primetime TV dramas. An important contributor to the accentuation of visual style that helped to differentiate American Quality Drama (AQD) from the 'regular drama' it gradually replaced (Thompson, 1996) was that network objectives around primetime TV drama came to include what Caldwell (1995: 88) calls "programme individuation", or the expectation that each show would "have its own 'look'" (ibid.). The AQD shows most credited with extending the stylistic parameters for American broadcast TV – including *Hill Street Blues*, *Miami Vice*, *Moonlighting*, *Twin Peaks* and *Homicide: Life on the Street* – all demonstrated how a distinctive 'look' could increase the cultural cachet of TV dramas and assist them to deliver the 'high value' audience segments for which advertisers were willing to pay more.

Following the stylistic trajectory of high-end TV drama after 2000, Robin Nelson (2007a: 109) registers that this has entailed an "increased emphasis upon visual style, an aspiration to be as close to cinema as possible, increased dynamism of image and sound (and the two in relation to each other) and a new configuration of the tension between credible illusionism and textual playfulness". Exploring TV drama's contributions to enhancing the cultural status of television, a project they describe as one of "legitimation", Michael Newman and Elana Levine (2012: 5) foreground an aesthetic trajectory through which it became possible for "certain kinds of television and certain modes of experiencing television content [to be] aligned with movies and the experience of movies", describing this as a process of "cinematization". Despite these developments, some scholars are still uncomfortable with the idea of 'cinematic television' because of its implicit suggestion that TV drama aspires to be something *other* than television, specifically to have a closer aesthetic relationship with the theatrical feature film. Accepting the rationale for this discomfort, it remains difficult to refute the changes highlighted by Nelson, Newman and Levine above, if we apply them to the specific case of complex drama serials. The stylistic complexity of these serials, which has contributed to the critical and industrial acclaim they have received, is evident equally in 'period' examples like *Deadwood*, *Boardwalk Empire* and *Mad Men*, as well as in those with contemporary settings, such as *The Sopranos*, *Breaking Bad*, *Dexter* and *Stranger Things*. So, even if the term 'cinematic' is sometimes applied incorrectly to productions, or scenes, whose aesthetics do not warrant this descriptor, the question remains of what label other than 'cinematic television' can as effectively acknowledge the increased stylistic proximity between high-end TV dramas and feature films that the above changes continue to effect.

Historically, TV dramas and theatrical feature films have been most distinguished by their narrative forms, production strategies and exhibition platforms, all three of which have shaped and differentiated their aesthetic objectives and stylistic outcomes. But, because there is no one style for either of these notably diverse categories, it is as difficult to argue that all feature films are equally 'cinematic' as it is to suggest that all TV dramas are equally 'televisual'. An outright rejection of the possibility of 'cinematic television' might be accused of the latter. Aside from the plethora of narrative differences between feature films and long-format TV dramas, the latter category has differed from the former principally on the basis of its design and capacity for renewal and longevity. Moreover, the meta-category of TV fiction comprises a large range of forms and genres, these distinguished from each other by their institutional roles, budgets, production processes and narrative structures. However, elements of convergence between the production processes and exhibition platforms of feature films and high-end TV dramas continue to reduce the traditional aesthetic and stylistic distinctions between them. With technological convergence and online streaming now impacting upon the commissioning of feature films, the historic separation of 'cinema' and 'television' platforms seems unlikely to be as pervasive in the future. Further development here is heralded by Netflix's interest in the origination of feature films (Pulver, 2017), a strategy that allows it to side-step still powerful Hollywood studios, but one that means the resulting films will debut on its own online network rather than in cinemas. While Netflix is but one of an increasing number of IDTV networks, as the largest and most widely available example internationally, its commissioning behavior may point to the possible trajectory of other IDTV networks as these develop.

TV Drama and the Convergence of Screen Production Technologies

Introducing convergence, Henry Jenkins (2006: 2) registers its broader facilitation of a "flow of content across multiple media platforms", "cooperation between multiple media industries, and the migratory behaviour of media audiences who will go almost anywhere in search of the kinds of entertainment experiences they want". The unprecedented ubiquity of television in an environment of convergence is reflected in Glen Creeber's observation that "you can now watch TV almost anywhere … while travelling in a car, train and aeroplane, or sitting in a bar with friends" (2013: 84). The increased mobility that new technologies have brought to TV viewing is perfectly complemented by significant improvements in the availability and transmission of programs through fixed monitors in domestic spaces. HD digital TV screens allow viewers to switch between different internet, broadcast and cable platforms with almost the same ease as they might switch between different channels or sites on any single one of these platforms. The domestic viewing experience has been greatly enhanced first by TV's shift to HD transmission and then by the rapid take-up of flat-panel HD, and now 'ultra HD', TV monitors. Working with these technologies to overturn historic perceptions of an inferior visual or aural quality for television as compared with cinema has been the availability and popularity of much larger domestic TV screens, along with the HD standardization of the medium's aspect ratio to the rectangular 16:9 format, this replacing television's traditional square-shaped 4:3 (Cardwell, 2015: 86). Enhancing the sensory experience of television through sharper images and clearer sounds, such significant improvements in television's aesthetic appeals have helped to incite perceptions of its "renewal and improvement as a technology and as a medium" (Newman and Levine, 2012: 102). Convergence, whose potentials have unfurled virtually in tandem with the rise of multiplatform television and the expansion of complex serial drama, has not only helped stimulate increased volume and diversity in TV drama production but also provided its audiences with a plethora of ways in which to view the finished programs. High-end TV drama has found itself better positioned than more modestly budgeted TV forms and genres to exploit HDTV's new opportunities. In turn, these opportunities have helped justify higher budgets for high-end TV drama.

While original high-end drama has always been a strategic asset for TV networks, convergence has invested this programming with unprecedented flexibility in terms of delivery, availability and exhibition. High-end TV dramas are time-shifted more often than other TV shows, have been integral to the take-up of cable channels and the expansion of network on-demand options and are currently fueling the growth of internet-distributed television (IDTV). While the origination of American high-end drama was once the preserve of commercial broadcast networks, a situation partly responsible for its over-reliance on episodic series devised for regularity and longevity, new dramas are increasingly commissioned for non-broadcast networks, and it is the different requirements brought by these non-broadcast networks that have most changed this drama's creative parameters. Today's multiplatform environment is encouraging TV drama's transition from episodic series toward serial narrative form, to higher episode budgets and a greater use of locations, and toward aesthetic and stylistic qualities that are closer than ever to those once exclusive to the theatrical feature film. Beginning with HBO, American cable networks led the way by permitting conceptual experimentation, in the process making commissioning decisions that prioritized a new drama's capacity for 'must-see allure' over its traditionally crucial capacities for schedule regularity and longevity.

Where the commercial function of TV drama was once limited to maximizing eyeballs for advertisers, convergence, having diversified the meta-genre's avenues for commercial return, is changing its forms, and, with this, its aesthetic characteristics and/or potentials. Highlighting how distinctions between TV and cinema have flowed from the specificities of each medium's image, Robin Nelson (2007a: 110) observes that:

> [E]ven in its digital format, the television image remains undoubtedly distinct from the 'cinematic' in being electronically configured rather than projected by light. The film image is physical and visible frame by frame in that the exposure of film stock to light chemically burns the image into specially treated material. In contrast, the magnetic configuration of videotape or the zeros and ones of digital recording are intangible and invisible until decoded.

These contrasts foreground longstanding differences in the recording and exhibition technologies used for TV shows, which are designed to be watched in domestic spaces, and theatrical feature films, which are designed for viewing in cinemas. Although these differences still separate cinema and television in the multiplatform era, convergence is bringing two main adjustments to the contexts that have maintained them to date. One is the alignment of the once distinctive technologies used to produce feature films and TV dramas, and the other, the alignment of viewing platforms for these texts, whereby both production forms can be consumed through the same range of devices. A new low for American movie ticket sales was reached in 2016, to which one observer responded by remarking that "the film industry is on pace to sell the fewest U.S. tickets per person of any year since perhaps before the 1920s and the fewest total tickets in two decades" (Thompson, 2016). While feature films have historically enjoyed an 'afterlife' as TV content, declining cinema attendance is indicative of the appeal and convenience of watching recently released movies through non-theatrical platforms, this change suggesting that more feature films may debut this way. Supporting this idea is Netflix's purchase of the rights to a Martin Scorsese-directed feature, in which Robert de Niro appears in the title role. Rights to *The Irishman*, purchased by Paramount Studios in 2016, were bought by Netflix in 2017, which is likely to mean that the completed film will debut on its own platform (Pulver, 2017) and not in cinemas.

As highlighted earlier this chapter, some scholars reject the idea of 'cinematic' TV drama, while others have cited stylistic developments and achievements in this same meta-genre to argue for increased 'cinematization' in television. Given such disagreement, it is worth underlining the continuing constraints on the potential for stylistic convergence between theatrical feature films and high-end TV dramas. TV drama production remains a different proposition to that of feature film because it is subject to a 'fast-turn-around' approach that is imposed on the back of requirements for a volume and continuity of completed episodes, a requirement that does not apply to feature films. Comparing the production time allocated to TV dramas and feature films, Robert Del Valle (2008: 7) explains that TV dramas "will produce perhaps 22 or more episodes over the course of a season. Each episode will be budgeted, scheduled, and shot separately. A two-hour feature film is a single project, scheduled and budgeted as an isolated production". As calculated by Del Valle, the minutes-per-day of finished screen time for feature film and TV drama, even though both figures are derived from shooting on 35mm film, is four minutes or less per day for feature film and seven to eight minutes per day for TV drama (Del Valle, 2008: 8). As these differences suggest, TV drama remains subject to a faster pace of production, which places more limits on its cinematography, mise-en-scène and editing than those applying to feature film. It is for this reason that, regardless of the conceptual ambition and stylistic sophistication that higher production budgets can certainly afford it, high-end TV dramas are unable to replicate the aesthetic properties of feature films, even if, as this chapter suggests, the conceptual and narrative complexity of the serials examined in this book extends to their aesthetics and style.

Notwithstanding the stylistic differences that are to be expected from the differing demands on theatrical feature film and TV drama production, technological convergence between their industries has accelerated in the last decade, key examples of which are their use of the same 35mm or HD digital cameras, and cross-deployment of cinematographers, directors and editors. As this industrial convergence continues, it ensures that "the original and significant differences between the two media are less pronounced than they once were" (Creeber, 2013: 85). While these changes are gradually impacting on most forms of American high-end TV drama, complex serials have provided a notably compelling and consistent exemplification of their effects.

One development that has increased the convergence between film and high-end TV drama at the level of production is the pervasiveness of HD digital cameras and capture. The inception of 'ultra HD' capacities for digital cameras (which allow shooting at four, six and even eight times the resolution of standard HD) is making its own contributions to reducing discernible differences between feature films and high-end TV dramas in terms of potential visual quality. Even though some cinematographers prefer 35mm film, others have found benefits in HD digital capture. Thus far, decisions about whether to use a 35mm or HD digital camera seem influenced by the specific setting and 'look' that is required. HBO's *Boardwalk Empire* (2010–14) is set in Atlantic City, New Jersey, in the 1920s and 30s, a place and period that, as considered by its showrunner, Terence Winter, and cinematographers, was ideally suited to the use of 35mm film (Heuring, 2010).[6] In contrast, its HBO contemporary *Game of Thrones* (2011–) – whose epic scale entails the deployment of multiple production units, shooting in remote locations and whose fantasy elements require extensive computer-generated imagery (CGI) – is the first HBO drama to be shot on HD digital.

The mixing of film and HD digital shooting for Showtime's *Dexter* (2006–2013) gave its initial cinematographer, Romeo Tirone (cited in Frazer, 2006), opportunities to compare the pros and cons of each:

> We shoot anywhere from seven to 10 [script] pages a day ... and it's a fran-
> tic pace. It's my job to make the days, but also keep the look and make it
> interesting ... I'm shooting five days a week for 12 to 16 hours, depending
> on what we're doing. It doesn't give me the luxury that I would have on a
> feature or even on a commercial to go and sit with the colorist and time it.
> A lot of [the footage] I see just as dailies ... It's a different kind of instinct
> with the HD, because the image is right in front of you. You can take more
> chances with it. With film, if I wanted to do a certain coloration I'd use
> filters and write notes to the colorist so they wouldn't just pull what I had
> done out ... And at any moment we can be switching to film. I pump up the
> light a little bit for film because we're shooting high speed. But I light the
> HD and film together the same way I would light the film. However, when
> I look at film and HD side by side, I always favor the film. There's something
> organic about a chemical reaction to light rather than an electronic one.

These assertions suggest that, from an artistic viewpoint, there are perceived
advantages and disadvantages for both of these shooting mediums. However, from
the perspective of studio and network bean-counters, HD digital may have an
edge over its celluloid rival. HD digital capture and post-production is faster and
cheaper than using 35mm film, Tirone suggests, and brings greater immediacy
for the viewing of 'dailies' (the footage captured on a shoot day). While 35mm
film has demonstrated its durability in terms of image storage, HD digital offers
a plethora of options for additional effects to be added after shooting, including changes to colorization and the addition of digital effects that can simulate
the texture of 16mm and 35mm film. A recent example is HBO's *Vinyl* (2016),
a high-end drama set in the American recording industry of the 1970s, whose
EPs included Martin Scorsese and Terence Winter. Although this setting made
Vinyl well-suited to using film, the decision to shoot it on HD digital was influenced by HBO's own preference. However, to achieve the period 'look' they
wanted, Scorsese and his cinematographer, Rodrigo Prieto, used a 'plug-in' called
'LiveGrain' to overlay their digital capture with a texture evocative of celluloid
(Thomson, 2016).

Recent developments suggest that HD digital cameras are beginning to replace
35mm film cameras as the medium of choice for the shooting of both theatrical
feature films and high-end TV dramas. The use of HD digital cameras (especially models produced by Arri, Red and Sony) has rapidly increased since 2010,
with some commentators estimating that up to 90 percent of the highest-earning
American feature films in 2015 were shot either entirely on HD digital or on a
mix of digital and film (Follows, 2016). Moreover, the availability of film stock
has reduced and the number of processing labs is declining (Stewart and Cohen,
2013). There is also an increasing preference, on the part of both Hollywood studios and American theatre owners, for digital formats and projection, which, mitigated by declining theatre ticket sales, they regard as the most cost-effective (ibid).

Style by Degrees: From Naturalism to Post-Modernism

> Television, it has often been argued, prefers the rhetorics of the 'narrative' –
> plot, conversation and character – over the aesthetics of the image. It has
> also frequently been said that it prioritizes straightforward and static com-
> position over more complicated arrangements, and operates through close-
> ups and two-shots rather than long shots. The so-called 'Quality Television'
> of the last twenty-five years is thought increasingly to have rebuffed these
> conventions, holding rhetoric and aesthetic in equal regard, adopting what
> is often (yet at times wrongly) called a 'cinematic style'.
>
> *Timotheus Vermeulen and Gry C. Rustad*[7]

The above assertions help to foreground a frequent problem for high-end TV
drama: that its stylistic register is vulnerable to misunderstanding or misrepresen-
tation if assessed in the context of the broader medium of television rather than
in direct relation to the aesthetic tendencies and stylistic potentials of its own
meta-genre. Although it is not at all inaccurate to suggest that television programming has a general tendency toward "straightforward and static composition
over more complicated arrangements" and the use of "close-ups and two-shots
rather than long shots" (Vermeulen and Rustad, 2013: 341), within TV fiction,
these conventions are considerably more applicable to continuing soap operas
and to sitcoms than they are to high-end TV dramas. The streamlined shooting
and post-production of soaps, for example, leaves them minimal opportunity for
"complicated arrangements" (ibid.: 341). Moreover, soap operas' deployment of
"emotional realism" (Ang, 1993: 61) *requires* the frequent use of close-ups and
two-shots because of their crucial function in enlisting the emotional engagement
of viewers. However, these same conventions are considerably less overt for high-
end TV dramas, which by definition use a single-camera mode of production and
aim to 'show' rather than 'tell' their stories through the incorporation of 'action'
and location scenes.

The upcoming discussions investigate the ways in which aesthetic objectives produce and differentiate style. Although complex serials provide the examples, the assertions and arguments are characteristic of high-end TV drama as
a larger category. As aesthetic traditions with an established importance to the
stylistic analysis of TV drama, the exploration of differences between 'naturalism', 'realism', 'modernism' and 'postmodernism' is crucial to the above purpose.
Moreover, 'naturalism', 'realism' and 'postmodernism', the three foremost aesthetic traditions, are important in creating the production contexts for 'zero-
degree', 'first-degree' and 'second-degree' style, as terms that have informed
scholarly discussions of TV drama style. An understanding of these, both as aesthetic movements in TV drama and as 'degrees' of style, can also explain the
significant aesthetic and stylistic contrasts between 'continuing soap operas'[8] and
complex serials.

Naturalism or Zero-Degree Style

> Scenes were played wide, with a dominance of two- and three-shots that emphasize conversation. If close-ups were used, they were typically reaction shots, underlining a character's internal point of view. There were no flourishes, canted camera angles, videographic ecstasies, or even bracketed montages. The sets were just that: spaces where quality actors could perform live.
>
> *John Caldwell*[9]

The above assertions highlight the production strategies and stylistic characteristics of 'zero-degree' style, which characterized American sitcoms from *I Love Lucy* in the 1950s to *Married With Children* in the 1980s, achieving much the same aesthetic effects regardless of whether film or video was the shooting medium. Its continuing deployment, in both continuing soap operas and studio-shot sitcoms since, underlines that 'zero-degree' style is neither the repercussion of technological limitations on TV production (even if these helped make it pervasive in the first place) nor the necessary companion of shooting on videotape. Instead, it is the aesthetic consequence of a multi-camera, studio-shot production mode. 'Zero-degree' style continues to function as the default aesthetic for shows whose studio shooting, dialogue-driven narratives and limited camera movements combine to enable the kind of streamlined, fast-turn-around production that responds most effectively to television's ongoing appetite for new episodes.

As such, 'zero-degree' style is not at all characteristic of complex serial dramas, which are shot and post-produced at a more leisurely pace, combine interiors with location scenes, and deploy a single-camera production mode. Yet 'zero-degree' style is important to clarify in this chapter because this helps to demonstrate that the stylistic differences between complex serials (as high-end productions) and continuing soap operas (as modestly budgeted productions) begin with their use of contrasting production modes. While the idea of 'zero-degree' style has informed American investigations of television style (see Caldwell, 1995; Butler, 2010), its equivalent in British TV scholarship has been 'naturalism' (see Caughie, 1981; 2000; Nelson, 1997). While both terms have informed aesthetic and stylistic analyses of TV drama, it is important to underline that, when applied to television (rather than to theatre or literature, in which both aesthetic traditions originated), they refer to precisely the same aesthetic and production conditions, which means that 'naturalism' and 'zero-degree' style (or ZD) are identical.

Naturalism is distinguished by a multi-camera, studio-shot mode of production and a consequent stage-like approach to performance. Its two foremost aesthetic characteristics are registered by John Caughie (1981: 338), his assertions incorporating ideas from former BBC dramatist Troy Kennedy Martin. One is "a preoccupation with 'people's verbal relationships with each other', and a consequent privileging of dialogue at the expense of action". The other is "a strict observance of natural time, which [means] that editing simply [follows] the characters rather than expressing a view of them". Helping to explain why naturalism and ZD are associated with a dearth of stylistic artifice is that their production mode leaves minimal potential for the camera and medium to be used subjectively. Instead, camerawork and editing are largely limited to observing and recording the facial expression and dialogue of the performing actors.

Naturalism/ZD's emphasis on the recording and coverage of performances can be contrasted with the ability of 'realism' to use the camerawork and editing to construct a point of view, a process to which dialogue need not contribute. Naturalism/ZD prefers to 'tell' rather than 'show' the details of a story, a situation in which dialogue is the foremost narrative device. This reliance on dialogue gives rise to other limitations on the mise-en-scène, camerawork and editing of TV dramas using it. When dialogue is the emphasis, the 'writer's voice' is the input that is privileged, reducing the creative agency of directors, since dialogue becomes the underlying framework for the narrative. Where a narrative is driven by dialogue there needs to be a fidelity to natural time, or the time in which lines are spoken by one character and responded to by another. Yet, because the scene hangs on an actor's ability to speak the words put in their mouth by writers, the director can do very little with that but photograph it in as interesting a way as possible. These constraints of naturalism/ZD, the aesthetic regime to which TV fiction was limited until the 1960s, underscore the critique that Troy Kennedy Martin (1964: 65) mounts against it, in which the following assertion is crucial:

> Since naturalism evolved from a theatre of dialogue, the director is forced into photographing faces talking and faces reacting. The director faced with a torrent of words can only retreat into the neutrality of the two- and three-shot where the camera, caged from seizing anything of significance, is emasculated and only allowed to gaze around the room following the conversation like an attentive stranger.

This interplay between dialogue and reaction means that the editor of a naturalist/ZD scene is literally "following the ball", as one editor, Nicola Smith, terms it (cited in Dunleavy, 1995: 88). In this process 'the ball', a synonym for the dramatic focus, determines where the visual emphasis should be. "When a piece of drama happens", Smith explains, "'the ball' moves between various characters. But 'the ball' isn't necessarily the delivery of information, it can be the receiving of that information" (ibid.). Accordingly, naturalism/ZD's emphasis on dialogue imposes an editing rhythm rather like that of a ping-pong ball bouncing back and forth over a net. Naturalism/ZD's "strict observance of natural time" (Caughie, 1981: 33) is a consequence of this emphasis on dialogue, since it is difficult to elide time or space if it means cutting into a piece of dialogue.

While naturalism/ZD is not at all characteristic of high-end TV drama, it remains the default aesthetic for continuing soap opera. Even though soap operas are now shot on HD digital formats, these are anchored in the aesthetics of naturalism/ZD on the basis of their fast-turn-around mode of production, as one designed to enable and sustain the production of what is usually five new episodes per week. Fast-turn-around production (see Dunleavy, 1995) requires the following basic strategies: (1) studio-based shooting, the pace of which (because of the controlled environment of a studio) is many times faster than shooting on location; (2) a multi-camera set-up, usually three to four cameras which move on dollies through an established range of mostly interior sets; (3) minimal time for set-up or rehearsal (a maximum of 15–20 minutes to record a scene); and (4) dialogue-driven storytelling, to which 'follow the ball' editing brings a coherent narrative line and dramatic focus. Although naturalism/ZD style has been derided on the basis of its stylistic simplicity, from the perspective of soap producers and directors, this absence of stylistic artifice is an advantage not a flaw. As one producer emphasizes, "[t]he clarity of line through an episode is the important thing for me. So you don't do a lot of fancy shots [or] camera moves" (cited in Dunleavy, 1995: 86). The camera must remain unobtrusive, with movements and cuts positioned to enhance the smooth flow of the central storytelling device, dialogue. Although a contrast with the sophisticated and subjective camerawork deployed for complex serials, naturalism/ZD remains an ideal aesthetic for soap operas, not only because of their faster pace of production than other TV fiction, but also because of the soap's discursive emphasis on reflection rather than action.

Realism or First-Degree Style

'Realism' is the aesthetic that has dominated screen fiction, both in theatrical feature film and in filmed TV drama. Echoing the stylistic equivalence between naturalism and ZD, the aesthetics of 'realism' can be considered to constitute 'first-degree' (FD) style. Although FD has evaded analysis in TV scholarship, its existence is nevertheless implicit in scholarly discussions of 'zero-degree' and 'second-degree' style; FD being the style that fills the yawning gap between them. While primetime TV drama was largely limited to naturalism/ZD until the late 1960s, it increasingly favored 'realism' thereafter. Realism/FD became the defining aesthetic for high-end TV drama as technological advances rendered it practicable and inter-network competition justified the higher production costs involved.

In high-end TV drama, mimetic realism is the foremost objective and 'realism' is the aesthetic through which this is pursued. Yet, as John Hill (1986: 57) underlines: "Realism, no less than any other type of art, depends on conventions, conventions which … have successfully achieved the status of being accepted as 'realistic'". The shared objective of 'realist' screen texts is to create a plausible, coherent diegetic world and to use camerawork, mise-en-scène, editing and soundtrack to foster and maintain audience belief in it. Constructions of 'the real' are also influenced by the conventions of 'verisimilitude' (which center on the evocation of and resemblance to a particular time and place). Yet since "each genre has its own particular conventions of verisimilitude over and above those of mainstream narrative fiction as a whole", as Stephen Neale (1981: 19) argues, the achievement of verisimilitude in TV drama is primarily a function of what Neale terms "systems of credibility" and "modes of fetishistic belief", rather than being simply a question of "fidelity to the real" (ibid.). Through the illusory potentials of camerawork and editing in particular, 'realism' aims to achieve what Caughie (1981: 343) calls an "invisibility of form" and a spectator who "forgets the camera". In concert with the many facets of mise-en-scène, the diegetic potentials of camerawork and editing are harnessed in 'realist' screen fictions via such camera, framing and editing techniques as the 'shot-reverse shot', 'eyeline match', '180 degree rule', 'cut on action' and the aesthetic construction of 'point-of-view'. Important to a TV drama's ability to engage viewers in a particular character and predicament is what Caughie (1981: 341-342) terms the "dramatic look", referring to the "system of looks and glances" (ibid.) that operates to privilege a particular perspective on the events depicted.

Requiring camerawork, mise-en-scène, editing and soundtrack to work together to produce its effects, realism aims to conceal all signs of its constructedness, this including its considerable capacity for subjectivity. Important to this is the ability of realism to create a "self-contained, internally consistent world which is real-seeming" (Fiske, 1987: 130) and to use the above techniques "to hide its nature as discourse" (ibid.: 131). As Fiske (ibid.: 130) elaborates:

> Realism imposes coherence and resolution on a world that has neither ... [The realist narrative's] internal coherence requires that the diegetic world must appear self-sufficient and unbroken: everything that we need to know in order to understand it must be included, and anything that contradicts or disturbs this understanding must be excised.

Hence realism, even though it supplies the subjectivity that is missing from naturalism/ZD, constructs a *preferred* meaning and reading on the basis of its ability to privilege particular ideas about and constructions of 'the real'. This capacity foregrounds Colin MacCabe's definition of the "classic realist text" (1981: 217) as "one in which there is a hierarchy amongst the discourses which compose the text" and this "is defined in terms of an empirical notion of truth". The key repercussion, according to MacCabe, is that the "realist text (a heavily 'closed' discourse) cannot deal with the real in its contradictions" (ibid.: 224). Instead, realism "fixes the subject in a point of view from which everything becomes obvious" (ibid.) placing "the spectator outside the realm of contradiction and of action" (ibid.: 232).

Although observing the tendency of realist texts toward ideological conservatism (1981: 217) as a consequence of the above limitation, MacCabe acknowledges how realism can exploit the subjectivity of the camera and/or its screen medium for progressive outcomes. It can, for example, use realist conventions to acknowledge contradictions "between the dominant discourse of the text and the dominant ideological discourses of the time" (ibid.: 225). Moreover, because it incorporates a hierarchy of discourses, a realist text can evaluate the truth claims of one of its discourses against those of other discourses in the same text. Even if realist texts cannot investigate contradictory versions of the real (a role that *can* be performed by the 'modernist' and 'postmodernist' aesthetics to be discussed later), viewers can still 'read between the lines' of their different and competing discourses. MacCabe (ibid.: 219) explains that:

> Through the knowledge we gain from the narrative we can split the discourses of the various characters from their situation and compare what is said in these discourses with what has been revealed to us through narration. The camera shows us what happens – it tells the truth against which we can measure the discourses.

A scene from *The Sopranos* demonstrates how this 'splitting' of discourses operates. This show's pilot episode opens by depicting the first meeting between stressed out mobster Tony Soprano and newly appointed psychiatrist Dr. Jennifer Melfi. Flashback cutaway sequences are inserted to introduce the moral dilemma constituted by Tony's conflicting roles as family man, mobster and patient. As Dr. Melfi struggles to find out what 'Mr. Soprano' does for a living, Tony chooses his words carefully when relating his workday as a 'waste management consultant'. In these scenes, the validity of the above discourse – Tony's first visit to Dr. Melfi, a challenging situation for both parties – is subverted by the discourse asserted by the cutaway scenes. Tony's response to Melfi's question about how he resolved the problem arising from a client's unpaid debt is simply that he did "Nothing. We had coffee". Tony is still completing this dialogue when the action cuts from Melfi's office to a scene depicting what happened during this 'coffee' meeting. As revealed by the images, sounds and dialogue that follow, Tony Soprano does everything but discuss the matter of the unpaid debt calmly. Instead, after Christopher Moltisanti spies the errant man, Tony hunts him down using Christopher's new Lexus, driving the car bonnet into the man's leg and forcing him to the ground. As Dr. Melfi listens to Tony's sanitized version of events, the camera shows Tony beating the errant man relentlessly, as oblivious to his victim's bloodstained face and sobs as he is to the crowd of onlookers now observing this very public attack. Contradictory versions of 'the real' in these first minutes of *The Sopranos* are foregrounded by the extreme (visual and verbal) contrasts between what Tony and Dr. Melfi tell each other and what the mise-en-scène, camerawork and dialogue of the cutaway sequences reveal.

Especially when created at a sufficient distance from the direct influence of commercial imperatives, notably of spot advertising, realism can produce discourses that directly challenge prevailing ideologies. As realism expanded to become the normative aesthetic for primetime TV drama, scholars observed some different approaches to it. One of these, labeled 'progressive realism' by John

Caughie (1981), recognizes how realism can expose and/or challenge dominant ideologies. Identifying key markers of 'progressive realism', Caughie (1981: 350) highlights the attempt to "confirm an identity (of sexuality or class)", to "recover repressed experience or history", or to "contest the dominant image with an alternative identity". As an approach that works in opposition to the objectives of advertiser-funded television, progressive realism has been most possible for TV dramas devised to progress 'public service' remits – from the BBC's *Boys From the Blackstuff* (1982) to the Danish (DR) network's *Forbrydelsen/The Killing* (2007–10). Yet, it is indicative of the political engagement of complex serials and the risk-taking of their commissioning networks that progressive realism has imbued some of them, beginning with HBO's *Oz*. A leading example of progressive realism, not only for American complex serials but for TV drama internationally, is *The Wire* (HBO, 2002–2008), which, in the ways discussed in Chapter 4, aims to show that Baltimore's problems, and by extension those of America itself, are rooted in the failure of public institutions.

Modernism

'Modernism' was a movement in art, literature and culture that involved the criticism of advanced commodification. Accordingly, its opportunities in TV drama have been extremely few due to the basic incompatibility of a modernist philosophy with the commercial objectives of most television. The consequent dearth of modernism in TV drama, despite the aesthetic influence of 'high modernism' on art cinema (see Stam, 2000b: 260-61), lies behind the disagreement evident among scholars about whether television – a predominantly commercial, populist medium – has ever been able to produce 'modernist' texts. Jim Collins (1995: 330-31), for example, contends: "Television, unlike architecture, literature, or painting, never had a modernist phase that could serve as a point of departure for post-modern television". Although Collins's assertion is not inaccurate if applied to American broadcast television, his argument underestimates the opportunities for modernist experimentation in TV dramas produced entirely outside the influences of commercialism. The foremost context for this has to date been in the high-end drama produced for British and European 'public service' TV networks, 'prestige' examples of which have enjoyed opportunities for stylistic risk-taking. On the other side of this debate, therefore, John Caughie (2000: 155) locates a 'modernist' strain in British TV drama of the 1980s, identifying BBC mini-serial *The Singing Detective* "as one of the significant works of twentieth-century British modernism".

While realism conceals its capacity to produce subjective discourses, 'modernism' deploys its aesthetic and stylistic elements in ways that seek to expose the constructed-ness and subjectivities of realism. Its characteristics in TV drama are exemplified by *The Singing Detective*, to which this discussion, in comparing modernism with realism, briefly turns. *The Singing Detective* constructs a multi-faceted diegesis, whose four story strands are separated by their settings in different British regions and historical eras, in opposition to realism's tendency to construct a coherent narrative world. Whereas realism uses mise-en-scène, camerawork, soundtrack and editing to solicit emotional identification and engagement, *The Singing Detective* uses all of these to encourage a degree of audience 'distanciation',[10] with examples in the deliberate mismatching of images and sounds, having the same actors playing multiple roles, and allowing characters to directly address the camera. Whereas realism deploys narrative coherence and flow as a way to maintain audience belief in its diegetic world, *The Singing Detective* not only offers a disrupted and fragmented narrative, but also fosters an additional sense of diegetic instability by allowing some characters to self-reflexively analyze their own roles and/or escape their designated story strand to intervene in the progression of another. Modernism's characteristic disdain for commercialism and commodification is reflected in *The Singing Detective* as a disdain for the popular TV drama product.

Postmodern Aesthetics

Common to naturalism/ZD and realism/FD, as they are used in TV drama, is their aim to 'make natural' a particular perspective on, or expression of, 'the real'. Hence both aesthetics operate on the assumption that "there is no doubt that reality can be depicted" (Thornham and Purvis, 2005: 159). As the aesthetic expression of postmodern theory's rejection of this kind of totalizing assumption, and reflecting its perceptions that discourse *constructs* rather than *reflects* realities and truths (ibid.), postmodern textuality, as with modernism, deploys style in ways that suggest that reality and truth are "relative and contingent" (ibid.: 155). Important to this achievement in TV drama, however, is that postmodern textuality operates within a realist/FD framework, since it is only through the mixing and juxtaposition of these different aesthetic modes that the "relative and contingent" nature of reality and truth can be demonstrated.

In contrast to the high culture and anti-commercial orientation of screen modernism, 'postmodern' aesthetics have flourished in fictional shows produced for commercial television and articulate their affinities with its populism in several ways. Postmodern TV dramas are overtly intertextual, this feature involving a tendency to incorporate and/or rearticulate earlier texts in ways that infer a self-awareness of their own status as texts. For Jim Collins (2000: 763) this extends to the extreme of "a hyperawareness on the part of the text itself of its cultural status, function and history, as well as of the conditions of its circulation and reception". Postmodern TV dramas reveal this hyperawareness, not only through their re-appropriation and re-articulation of earlier tropes, genres and styles, but also through their incorporation of frequent self-reflexive references to other texts.

A striking example of the hyperawareness identified by Collins is evident in the pilot episode of *Six Feet Under*, whose family funeral parlor business provides the main vehicle for the critique of the commodification of death and grief that (as explained in Chapter 2) was important to its creator-showrunner, Alan Ball. In this episode, however, postmodern aesthetics operate to effect a broader critique of the commodification of American TV drama. As with some other *Six Feet Under* episodes, the pilot makes reference to the ideas and aesthetic strategies of Dennis Potter, an ardent critic of commercial television. Highlighting Potter's own unease about the capacity of commercial schedules to foster a dialogue between advertisements and TV shows, John Cook (1998: 143-44) explains Potter's sense that their juxtaposition in TV schedules encourages a "complex exchange of mutual values" which favors consumerism whilst profoundly shaping the TV shows created to co-exist with them. As Cook (ibid.) observes:

> Not only do most programme styles ape those of the commercials (and vice versa), it also feels as if they are all *selling* something ... The result is that TV plays and drama series come to merge with the rest of the programmes – trying to 'sell' themselves as technically innovative or exciting and in the very process, losing all sense of distinctiveness from the rest of the schedule.

Influenced by Potter's TV drama (Ball, author interview, 2013), Ball's own irritation at the many textual consequences for American TV fiction that arise as a direct consequence of its function as 'bait' for advertisers is articulated through the embedding of three different faux 'commercials' (for embalming and funeral service products) into the narrative flow of *Six Feet Under*'s pilot episode. Appearing suddenly, their mise-en-scène evocative of 1950s-era TV naturalism and in striking contrast to the visual style of the events on either side of them, these mini-texts interrupt narrative flow to mount an effective critique of the way in which commercials profoundly shape, as well as merely interrupt, the TV narratives that host them.

These intertextual strategies may also function as TV drama's equivalent of the "ironic articulation of the 'already said'" that Umberto Eco considers to be "the distinguishing feature of postmodern communication" (cited in Collins, 2000: 761). The appearance of the word 'ironic' is important in clarifying the intentions behind postmodern textuality's use and referencing of other texts. Postmodern aesthetics, Collins suggests, cultivate an ambivalent relationship with these other texts, as evident through the "very different perspectives" that may be deployed, "ranging from nostalgic reverence to vehement attack or a mixture of these strategies" (ibid.). It seems important that AQD and complex serials, both of which have deployed postmodern aesthetics, have entailed somewhat different strategies. The use of self-reflexivity as an "ironic articulation of the already said" (ibid.) has long been an important feature of the AQD paradigm, from *St. Elsewhere* and *Moonlighting* in the 1980s to *Boston Legal* and *House MD* in the 2000s. All these examples reflect AQD's enthusiasm for generic mixing, for the kind of self-reflexive play that foregrounds a text's acknowledgment of its own textuality and for the direct referencing of shows with which the text is claiming some kind of relationship. Yet in AQD productions, these activities and references have more often involved other TV shows.

AQD's tendency to make references to TV rather than to non-televisual texts is mitigated by their design for linear broadcast schedules within which many different forms, genres and styles are juxtaposed. When *House MD* references reality series *The Apprentice*, for example, an ongoing occurrence through Season 4, it does so with an awareness that its viewers know of, if they have not actually watched, this show. When *Boston Legal* (ABC, 2004–08) references the 50-plus 'baby boomer' generation in 'Juiced' (5:11), it understands its own position as a TV drama whose stars and following are themselves 50-ish and the demographic problem that this entails for ABC, which, when this episode aired in 2008, was moving to cancel this show. In a notably self-reflexive speech and address in 'Juiced', a regular character, lawyer Carl Sack, mounts an indirect protest about *Boston*'s cancellation, citing the unrivaled disposable income and regular TV viewing habits of his own cohort, the baby boomers.[11]

In their own use of intertextuality and self-reflexivity, complex serials have been less focused than AQD on other TV dramas and more consistently interested in feature films. One contributor to this difference is that complex serials are without direct conceptual precedent in TV drama, though may have antecedent relationships with either feature films, as with *The Sopranos*, *Deadwood* and *Stranger Things*, or literature, as with *True Blood*, *Game of Thrones*, *Dexter* and *The Handmaid's Tale*. There is another explanation for these tendencies in the complex serial's origination for non-broadcast networks. Although these are differentiated from broadcast networks by their cable or internet platforms, common to them is their market position as optional TV services. Influenced by this, their commercial strategies have included attempts to disavow their status as television (as HBO did with its 'Not TV' tag-line), rather than to foreground this through the intertextual referencing of other TV shows. Instead, complex serials have claimed cultural cachet for themselves and their networks through the use of self-reflexive references to films and/or literature, both of which have traditionally enjoyed a higher cultural status than television.

This broader intertextual frame of reference for complex serials is exemplified by *The Sopranos*. Generic mixing, or the blending of different genres in the creation of a TV show (Mittell, 2004), has been an element of concept design for complex serials. While *The Sopranos*' generic mix combines psychodrama, family melodrama and the mafia film, its generic self-reflexivity is the focus here. In Tony Soprano's very first voiceover, he tells viewers: "It's good to be in something from the ground floor. I came too late for that, I know. But lately I've been getting the feeling that I came in at the end, the best is over". Delivered just a few minutes into the pilot, Tony's statement can be read as an articulation of a broader 'postmodern condition', anchored as it seems to be, in a mobster's experience of mid-life crisis. Yet as Glen Creeber (2002) observes, it also registers something else: a drama that longs to be 'golden age' Hollywood cinema rather than contemporary television, specifically, a gangster film in the tradition of *The Godfather* trilogy. Reflecting Chase's own belief that "TV ruined the movies" by gradually imposing its institutional tendencies toward "pandering, cheerleading, family entertainment shit" (cited in Creeber, 2002: 124), Tony is characterized as a depressed, Prozac-dependent modern Don who pines for the past because he feels that the "best is over" and he has missed it. Although his fascination with history is broader, Tony most laments the lost "standards and ... values epitomized by an earlier generation of gangsters" (Creeber, 2002: 126). Even though Tony can remember the 'glory days' of the Mob – albeit more as they were represented in the movies than as he experienced them at the elbow of his gangster father, Johnny-Boy – his inability to emulate these fuels his psychological angst. Tony's most treasured movie is Francis Ford Coppola's *The Godfather* trilogy, which he watches "all the time", according to Carmela (ibid.). Whilst *The Godfather* trilogy works as a kind of aspirational training manual for Tony, its pivotal mentor/protégé relationship between Don Vito Corleone (Marlon Brando) and his son and heir, Michael (Al Pacino), is invoked in *The Sopranos* by the two equivalent relationships in which Tony finds himself. Equally unsuccessful, one is with his 'Uncle Junior', the failing former Don who shoots and nearly kills his nephew in a moment of senile diso-rientation (6:1), and the other, with Tony's own protégé, Christopher Moltisanti, who represents the Mafia's future. However, the greatest obstacle to Christopher's leadership is shown to be his lack of respect for Mafia tradition, Tony's realization of which motivates the younger man's demise. The catalyst for this – which is also *The Sopranos'* most pointed reflexive reference to the decline of cinema's gangster epic – is the artistic failure of *Cleaver* (6:14), Christopher's soulless (*Saw* meets *Reservoir Dogs*) feature film.

Second-Degree Style

A longstanding option within postmodern textuality is the manipulation of subjectivity. As a striking departure from realism, which produces a "heavily closed discourse" (MacCabe, 1981: 224), such manipulation opens textual discourses through the juxtaposition of opposing truths. The aesthetic complexity of this strategy is most pronounced when the alternative truths asserted are in conflict with the text's dominant discourse, this generating moral ambiguity and demanding moral engagement and judgment from viewers. This approach exemplifies what Pierre Barrette and Yves Picard (2014) identify and label 'second-degree' style, as one that originated in literature, there termed "literature in the second degree" (Genette, 1997). As Barrette and Picard (2014: 124) explain:

> [S]econd-degree style is a form of double meaning: a style, which demonstrates its subjectivity ... Second degree style is even more *encunciative*, when it mocks conventions, fails to deliver on expectations and destabilizes;

when it is opaque, hermetic, or even abstract. In journalistic terms, second-degree style takes the form of a commentary, editorial, or critique: a point of view that stands out, evaluates and judges and thus contributes to public debate. In cinematic terms, it is an individual perspective, if one likes, which interposes a gaze between reality and the audience in order to change both attitudes and form.

A defining feature of second-degree style (SD), therefore, is its capacity to *investigate* as well as demonstrate the "relative and contingent" nature of reality and truth (Thornham and Purvis, 2005: 155). It requires viewers to weigh up the alternative depictions of reality and truth that the text offers, which in screen narration may arise, for example, from the divergence between the revelations of dialogue as opposed to those of mise-en-scène and/or camerawork, or between different (juxtaposed or contiguous) story strands. Foregrounding its ability in screen texts to work beyond dialogue and related narration through images alone, Barrette and Picard observe that SD is both "the point of view that reflects its presence in the visual field by self-reflexive constructions" and "the image that bends toward less orality or even silence" (2014: 125). While the use of SD is by no means exclusive to complex serials, its compatibility with them is that it makes unusual demands of viewers. As Barrette and Picard underline, SD "requires a maximum level of effort" demanding that viewers "carry out a dual reading" and demanding that they "*recognise* the style" (ibid.: 124). The operation and impacts of second-degree style can be demonstrated through examples from *Mad Men* and *Breaking Bad*.

The first SD example works in *Mad Men*'s 'The Other Woman' (5:11) to sharpen this serial's larger critique of the continuing subordination of working women in the 1960s, which foregrounds the arising serious problems for core characters, Peggy Olsen and Joan Harris. For Joan, a long-serving and married employee, this is initiated in 'The Other Woman' by an indecent request from Jaguar senior executive, Herb Rennet, who tells Peter Campbell that a night with "that hot redhead, built like a B-52" will turn a possible failure for the firm in securing the Jaguar account into a likely success. Echoing the assumptions behind Rennet's request, the Jaguar 'pitch' asserts that even if it's expensive, the purchase of a beautiful car returns greater value for the financial outlay than the acquisition of a beautiful woman, because a man can "really own" the former. *Mad Men*'s use of the Jaguar story to foreground the subordination of female employees gains force from the intercutting of two scenes – one in which Don Draper delivers the Jaguar pitch to Rennet and his executive team, and the other in which Joan visits Rennet's apartment and tolerates the unwanted encounter with him. Importantly, these juxtaposed events take place some 12 hours apart, allowing Rennet to appear in both scenes. As Don attempts to sway Rennet and his team, by likening the "natural longing" of aspiring Jaguar owners to male desire for what he terms "unattainably, beautiful" women, Joan is treated much like a prostitute by Rennet as he commands "Let me see 'em", whereupon Joan, in close-up and gazing into the camera, unzips her dress. Allowing Don's monologue and pitch to male Jaguar executives to be set against the camera's witnessing of Joan with Rennet, SD's effect is to place these two events in a causal relationship, in which women and cars, however unattainable they may seem, are both (in this diegetic world, at least) commodities.

A second example occurs in the *Breaking Bad* episode 'Face Off' (4:13), as one of several key scenes in which viewers confront Walter White's duplicity and criminality, important to which is the offer of alternative discourses, from Jesse and Skyler, in particular. Earlier in the episode, Walter and Jesse have exchanged important new information: Walter reveals that Gus Fring is dead and Jesse that the poisoned Brock (the young son of Jesse's new girlfriend, Andrea) was given lily-of-the-valley rather than ricin, and doctors expect him to recover. As with earlier scenes in which Walter's behavior encourages viewers to "question their allegiances" to him (Gilligan, Brooker interview, 2013), viewers are positioned on a higher plane of awareness than other characters, and moral judgment about what is shown or inferred is left to them. Jesse's affinity with children (a legacy of the parental rejection that plagued his own childhood) has been established by Season 2's 'Peekaboo' episode (2:6) in which, during a mission to avenge the theft of money by a meth-addicted couple, Jesse is horrified to discover their tiny malnourished son. Nuanced by this backstory, which also highlights Jesse's attachment to Brock and shows that Brock's poisoning is fueling the competition between Walter and Gus for Jesse's loyalty, it can be surmised that either Walter or Gus has poisoned Brock. Yet, as active viewers understand, only Walter knows Jesse sufficiently well to anticipate how strongly he will react to Brock's poisoning. Hence, even though this episode's dialogue implicates Gus, the backstory evidence points to Walter. It is in the context of Walter's duplicity and unreliability as primary character that SD offers an effective, yet subtle, way to expose him. The final shot of the episode, musically underscored, offers a slow but purposeful pan left and zoom in to close-up. The object of the camera's focus is one of the potted plants beside Walter's swimming pool. In the absence of characters or dialogue, the camera controls the 'truth' that is ultimately revealed. After zooming in on the plant, it lingers on the label, 'Lily-of-the-Valley', thereby effecting a silent but unmistakable rejoinder to Walter's vehement denial that he could ever murder a child.

Case Study of *Stranger Things*

> We came from a neighbourhood that was aesthetically very, very similar to [the one in *Stranger Things*] … We hung out with a group of nerdy friends, playing games … There was this sense [if we went into the woods] that we might find a treasure map or whatever and go on this huge adventure. It's autobiographical in the sense of we wish something like this had happened and we wish we had found something in the woods. Our imagination would always take us there.
>
> *Ross Duffer* [12]

While other complex serials examined in this book were all commissioned by American cable networks, *Stranger Things* (2016–) was devised for the streaming service Netflix. Its selection as a case study in this chapter underlines that, having emerged on cable television, complex serial drama is among the options for the serial drama being originated by IDTV networks.

As a story in which a community's search for a missing boy unfolds in tandem with the arrival of a terrified, shaven-haired girl, *Stranger Things* stands out within TV drama for its innovative blending of 'coming of age', science fiction and horror traditions and tropes. Consistent with a broader tendency for complex serials, *Stranger Things* has looked more to cinema than to television for conceptual and aesthetic inspiration. As with most other complex serials *Stranger Things* combines the aesthetics of 'realism' and 'postmodernism', pairing its references to earlier texts with painstaking verisimilitude to effect a celebration of the look, feel and popular culture of the 1980s, which brings the capacity to induce nostalgia. But, deviating from the tendency of complex serials to foreground a particular genre (as *The Sopranos* does with its references to the mafia film), *Stranger Things*, having been influenced by such different generic traditions as those above, pays dutiful homage to all three. While its 'coming of age' theme incites frequent nods to *ET* (1982) and *Stand by Me* (1986), *Stranger Things*' science fiction and horror elements ground themselves in 1980s popular culture via references to films like *Alien* (1979), *Aliens* (1986) and *The Thing* (1982). While some critics have cited *Stranger Things*' intertextuality as an indicator of its creative debt to earlier texts, Jean-Luc Godard's advice to film-makers, "It's not where you take things from – it's where you take them to" (cited in Jarmusch, 2013), provides a more useful frame within which to assess its originality.

Stranger Things tells an original story that bristles with a sense of encroaching yet irreparable danger, arising from the collision of 'ordinary' and 'extraordinary' occurrences in the fictional Hawkins, Indiana, in 1983. Despite Hawkins' potential to be the kind of sleepy little town in which nothing much happens, it hosts a monolithic research facility, the Hawkins National Laboratory, images of which open the first episode. Implicating this government-owned facility in the supernatural occurrences to which the wider community is vulnerable, its mind control experiments have accidentally opened a portal to a supernatural, subterranean realm called 'the Upside-down', a perennially dark, slime-covered and cold version of the 'natural' world. While inhospitable to humans, especially since its giant slug-like life forms are apt to invade their bodies, the Upside-down (USD) is most immediately troublesome as the home of a single terrifying creature, the 'Demogorgon', with the agility and incentive to traverse these supernatural and natural dimensions to endanger Hawkins' townsfolk.

At the center of *Stranger Things*' 'ordinary' domain are four *Dungeons and Dragons*-obsessed pre-teen boys, Mike, Will, Lucas and Dustin, and their families. Of the two families depicted, one is the Byers, comprising Will's mother, Joyce, and brother, Jonathan, and the other, the Wheelers, the parents of Mike and his sister, Nancy. Also important to the 'ordinary' are the town sheriff, Jim Hopper, and high-school seniors Steve and Barb (Nancy's boyfriend and best friend, respectively). Disrupting this 'ordinary' domain is the menacing world of the 'extraordinary'. Two interconnected events comprise the serial's first long cold open in which the clash between opposing domains begins, this incited by the marauding Demogorgon. First, in a scene which establishes the Hawkins National Laboratory, a white-coated researcher runs for his life through the corridors, pursued but soon taken by the unseen creature. Second, after the boys' lengthy *Dungeons and Dragons* 'campaign' finishes, Will reflects on his own performance, telling Mike, "the Demogorgon got me". As viewers soon realize, this self-reflexive admission foreshadows Will's immediate fate. As he cycles home, Will is identified, pursued and finally abducted by the still unseen Demogorgon. Although a publicly funded Department of Energy research facility and program, the Hawkins Lab is implicated in Will's abduction, if only because its activities have left the town vulnerable to supernatural threats. Yet, as discovered in the first episode, the Hawkins Lab portal is but one of several access points between the town and the USD. With the pursuit of Will, a new rift, between the walls of the Byers' home, has been opened. The Hawkins Lab is finally crucial as the place of origin, incarceration and suffering for the serial's most intriguing and mysterious character, a pre-teen girl with minimal language, yet well-developed telekinetic abilities, who reaches out to the boys and identifies as 'Eleven'.

Stranger Things began as a 20-page pitch document, conceived by twins Matt and Ross Duffer. Indicative of the risk that Netflix seemed more than willing to take in 'greenlighting' their idea, the very feature that most distinguishes *Stranger Things* within high-end TV drama – the narrative predominance of pre-teen rather than adult characters – was the primary deterrent for the many cable networks (reputedly 15–20) which 'passed' on the Duffers' pitch (Grow, 2016). As Matt Duffer recalls, these networks disliked their foregrounding of child characters, advising the brothers to either turn their idea "into a kids show" (cited in ibid.: 2016), or to adjust the story to focus on the Sherriff Hopper character and the investigation of paranormal activity. Instead, the Duffers continued searching for a network that might allow them to retain the child-like perspective they wanted for this story. The conduits for finding this were Shawn Levy and Dan Cohen, CEO and VP respectively, of a studio called Twenty-One Laps Entertainment. Beginning when Cohen brought the script to Levy, the pair saw sufficient potential to bring the Duffer brothers in to discuss the project, buy the rights to their idea, offer the show to Netflix and assemble the additional creative personnel that would be required. Within this creative team, and while the Duffers did direct some of the episodes, Levy and Cohen felt it important that the brothers (who would also be EPs and showrunners) lead the writers' room.

Shot on an Ultra HD digital camera,[13] *Stranger Things* exemplifies the effects of the industrial convergence between feature film and high-end TV drama production examined earlier in this chapter.[14] The shooting of two episodes at a time for

Stranger Things to which 21–22 days were allocated (Zimmerman, cited in Hullfish, 2016) is a point of contrast with broadcast TV dramas, which tend to be shot one episode at a time, not necessarily in order of their screening, each receiving seven to nine days (Del Valle, 2008: 10). Another deviation from broadcast drama in the workflow devised for *Stranger Things* was its approach to post-production. Whereas each episode of a broadcast drama is post-produced individually (while other episodes are being scripted, filmed or edited), the first season of *Stranger Things* was post-produced in one continuous stretch. Dean Zimmerman (cited in Hullfish, 2016), one of its two editors, suggests that this approach strengthened the serial's narrative and aesthetic continuity:

> [W]e did all our mixing and color-timing on the back end once all the episodes were locked and completed and all the visual effects were done. It allowed us that flexibility of being able to watch the entire series and go back into respective episodes and really fine-tune this basically eight-hour movie, which I think paid huge dividends in the storytelling.

Kevin Ross (cited in Hullfish, 2016), the other editor, underlines that the above strategy allowed "twenty-eight straight days of mixing", something "that just never happens in television". These differences highlight the broader attempt with *Stranger Things*, enabled partly by its limited number of episodes relative to a broadcast drama season, to "make [its production] as much like a feature [film]" (ibid.) as possible.

Although many commentators and viewers have registered the particular influence of 1980s films on the narrative and aesthetics of *Stranger Things*, its tapestry of cultural influences and references is far broader, incorporating, in addition to the films mentioned, popular novels, posters, video and board games, music and clothing from 1983. Distancing *Stranger Things* from the many texts to which it refers, however, is that, whereas these are mostly cultural products of the early 1980s, it is a twenty-first century production that references 1980s texts as part of its larger effort to evoke the look, feel and culture of the decade. An additional contributor to this is the serial's meticulous attention to the construction of verisimilitude, one element of which is the technological idiosyncrasies of a pre-digital age. In addition to the rabbit-eared TV set that Mike's father struggles to adjust in one scene, Matisse (2016) finds examples in the "vinyl records and cassette tapes, single-speed bikes providing endless freedom, and AV Club devotees with ham radios and walkie-talkies".

The 1983 setting for *Stranger Things* is also important in representing the historic moment by which an earlier (1960s and 1970s) transition from social modernity to social postmodernity was being completed, a process whose key change agent was rampant neoliberal ideology. A sense of community unease about era-specific government priorities resounds in *Stranger Things* through the unethical practices occurring inside the Hawkins Lab, which, as its narrative asserts, have a longer history. Two characters in particular, even though they barely interact, effect a probing investigation of this laboratory, a politically charged thread within *Stranger Things* because the state-sanctioned research program that it reveals has a real-life precedent in CIA project MKUltra, circa 1950–1973 (Drell, 2016). One character important to this thread is Sheriff Jim Hopper, whose search for Will leads to his discovery that the Hawkins Lab has conducted mind-control research in which human subjects were used as guinea pigs for experiments in telepathy and telekinesis. The other is the gifted but damaged Eleven, whose backstory – as a child victim of these experiments – is narrated in flashbacks.

While the USD and Demogorgon provide it with rich sources of mystery, intrigue and spectacle, *Stranger Things* accrues narrative and aesthetic complexity in its investigation of the identity and deeply troubled backstory of Eleven. Initial answers are provided by her interaction with Dr Martin Brenner, the senior Hawkins Lab researcher Eleven calls 'Papa'. Under pressure to perform increasingly difficult and morally questionable tasks, and punished when she falls short of expectations, Eleven's abject relationship with Brenner is overtly reminiscent of 'Stockholm Syndrome'. Only partially resolved by the end of the show's first season is the question of how Eleven – a character whose flashbacks are all located within the Hawkins compound, suggesting her history of incarceration – became the subject of Brenner's experiments.

Important to the narrative and aesthetic complexity of *Stranger Things* is the expectation that viewers will re-watch its text so as to mine it for additional understandings. The mystery surrounding Eleven provides a strong example of how viewers are motivated to do this and the additional details that are available to those who undertake repeated viewings. While it is not at all unusual for complex serials to incite and reward the re-watching of their episodes, the distinction of *Stranger Things* is not only that it constructs the kind of complexity that invites and rewards this re-watching, but also that Netflix's online platform opens the text fully to this very activity. Two threads demonstrate how narrative and aesthetic complexity work together to effect the investigation of Eleven.

The first involves the discoveries of Sheriff Hopper. The resistance of Hawkins' Lab personnel to his investigation of Will's disappearance leads Hopper to suspect that Will was taken by Lab personnel and to research its institutional history. As with all other main threads in *Stranger Things*, Hopper's investigation unfolds through multiple interweaving storylines, and its key narrative kernels are dispersed across several episodes. Together, kernel scenes establish an elaborate connection between Eleven, Brenner and a woman called Terry Ives. The experience that links them is a historic research project named MKUltra, named after the real-life research program on which the Hawkins Lab is modeled (Drell, 2016). Hopper uncovers this connection in microfiche news articles, whose details can only be fully deciphered by viewers who are willing to use the freeze frame button to read them. His findings lead Hopper to visit Ives and her sister, Becky – this visit supplies further revelations. Although the text refrains from confirming that Eleven is none other than Jane, the daughter who was taken from Terry Ives during her own incarceration at the Hawkins Lab, it reveals that Eleven is Jane by showing rather than telling viewers. As Becky Ives explains what happened to her sister and the special abilities that saw baby Jane retained by Hawkins, the camera cross-cuts to images of Eleven using these same abilities. In this way, even though most other characters are unaware of it, Eleven's identity is revealed to viewers.

The second thread narrates the backstory of Eleven in a succession of flashbacks. Together, these depict an increasingly traumatic series of experiments designed to develop her telekinetic and telepathic abilities. Whereas in the first flashback she is powerless, screaming and kicking as Brenner's assistants drag her away, her telekinetic prowess is seen to develop. As is characteristic of complex serials, these flashback scenes are delivered out of chronological order, are summoned by related anxieties experienced by the character in the narrative present and are scattered throughout the narrative, with each one providing vital 'kernel' information.[15] In successive references to *The Men Who Stare at Goats*, a 2004 novel and later film about DIA research project Stargate (ibid.), whose subjects were trained to kill animals with their minds, Eleven crushes a Coke can (1:2) and is later forced to will the death of a caged cat (1:3). It is as loyal friend to the boys and traumatized Hawkins' Lab escapee that Eleven demonstrates the extent of her telekinesis. First she flips a Hawkins van up in the air to allow the gang's escape from a convoy of Lab vehicles (1:7), second she wills the death of a team of approaching Hawkins staff (1:8), and finally she wills the disintegration of the Demogorgon (1:8). It is because of the mind-control abilities that Eleven has developed that she alone can defeat the Demogorgon. She meets and briefly touches this creature in the blackness of the arena that Brenner calls 'the bath', a sensory deprivation tank and procedure through which Eleven enters her own mind and develops the ability to communicate telepathically. It is her increasing telepathic and telekinetic powers to which the Demogorgon seems attracted, as inferred when Brenner tells her: "It's reaching out to you, because it wants you, it's calling you. So don't turn away from it this time, I want you to find it" (1:5). Easily the most frightening of Eleven's memories, the supreme terror that is her response to touching the creature (1:6) induces a powerful scream. As registered by the cracks that immediately appear in one wall of the Laboratory theater in which 'the bath' is located, it is Eleven herself who produces the exceptional force which opens the portal to the USD, an effect she understands and for which she feels solely responsible.

Stranger Things debuted on Netflix in July 2016 and was soon being labeled both a "cultural phenomenon" (Hullfish, 2016) and the "biggest TV hit" of the Northern hemisphere summer (Grow, 2016), underlining its blend of critical and popular success. Indicating a favorable industry response, *Stranger Things* received two nominations for the 2017 Golden Globe awards and its actors won a coveted Screen Actors Guild Award (for 'Outstanding Performance by an Ensemble Cast'). Yet the reception of *Stranger Things* is difficult to directly compare with that of other TV dramas because Netflix has not released any ratings data, consistent with its view that "ratings are not germane to its business model" (Holloway, 2016). Also different from the reception of TV dramas originated by cable networks is the rapidity of audience response to IDTV network originals, a facet important to *Stranger Things* because all eight episodes were released on the same day, July 15, 2016. Despite these differences, it has clearly been a very popular Netflix original, as indicated by data returned by newer measurement technologies designed for IDTV networks (ibid.). Although, as with traditional ratings, these figures are limited to the American market, they indicate that *Stranger Things* is among Netflix's most successful original productions to date. It took just 35 days for it to be viewed by an estimated 14.07 million U.S. domiciled 18–49-year-olds (ibid.) and *Stranger Things* was the third most watched Netflix original to debut in 2016 (ibid.).

Conclusions

The aesthetic and stylistic qualities of complex serials, as suggested at the outset of this chapter, are not specific to this form, instead being indicative of the capacities of high-end TV drama more broadly. However, this chapter's foregrounding of complex serials has allowed it to detail some specific ways in which creative ambitions and personnel, along with certain production strategies, combine to maximize the aesthetic objectives and stylistic achievements of these dramas. While they do not produce any consistent stylistic characteristics for complex serials, the above conditions have enabled greater attention to visualization than has generally been possible in long-format American TV drama. This is evidenced by the following four tendencies – as revealed by this chapter's investigations – of the production strategies and aesthetics of complex serials.

First is the deployment of a single-camera, film-like approach to mise-en-scène, cinematography, editing and post-production, important to which is a greater allocation of production time, usually paired with higher per-episode budgets than is usual for long-format TV drama. In addition to producing fewer episodes per season, complex serials usually receive a more generous allocation of production time per episode, this averaging eight to 12 shoot days,[16] as opposed to around seven to nine days for most other hour-long TV drama episodes (DelValle, 2008: 10). These additional resources assist complex serials to incorporate more location scenes than is conventional for long-format broadcast dramas, as evidenced by *Boardwalk Empire*, and to take longer over editing and post-production, as outlined in relation to *Stranger Things*.

Second, an approach which flows from the first, is the tendency to use the same shooting mediums (either 35mm or Ultra HD digital) and to emulate the visualization strategies deployed for feature films more closely than most other long-format TV drama can. Exemplified here by *Boardwalk Empire*, this situation is supported by the cross-deployment of cinematographers, directors and editors with experience in theatrical feature film. However, rather than yielding the equivalent of the 'cinematic look' of theatrical feature films, complex serials remain subject to a volume and continuity of completed episodes in striking contrast to feature films, whose two-hour narratives allow them to be visualized, shot and edited as one production (Del Valle, 2008). While this does not rule out the inclusion of more ambitious set-ups and potentially 'cinematic' scenes or moments, complex serials must intersperse these with other scenes whose "straightforward and static composition" (Vermeulen and Rustad, 2013: 341) helps to ensure that episode budgets and shoot-day targets can be met.

Third is that the settings for complex serials are subject to greater diversity if compared with those of broadcast TV's procedural crime series, a notably more prolific form of high-end drama. As an opportunity arising from the creation of concepts without direct precedent in TV drama, complex serials utilize aesthetics and style to cultivate a distinctive 'look' for each show, pivotal to which, as exemplified by *The Sopranos*, *Mad Men* and *Stranger Things*, is the construction and visualization of a *particular* sense of locale and verisimilitude. In the content of their idiosyncratic concepts and stories, their adoption of a specific 'point of view' on these, and their greater use of locations, complex serials deploy style in ways that can directly articulate their key narrative tensions and thematic concerns.

Fourth is the interplay in complex serials between the aesthetics of realism and postmodernism, a combination which, as evident in *Six Feet Under*, *Mad Men* and *Breaking Bad*, imbues these serials with stylistic complexity. While their use of postmodern aesthetics frequently involves the self-reflexive referencing of other texts (though more often film or literature than television), the hyperawareness (Collins, 2000) shown by complex serials as to their own status as texts begins, as we see in *The Sopranos*, with the generic mix that informs their concept design. A facet that has helped to distinguish complex serials within high-end TV drama, the former's postmodern aesthetics include the capacity for second-degree style. Deployed to facilitate the juxtaposition and investigation of opposing discourses and truths, as demonstrated in the examples from *Mad Men* and *Breaking Bad*, second-degree style "requires a maximum level of effort" from viewers (Barrette and Picard, 2014: 124), demanding not only that they "*recognise* the style" (ibid.), but also that this recognition informs the moral judgments that complex serials devolve to their viewers.

Notes

1 For a useful outline of the range of scholarly interests that comprise this field, see Sarah Cardwell (2006) "Television Aesthetics" in *Critical Studies in Television*, Vol. 1: Issue 1, pp. 72–80.

2 Since the 1970s, feature films have regularly been produced for American television and this has continued up to the present, with cable networks (beginning with HBO and Showtime) joining broadcast networks in commissioning successive feature films. In the multiplatform era, however, feature films are being commissioned for broadcast, cable and internet networks, as well as for cinema release. For increased clarity as to the platform of origination for feature films, this book and the current chapter

use the term 'theatrical feature film' for examples produced to debut in cinemas and the term 'feature film' for examples produced to debut on either broadcast, cable and internet networks.

3 All three terms will appear frequently in this chapter. 'Cinematography' combines the artistry of camerawork with the specific shooting medium deployed (either 35mm film or HD digital for complex serials) and related decisions about framing, lighting and texture. 'Mise-en-scène', although a larger domain, refers here to performances, dialogue, settings, sets and locations. 'Editing' refers to the processes through which the captured footage is selected and arranged within a scene or episode.

4 This term refers to the set of conditions and processes by which TV programming is performed and recorded.

5 See, for example, Christine Geraghty (1991), John Caughie (1981; 2000), John T. Caldwell (1995), Jane Feuer (1984b; 1994; 1995; 2007), Robin Nelson (1997; 2007a), David Lavery (2005), Trisha Dunleavy (2009), Jeremy Butler (2002; 2010), and Glen Creeber (2004; 2013).

6 The first season of *Boardwalk Empire* was crucial to the inception of this serial's period verisimilitude, and the team of key creative personnel contributing to this first season demonstrates a broader tendency for complex serials to deploy some cinematographers and directors with experience in theatrical feature film. Receiving an average of 12 shoot days per episode, this serial's showrunner was Terence Winter. Three cinematographers, Stuart Dryburgh, Kramer Morgenthau and Jonathan Freeman, established the 'look' of the show, beginning with the pilot, which was directed by Martin Scorsese (Thomson, 2010).

7 Timotheus Vermeulen and Gry C. Rustad (2013) "Watching Television with Jacques Rancière: U.S. 'Quality Television', *Mad Men* and the 'Late Cut'", *Screen*, Vol. 54, No. 3, p. 341.

8 The 'continuing soap opera' can be distinguished from all other serial TV drama (as well as from the 'supersoap' referred to in Chapter 4) by its unrivalled regularity, continuity and longevity. Produced for television since the early 1950s, it remains a broadcast form whose commercial attributes include its capacity to be produced at a rate of five new episodes each week, its lower production cost than most other drama, and its capacity for longevity through several decades. With the notable exception of *Peyton Place* (ABC, 1964–1969), it has remained a daytime form on American television. This is a point of contrast with a range of non-American countries and territories (including Britain, parts of Europe, Ireland, Australia and New Zealand), in which the continuing soap opera has operated as an early evening and mid-evening form.

9 John Thornton Caldwell (1995) *Televisuality: Style, Crisis and Authority in American Television*, New Brunswick and New Jersey: Rutgers University Press, p. 56.

10 *The Singing Detective* and other TV dramas created and written by Dennis Potter bore the aesthetic influence of German playwright and dramaturg Bertolt Brecht. Introduced in the 1920s, Brecht's influential approach to theatre entailed the use of four key devices of which 'distanciation' was one. Together, these 'Brechtian' devices aimed to expose the constructedness and artifice of the theatre text, to 'make strange' its apparent connections with the lived social world and to ensure that audiences knew they were watching a play.

11 Carl Sack (John Larroquette) describes the frustration of American 'baby boomers' at television's failure to provide shows that target them. During a longer address in which he mentions the show in which he is a character, he complains: "All the networks want to do is *skew younger* ... The only show unafraid to have its stars over fifty is *B*". Looking directly into the camera at this point, Sack admits: "Gee, I can't say it, it would break the wall".

12 Cited in Emma Thrower (2016) "*Stranger Things*: The Duffer Brothers Share the Secrets of their Hit Show", *Empire*, 27 July. Accessed 5 March 2017.

13　For Season 1 of *Stranger Things*, the camera was a Red Epic Dragon with 4x HD.

14　Season 2 of *Stranger Things* was shot on the newest Ultra HD digital camera and format, the Red Weapon with 8x HD.

15　The functions of and distinctions between 'kernel' and 'satellite' scenes are examined in Chapter 4.

16　The range of shoot days allocated per episode varies between different examples of complex serial drama, with those involving historical settings requiring the largest number overall. Indicative examples include *Six Feet Under* and *Mad Men*, (both shot on film and allocated nine shoot days per episode), *Boardwalk Empire* (shot on film and allocated 12 days per episode) and *Stranger Things* (shot on Ultra HD digital and allocated 10–11 days per episode). With just eight days per episode, *Breaking Bad* and *Dexter*, the former shot on film and the latter combining film and HD digital, are indicative of the low-end of the shoot day allocation for complex serial dramas.

CONCLUSION

The Sopranos, Oz, Six Feet Under, The Wire, Mad Men, Dexter, Boardwalk Empire, Breaking Bad and *Stranger Things*, all of which feature in the preceding chapters, are leading examples of the complex serial form that this book has identified and examined.[1] As a form of TV drama that first appeared in HBO examples, it has continued to flourish on American cable television and is now being originated by additional internet-distributed television (IDTV) networks; its hallmarks of conceptual novelty, long-format seriality, narrative complexity, aesthetic idiosyncrasy and morally conflicted, potentially villainous, primary characters have been integral to the attention and acclaim that its leading examples have received. Locating this complex serial form within American multiplatform television – the post-millennial context that facilitated its emergence and continues to encourage its expansion – this book has investigated the institutional and industrial contexts, conception and authorship, narrative strategies and stylistic tendencies that together distinguish it within the totality of American TV drama.

Although it is possible to create complex serials for broadcast networks (with ABC's *Lost* a notable example), they have proved well-suited to the non-broadcast sector of American television, being successfully established on premium and basic cable networks (beginning with HBO, FX, AMC and Showtime) before expanding to include origination by IDTV providers, notably Netflix, Amazon Prime and Hulu Plus. In addition to the unusual tolerance for creative risk-taking and experimentation that has been exhibited by the above networks, crucial in sustaining this drama's shared characteristics have been, first, the capacity of non-broadcast networks to originate high-end drama for narrower audience segments than those served by American broadcast networks, and, second, the non-traditional revenue streams that, to a larger or smaller degree, these networks deploy, which inform and shape their commissioning decisions.

While the impacts of convergence on the delivery and exhibition of complex serials are highlighted below, the ability to watch these dramas on non-traditional devices and to re-watch them, if desired, has been highly conducive to the 'complex seriality' that formally unites these shows. Important in justifying the high levels of per episode investment that has facilitated their conceptual, narrative and aesthetic ambition, despite their niche-orientation and sometimes narrow appeal, is the capacity of complex serials to exploit the context of multiplatform television not only to return value to their investors in traditional ways through the viewers they attract and the reputational benefits they return to their commissioning networks, but also to amortize their deficit financing and significant production costs through a succession of exhibition 'windows'.

This final chapter draws conclusions in relation to the four areas of this book's exploration that have been most pivotal to the emergence, expansion and innovation of the complex serial drama form. Accordingly, the rest of this chapter is structured into four sections, the first dealing with relevant features of the multiplatform environment and the second with the authorship of complex serial drama. The third and fourth sections foreground the textual distinctions of complex serial dramas, focusing on their narrative and stylistic characteristics.

'Peak TV', Multiplatform Television and Complex Serial Drama

In August 2015, FX president John Landgraf claimed that "there is simply too much television" (Littleton, 2015), coining the notion of 'peak TV' in acknowledgment of an unprecedented spike in the number of original scripted shows being produced for American television. In the period since Landgraf's assertion 'peak TV' has not abated, but intensified. With repercussions for the American screen production industry, for TV networks and services, and for the millions of viewers (both domestic and foreign) who watch these shows, the continuation of 'peak TV' is reflected in the exponential increase – from 182 in 2002 to 266 in 2012, 349 in 2013 and 455 in 2016 (Ryan, 2016) – in the annual total of scripted shows (both dramas and comedies) in production.

Directly attributable to the seismic environmental shifts that have either accompanied or have constituted the burgeoning of multiplatform television, 'peak TV' is a broader institutional and creative response to the proliferation of TV services and platforms that differentiate multiplatform television from earlier eras of American TV. While multiplatform television is a striking contrast with the broadcast-only era (the 1960s and 1970s), it is also a significant departure from its immediate predecessor, the era of 'multi-channel transition' (Lotz, 2007a) in the 1980s and 1990s. This departure is all the more significant if we focus on the origination of long-format TV drama, a production category whose prohibitive costs have historically favored the most established and profitable networks in a given TV market. In these terms, a key difference between multi-channel and multiplatform eras is that while TV drama continued to be dominated by broadcast networks throughout the former, the multiplatform era, which emerged after 2000, is one in which TV drama is produced for an unprecedented range and volume of institutional providers, combining broadcast, cable and internet networks.

This explosion of original scripted television foregrounds an increased commercial and cultural value for fictional material in television's multiplatform environment. That 'peak TV' has occurred in tandem with the inception and expansion of multiplatform television, rather than before or after this, suggests that this 'peak' is itself being fueled by the commissioning activity of an expanding number of non-broadcast networks. While IDTV networks comprise the fastest-growing area of the increased production that is sustaining 'peak TV' – their total rising from just four shows in 2010 to 93 in 2016 (Ryan, 2016), more responsible for it, to date at least, have been cable networks. The number of scripted shows originated by American cable networks rose from 47 in 2002 to 217 in 2016 (ibid), this foregrounding a direct linkage between their commissioning activity and the increased annual production totals that constitute 'peak TV'.

In general, 'peak TV' is the response of non-broadcast networks to the particular challenge of how to attract viewers and build audience markets in an era of unprecedented television supply. In particular, however, it was stimulated by the commissioning behaviors of cable networks, beginning with HBO in the late 1990s and expanding to include other cable networks, basic as well as premium, in the ten years to follow. As the number of entertainment-oriented cable networks increased in the first decade of the new century, both premium and basic cable providers responded by commissioning high-end long-format drama, albeit with slightly different motivations for doing so, precipitating the expansion of the complex serial form.

Exemplified by HBO, premium cable networks were motivated into original long-format drama by a perceived necessity not only to turn their businesses from "occasional use" into "regular-use" services (Carter, 2002), but also to offer TV dramas whose novelty, quality and seriality could provide additional enticement to their well-heeled subscribers, so as to expand these, and also to sustain their monthly commitment. In HBO's case, this flagship drama needed to provide an aesthetic complement to its existing feature film offerings and specifically target "the better-educated slightly older men and women aged 35 to 55" that were its existing subscribers (Albrecht, cited in Meisler, 1998: 48). In a well-established position when it began commissioning long-format drama, yet initiating this high-stakes venture earlier than most other cable networks were able to, HBO's commissioning executives proceeded with the kind of 'devil may care' attitude that Carolyn Strauss describes as "black-box theater, rather than the main stage", a position that conferred "a tremendous sense of freedom" (cited in Sepinwall, 2012: 24). HBO's tolerance of creative experimentation combined with other elements of its institutional position and motivations to yield the first examples of complex serial drama, which were *Oz, The Sopranos, Six Feet Under, The Wire* and *Deadwood.*

The motivation for basic cable networks was somewhat different. Unlike HBO, which from inception had sought a point of difference through the offer of alternative fare to that provided by the broadcast networks, entertainment-oriented basic cable networks had initially been heavily reliant on flows of ex-broadcast programming, the established popularity of which rendered them relatively low-risk as acquired flagship dramas (Mullen, 2003; 2008). However, as the number of cable channels continued to expand, a reliance on acquired dramas came to seem an increasingly limited strategy for basic cable channels for two reasons. One was that acquisition prices of ex-broadcast dramas rose to new heights in the context of increased inter-network competition for them (Albiniak, 2010). The other, a rising problem as brand distinction became a necessary strategy in a crowded multi-channel environment, was that it was increasingly difficult to build a distinctive identity on the basis of acquired shows. As the potentials of multiplatform television unfolded to foreground the commercial dangers of a continued reliance on acquired material, basic cable networks followed the example of premium cable networks to commission long-format drama that could be "tailor-made to the individual specifications" of their audiences (Edgerton, 2013: 9). When FX became the first basic cable network to commission complex serials, the capacity of this drama form to bestow reputational benefits and return additional value beyond its debut play had been established by the first HBO examples. Yet FX, as the first cable network to deploy its characteristically 'edgy' and explicit content in a mainly advertiser-funded economy, also took significant risks. However, with the success of *The Shield*, crucial to which was the realization that some advertisers were willing to support TV dramas that "violated [the] norms of acceptable content" (Lotz, 2007a: 185), it was possible for other basic cable networks to follow FX into complex serial drama.

Although they had different reasons for entering the costly, risky business of original high-end drama, and notwithstanding the larger range of TV drama forms and shows that American cable networks were individually commissioning, it is revealing of their common objectives that premium and basic cable networks both opted to invest in complex serials. As a particular kind of serial drama and one that deviates not only from the historically dominant procedural series but also from the earlier forms of high-end serial drama produced for American television, the deployment of complex serials by American cable networks has entailed two common imperatives. One is that, seeking to increase their subscriber numbers and also to secure their audience profile through the offer of distinctive programming that would make them "undroppable" to cable system providers (Sorcher, cited in Sepinwall, 2012: 303), they have been strongly motivated to deploy serials, a fiction form with a well-proven capacity to build and sustain audience loyalty (see Hagedorn, 1995). The other is that as optional TV services for which viewers pay either a monthly subscription direct to the network or a smaller charge to cable system operators, cable networks are incentivized to provide flagship dramas whose qualities can articulate their difference from broadcast channels and thereby mitigate this extra cost. While their distance from Federal Communications Commission (FCC) content rules allows them the regulatory freedom to incorporate explicit content, cable networks are also obliged to deploy it because "chance-taking is a must" for them (Goodman, 2005). Even though in this process, basic cable networks must remain responsive to their advertisers and premium cable networks to the possibility of subscriber churn, the position of cable networks contrasts with the necessity for broadcast networks to offer shows whose broad appeal can maximize audience size and thus advertising revenue.

Internet networks are increasingly important to the dissemination, exposure and commissioning of complex serials. However, their business model and incentives in respect of risk-taking place them in a slightly different position to that of cable networks. As the longest-standing and largest example, Netflix provides a useful exemplar of these differences. Notwithstanding its capacity to commission complex serials – whose examples include *Orange Is the New Black* (2013–), *House of Cards* (2013–) and *Stranger Things* (2016–) – Netflix differs from American cable networks in ways that, taken together, may mitigate against the extent of complexity – especially of the kind of narrative strategies examined in Chapter 4 – that its original dramas are able to incorporate. As an IDTV network, Netflix substitutes the linear schedule of a cable network with a menu (including feature films, TV dramas, comedies and documentaries) from which viewers can choose. Yet as with the function of a 'menu' for any of the services that use one, Netflix needs to be able to deliver to a range of tastes. Whereas cable networks target niche or specialist audience groupings, Netflix serves a larger volume and broader range of viewers, since its profitability is reliant, above all else, on the size of its subscriber base. Although within this domestic and international subscribership there remain opportunities to acquire and originate niche-oriented dramas, Netflix is somewhat less motivated than HBO, FX and AMC have all been to invest in dramas with relatively narrow appeal. Netflix is obliged to provide a mix of TV dramas, both acquired and original, that can allow it to cultivate broad appeal as well as catering to smaller or specialist audience segments. In consequence, and although Netflix prefers to commission dramas in serial form, some of its original shows eschew narrative and/or aesthetic complexity in favor of well-established and/or conventional approaches.

As an early and ambitious IDTV exhibitor of drama, Netflix has sought a point of difference from linear networks (both broadcast and cable) through the offer of 'binge viewing', a practice facilitated by the network's delivery of complete seasons as opposed to a weekly drip-feed of new episodes, a provision that applies only to those shows it solely owns or to its older acquired shows. Netflix subscribers can access hundreds of screen productions. These remain dominated by acquired shows, but include a diversity of properties either commissioned by Netflix alone, or which it has co-produced with other networks. However, the tendency of Netflix has been to obfuscate the origin of these shows, to label them 'Netflix originals' regardless of the institutions and arrangements that brought them into being. Accordingly, a potential problem for networks who have taken the risk of investing in complex serials as a way to articulate their brand identity and raise their cultural status, but have then sold them to Netflix, is that when streamed on Netflix's portals these properties are vulnerable to being perceived as 'Netflix' originals, with their identity as productions created for a particular TV network either reduced in profile or simply elided.

Notwithstanding this issue, its large and still growing international subscriber base has made Netflix potentially important to the circulation and exposure of any TV dramas offered on its portals. The rapid international expansion of Netflix highlights the capacity of IDTV networks to operate globally, which means that any TV shows such networks do produce or acquire can be speedily circulated around the world, raising the international cultural profile of these shows in unprecedented ways. It is this facet of Netflix to which Vince Gilligan alluded when accepting *Breaking Bad*'s award for best drama at the 2013 Emmy Awards. Gilligan's acceptance speech includes the speculation:

> Netflix kept us on the air. Not only are we standing up here [but also] I don't think our show would have lasted beyond Season 2. It's a new era in television and we've been very fortunate to reap the benefits.
>
> *(Acuna, 2013)*

As demonstrated by the international responses to the Netflix-commissioned *Stranger Things* (2016–) and Hulu's *The Handmaid's Tale* (2017–), IDTV networks with global reach and/or TV dramas that are distributed through foreign IDTV services can achieve more rapid international circulation and exposure than is possible when these air in non-American markets as acquired programming for national broadcast or cable networks.

Having placed complex serial drama within the multiplatform context that continues to encourage its origination for American non-broadcast networks, the remaining sections of this chapter examine the textual distinctions of complex serial dramas and the creative strategies considered to contribute to these. These discussions begin with the area of authorship.

Authorship Discourses and the Writing of Complex Serial Drama

The authorship strategies that have distinguished and sustained complex serials have been an important area of investigation for this book for two main reasons. One is that this drama form has been unusually subject to the construction and dissemination of auteur-like discourses, a process that Robin Nelson (2011) terms 'author[iz]ation'. The other is that their conceptual and narrative complexity has been supported by a more nuanced approach to authorship than either the director-centered model celebrated by cinema's auteur theory or the collaborative 'team-writing' model (Wells, 1996) that developed around American Quality Drama (AQD). Yet, for reasons detailed in Chapter 3, complex serial authorship is neither purely collaborative nor is it consistent with the requirement for 'authored' literature, theatre or art to demonstrate "an integrity sustained by the controlling vision and execution of an individual artist" (Nelson, 2011: 52). Instead, the writing and creation of complex serial drama is distinctive for its blending of creator-led and collaborative authorship. Chapter 3's analysis of the strategies most important to this offers an instructive example of how the achievement of narrative complexity in serial drama should not be perceived as the product of individual creativity or control, but rather as the consequence of a push-and-pull interplay between individual and collaborative authorship contributions.

Distinctive TV drama has often emerged as the product of individualized and authorial contributions. Indeed 'authored drama', institutionally facilitated by public service ideals and funding, has been a longstanding possibility within the larger totality of British (especially BBC-produced) TV drama. Yet, as Chapter 3 argues, this model of authorship is most achievable in short-format TV drama, especially in 'one-off' and 'mini-serial' forms, whose onscreen duration is sufficiently limited to allow the authorial control of a single writer-producer. Albeit few, there have been opportunities for this kind of drama to be produced for contemporary American television, these centering on the mini-serial form. Outside of this form, and mitigated by the dominance of TV drama genres and forms that can respond to network requirements for a high, ongoing episode output, individual authorship for drama has often been a tactical impossibility. Despite this, American television has frequently been subject to the construction of authorship discourses as a means to demarcate 'quality' in TV drama. This began with the valorization of individual playwrights whose acclaimed one-off teleplays occasioned the considered 'first golden age' of American television in the 1950s. Authorship discourses re-emerged in American television with the inception of the AQD paradigm, assisted by the rising status of writer-producers in an era of multi-channel competition (a change personified by Steven Bochco and David E. Kelley), as well as by the critical acclaim achieved by successive AQD examples (Thompson, 1996). As an achievement of the AQD paradigm and its leading shows, the attribution of authorship to individual writer-producers – despite the fact that team-writing remained the only sustainable practice for what were predominantly long-format, high-output shows – provided an effective way for networks to mark these shows as 'quality'.

Although a broader tendency of the AQD paradigm, the most striking example of the use of authorship discourses for the purposes of 'cultural legitimation' (Newman and Levine, 2012) occurred with AQD serial *Twin Peaks* (1990–91). Although jointly created, written and executive-produced by David Lynch and Mark Frost, *Twin Peaks* was promoted as 'art television' and 'authored drama' on the basis of the 'auteur' status that Lynch had achieved as a director of theatrical feature films. The example of *Twin Peaks* provides a compelling demonstration of the extent to which 'author[iz]ation' is, above all, a construct, the accuracy of which should not be accepted at face value but rather subjected to a process of careful investigation (see Prys, 2006). There is more evidence of such construction in a comparison between the authorial contributions of David Chase to *The Sopranos* and those of Tom Fontana to *Oz*, both of whom had lengthy careers as writer-producers and/or showrunners of TV dramas produced for broadcast networks. As the creator, head writer, co-EP and showrunner of *Oz*, the HBO drama that pioneered complex serial form, Fontana, who wrote or co-wrote all of *Oz*'s total of 56 episodes, was not subject to valorization as 'author' of this production. Yet *The Sopranos*, which comprises some 86 episodes and was written by a team of writer-producers, entailed the 'author[iz]ation' of Chase (Nelson, 2011). Notwithstanding Chase's significant contributions to *The Sopranos*, whose concept represented an unusually personal vision derived from his Italian-American background and experience, he "did not write (or author) all the episodes" (Nelson, 2011: 41). Despite this, and underlining the function of 'author[iz]ation' in promoting cultural legitimation, Chase was subject to an elaborate process of individual valorization in which he was constructed and celebrated as the individual 'author' of *The Sopranos*.

Whilst demonstrating the longstanding linkages between original drama, 'author[iz]ation' and cultural legitimation, the above examples do not directly connect with the environment of multiplatform television. As suggested by the attainment of 'peak TV' at a relatively early point in the multiplatform era, this era has been characterized by an unprecedented abundance of providers and shows, a context in which authorship discourses provide ways "to distinguish certain kinds of television from others" (Newman and Levine, 2012: 38). Whilst networks themselves have instigated authorial discourses and 'author[iz]ation', the multiplatform era has brought with it some new avenues through which to disseminate ideas about authorship, including the capacity for these to be instigated by viewers themselves. New in the multiplatform era is that the debut screening of TV dramas is supported by what can be a large array of multimedia paratexts (Gray, 2010), these combining fan-initiated with institutional websites, discussions and details about the show. Because they combine behind-the-scenes footage and interviews with creator-showrunners, in particular, these paratexts have demonstrated the capacity not only to frame discourses of authorship on behalf of audiences but also to incentivize fans themselves to "mobilize, build, and disseminate worldwide [the] valorization of a TV show" (Nelson, 2011: 43).

A situation somewhat at odds with the tendency for complex serials to involve the construction and valorization of a single creator-showrunner is that their authorship model is one that relies on what is ideally a small team of writers, these handpicked and led by the creator-showrunner but working collaboratively. Important to the narrative complexity and the risk-taking inherent in the stories and characterizations of complex serials are the processes of 'breaking story', which precede any writing of full scripts by individuals within the writing team and are focused on 'pitching', debating and negotiating both seasonal storylines and individual episode beats at the writers' room table. Writers' rooms were introduced to high-end American drama, as explained in Chapter 3, by the requirements of often long-running AQD shows to maintain a high episode output and to incorporate serial subplots. Together, these two demands made it unviable for individual writers, as they had historically done with long-format dramas, to simply retreat to their offices and script whole episodes, in consultation with their head writer and EPs. The solution that AQD productions found was 'team-writing', a process in which it became commonplace "for the stories to be created as a group, for a writer to be assigned one script to write, then a different one to rewrite, while someone else might be rewriting the script that you wrote the teleplay for in the first place" (Wells, 1996: 196).

Although complex serial drama has also deployed team-writing, its operational processes have entailed differences from those deployed for AQD, these necessitated by two elements of this form. First, mitigated by their basis in serial form, is that each member of their ideally small team of writers brings with them into the 'room' an encyclopedic knowledge of backstory. Second, because new story beats for complex serial episodes always have an inter-relationship with those of earlier episodes, it is necessary for seasonal arcs and episode beats to be 'broken' in detail at the writers' room table, a process that needs to precede the scripting of episodes. Foregrounding the consequent differences between the authorship of AQD shows and complex serials is the extended time devoted and the higher expectations attached to the processes of 'breaking story' in the writers' room, which are outlined in Chapter 3. Underlining the significance of these 'breaking story' processes to a complex serial's authorship, Gilligan (*Emmy Legends* interview, 2011) characterizes them as "heavy lifting". 'Breaking story' is more significant to the authorship of complex serials, Gilligan suggests, than the writing of scripts by individual members of the writing team. While the former is characterized as 'heavy lifting', the latter is relatively "carefree because I've got this outline … and I know what happens next" (ibid.). The extended time devoted to 'breaking story', which for *Breaking Bad* involved the determination of episode beats "in excruciating detail" (Walley-Beckett, cited in Connor interview, 2014), is a direct response to the creative challenges of the 'complex seriality' that distinguishes these dramas in narrative terms. Linking the necessity for an increased proportion of time devoted to direct collaboration between writers in the 'room' to the formal commitments of these dramas to both serial storytelling and unusual narrative complexity, Gilligan observes: "The shows I've worked on have been very complex, plot wise … And to that end you've got to know, you can't just sit down and write just a vague inspiration for an episode" (*Emmy Legends* interview, 2011).

The Narrative Distinctions of Complex Serials

The label 'complex serial', as demonstrated in Chapter 4, identifies a specific type of TV drama. Two initial characteristics of this form attest to its deviation from longstanding narrative tendencies in American TV drama. One is its persistent seriality, which, as a departure from the predominant episodicity of broadcast drama, reflects the strategic necessity for non-broadcast networks to deploy the kind of original drama that can most effectively build and maintain audience commitments to optional TV services. The other is the multi-season longevity of these shows which, averaging 50–80 episodes each, involves a narrative canvas that is considerably larger than that of high-end mini-serials, the complex serial's closest formal precursor. While this mini-serial form has long been a site for narrative complexity, as exemplified by iconic British example *The Singing Detective* (BBC, 1986), the extended narrative canvas of complex serial drama has proved highly conducive to the building of a distinctive 'mythology' (the ideological framework that underpins the diegetic 'world' of the show) and to the accrual of a comprehensive narrative memory as they develop and endure over the seasons.

While narrative complexity in TV drama is by no means exclusive to serial form, important to its achievement in complex serials have been the potentials that serial form and narration bring to the conception of story, character and setting. In their own approach to these three elements, complex serials have adapted the narrative conventions developed by high-end mini-serials, a form introduced in the 1970s as event-oriented 'prestige' programming, yet distinguished from other TV drama by its limited number of episodes and single-season duration. As 'closed' serial form, the mini-serial has been a conceptual, narrative and aesthetical contrast with the more prevalent 'open' serial form or soap opera, unique to which is the capacity to endure indefinitely. With 'closed' and 'open' serials conceived to serve quite different institutional and schedule roles, the narrative conventions of high-end serials deviate significantly from the multiple, interweaving stories and evasion of closure that are longstanding narrative conventions for soap opera. Accordingly, it is the narrative conventions of high-end serials, rather than those of soap opera, which have provided the structural framework for the conception of story, character and setting in complex serials. The narrative strategies that complex serials have drawn from this mini-serial form are briefly outlined below.

High-end serials foreground a single overarching story that spans all the episodes, requiring narrative progression, unavoidable change and an inevitable end. It is because of the dominance and the progressiveness of this story that high-end serials cannot be viewed casually nor does casual viewing serve their institutional function as 'prestige' drama. Instead, high-end serials accumulate a potentially detailed narrative memory, and on this basis their episodes need to be viewed in entirety and in the intended order. High-end serials are character-driven narratives in that their characters articulate this overarching story, demonstrate its progression and reveal its consequences. Pursuant to this, high-end serials deploy a hierarchy of characters, at the top of which are distinctive, well-drawn individuals. As the subjects of ongoing development and investigation, these characters are present in all or most episodes and are vital to resolving the overarching story. It is because of the narrative progression of serials, from one episode to the next, that their core characters are obliged to remember their history, be affected by narrative developments and embody the consequences of change.

Complex serials deploy the above narrative conventions of high-end serials, the larger category in which their own form is located. What distinguishes them within this category, however, is their deployment of the set of specific narrative features and strategies that Chapter 4 identifies as 'complex seriality'. While narrative complexity is a broader tendency in American TV fiction (see Mittell, 2015), 'complex seriality' refers to the six facets of complexity that unite these serials in narrative terms and distinguish them within the larger category of long-format TV drama.

The first is conceptual originality, specifically the exploration of subjects or topics without direct precedent in TV fiction, important to which is the adoption of a particular point of view. Albeit equally applicable to all other complex serials examined in this book, an important example is *The Wire*. Foregrounding the intentions of its co-creators David Simon and Ed Burns, Simon's assertion that "It could have – if we'd done everything wrong – been a cop show" ("The Game Is Real", 2007) underlines that *The Wire* is definitively not a 'cop show', even if police characters and police procedures are incorporated into its narrative. Instead, the central 'character' of *The Wire* is the city of Baltimore, the ongoing and probing investigation of which reveals a multi-layered, though dysfunctional, community and society. As such, *The Wire* represents in microcosm the neglected communities and citizens that post-industrial, post-neoliberal 'functional America' has marginalized and left behind.

Though not utilized in every example of complex serial drama, the second facet of complex seriality has proved invaluable to maximizing the longevity of this form. It entails the incorporation into the show's concept of a series-like problematic which complements, but is also secondary, to the character-driven overarching story on which the show's concept centers. By providing for a flow of guest characters and additional stories that intersect with those that are more prominent and enduring, this 'series-serial' strategy – as demonstrated by the Mafia business in *The Sopranos*, the homicide unit in *Dexter* and the advertising agency in *Mad Men* – helps to sustain the larger volume of episodes that differentiates complex serials from mini-serials. Set in a family-owned funeral home, *Six Feet Under* provides an indicative example. The overarching story of *Six Feet Under* follows the Fisher family and their struggle to retain the business following the death of their patriarch, Nathaniel Fisher Sr. Complementing this serial narrative with a succession of 'deaths-of-the-week', this series-serial strategy articulates Ball's desired critique of the commodification of grief; ensures a flow of guest characters, enabling a diversity of representations of death, loss and grief; and allows for the additional 'magic realist' featuring of 'talking dead' characters whose perspectives connect and help externalize the private concerns of the living core characters.

The third facet of complex seriality is an unusually close integration between the dilemma of the central character/s and the overarching story that the serial tells. A point of difference between complex serials and conventional serials and series, this third facet foregrounds the way in which complex serials are created not as situation-driven but as character-driven narratives. This third strategy confirms that the concept design of a complex serial begins with the conception of a conflicted character rather with the conception of situations of conflict (such as police stations, hospitals and law firms) that characters are subsequently created to inhabit. It is the character-driven tendency of complex serials in concert with narrative prominence of conflict-riven lead characters that makes it possible for their personal conflict/s to embody those of the overarching story that is developed around them. An indicative example is *Mad Men*, a drama whose setting is Madison Avenue's advertising world in the 1960s, but whose overarching story is that of Don Draper/Dick Whitman. Having successfully reinvented himself, Whitman/Draper is the personification of what a successful advertising campaign can achieve. Underlining the complexity of this integration of story and character, Don Draper embodies the former in two ways. First, Don embodies *Mad Men's* interest in the difference between what is on the surface and what lies underneath; this theme is central to this show's concept and is interrogated through its advertising agency milieu. Second, the backstory of this character, the story of Dick Whitman, former soldier, furrier, car salesman and unloved 'whore's child', is anything but the kind idealized past that nostalgia tends to celebrate. The story of Dick Whitman, narrated in fragments scattered across *Mad Men's* seven seasons, is summoned to the narrative surface quite literally as "the pain from an old wound" Don feels in the narrative present (1:13), supporting and contributing to *Mad Men's* broader critique of nostalgia.

Fourth is the deployment of morally conflicted, usually transgressive lead characters. While it is not obligatory for these characters to be seriously transgressive, they can be so – the sometimes criminal nature of these transgressions being a departure from the longstanding tendency of broadcast dramas to create lead characters who, albeit flawed, are not so deviant that they risk rejection by viewers. Even though flawed lead characters have a lengthy history in broadcast TV drama, their niche orientation has allowed cable networks, in particular, to commission dramas whose lead characters can exhibit more serious deviancy than has ever been possible on broadcast television. In fact, the degree of transgression and/or villainy shown by lead characters in American TV drama has been sufficiently differentiated, as Lotz (2014) suggests, to itself point to a show's origin as either a broadcast or cable drama. While it is too early to be sure whether IDTV networks will be as tolerant of complex serials with villainous lead characters as cable networks have been, the deployment of complex serial form on cable networks highlights the influence of the following considerations in the construction and deployment of villainous lead characters. The character-centered concepts of complex serials, as distinct from concepts devised around precincts, workplaces or character communities, generate narratives with the scope to subject different features of these characters, both redeeming and despicable, to ongoing investigation. As one consequence, the transgressions of complex serial characters, whether minor or serious, are shown to be motivated by the particular moral dilemma being suffered by the characters who perpetrate them. Assisting the moral evaluation of these transgressive lead characters has been the deployment of 'relative morality' (Mittell, 2015), whereby these transgressions occur in the context of the significantly greater villainy of other characters in the same show. 'Relative morality' has been important to the appeal, despite their transgressions, of mafia boss Tony Soprano, serial killer Dexter Morgan and meth cook Walter White in turn. Although all three characters exemplify the extent of lead character villainy in complex serials, Walter White stands out on the basis of his radical transformation from financially struggling high-school chemistry teacher to proficient meth cook and unrepentant killer. A point of difference from Tony Soprano and Dexter Morgan, whose transgressive tendencies do not radically change as the narrative progresses, is the extent of Walter's transformation as the most significant creative risk taken by *Breaking Bad*. Important to its successful mitigation was the resolve of *Breaking Bad*'s writers to enlist audience sympathy for Walter before gradually eroding this over time. Beginning in Season 2, this strategy involved offsetting Walter's increasingly evil persona against Jesse's contrastingly positive transformation, the objective of which was to encourage viewers to reconsider their allegiances.

The fifth and sixth facets of complex seriality are closely interrelated in complex serials that foreground the problems and progress of one character. While the sixth facet involves the subjection of these troubled characters to probing psychological investigation, the fifth contributes to this investigation through the provision of additional embedded scenes, most often flashbacks, which extend understandings of a character's history, current dilemma and behavior in the narrative present. Deepening the narrative complexity of these dramas, the additional scenes appear out of their chronological order, which highlights their manipulation and extension of the narrative's syuzhet dimension (the order in which events are narrated and revealed to viewers, as distinct from the chronological order of their occurrence in the narrative's fabula). Dispersed widely across the show's larger narrative, these scenes deliver unique and vital information, demanding that viewers watch and listen closely. Contributing significantly to the psychological investigation of conflicted lead characters, these scenes are also placed at moments of indecision or crisis in the unfolding main story. This placement underlines that the function of these additional scenes is not simply to deliver backstory information but rather to connect the lived experiences of conflicted lead characters with their problems and behaviors in the narrative present. There is an example in the use of flashbacks to effect the psychological investigation of Eleven in *Stranger Things*. Together, a succession of flashbacks reveals that Eleven has been subjected to traumatic series of experiments designed to develop her telekinetic and telepathic abilities. As is characteristic of complex serials, these individual flashbacks are delivered out of chronological order, are summoned by related anxieties experienced by the character in the narrative present, and are scattered throughout the eight-episode season. As these strategies underline, complex serials use a distinctive approach to the psychological investigation of central characters which is facilitated by the interconnection and interdependence between the fifth and sixth facets of complex seriality outlined above. Working together, these last two facets of complex seriality increase the overall complexity of these dramas, privilege the understandings and readings of viewers who can remember and piece together the revelations provided by the fragmented additional scenes, and may encourage viewers to re-watch a show in order to glean all the information the text makes available.

Aesthetic and Stylistic Strategies in Complex Serial Drama

Notwithstanding the continuing aesthetic differences between cinema and television, Chapter 5's examination of the aesthetic and stylistic tendencies of complex serial drama highlights its contributions to perceptions of increased "cinematization" in television (Newman and Levine, 2012: 5). Yet complex serial drama is not an aesthetic equivalent to the cinematic feature film. Most important to maintaining a sense of aesthetic differences between the two forms is that feature films and high-end TV dramas are subject to different commercial functions, exhibition spaces and regimes for production and post-production. Notwithstanding this, Chapter 5 highlights evidence of technological convergence between film and TV drama production industries, key examples of which are their use of the same 35mm or HD digital cameras, and their increasing cross-deployment of cinematographers, directors and editors. In addition, as Chapter 5 acknowledges, the aesthetics and style of complex serials is not in itself distinctive, but rather is indicative of the aesthetic capacities of high-end drama as a larger production category.

Important to maximizing the perceived aesthetic sophistication of complex serial dramas has been their deployment of a meticulous approach to mise-en-scène, cinematography, editing and post-production. This approach has been encouraged by the more generous allocation of production time, usually paired with higher per episode budgets, than is usual for long-format TV drama. These additional resources have assisted complex serials to incorporate more location scenes than is conventional for long-format broadcast dramas and to take longer over editing and post-production. Assisted further by a reduced number of episodes per season than for long-format broadcast dramas, these additional resources for complex serials have allowed more time for the visualization of their narratives and facilitated an increased interest in visual storytelling. Although it does not receive detailed analysis in this book, HBO's *Game of Thrones* (2011 –) has regularly featured scenes – indicatively 'Battle of the Bastards' (6:9) – that demonstrate the accentuated interest in visual storytelling that is more broadly characteristic of complex serials. Two tendencies of complex serials foreground the areas in which this form demonstrates the capacity for aesthetic complexity.

One is their approach to the construction of 'realism' (or first-degree style). Requiring camerawork, mise-en-scène, editing and soundtrack to work together to produce its effects, realism aims to conceal all signs of its constructed-ness, including its capacity for subjectivity. Yet as a consequence of realism's ability "to hide its nature as discourse" (Fiske, 1987: 131), its key limitation, as Colin MacCabe suggests, is an inability to investigate contradictory versions of the real (1981). Yet, in their deployment of realism, complex serial dramas have been progressive. While there are representational indicators of this progressiveness, as demonstrated by *The Wire*'s depictions of a neglected, dysfunctional and under-represented Baltimore, there are also ideological consequences, as evident in the splitting of realist discourses (1:1) by which TV dramas can juxtapose and thus evaluate the truth claims of one of the discourses within their text against those of another. In the pilot episode of *The Sopranos*, as examined in Chapter 5, this splitting of discourses establishes the morally conflicted position in which Tony Soprano finds himself as a mobster in therapy. Pivotal to the unfolding drama because of its role in introducing such a complex character, this sequence divides its realist discourses as a way to resolve the contradictions between the kind of workday that Tony describes during his first meeting with Dr. Jennifer Melfi and the revelations about what really happened that are provided by its cutaway scenes.

The other involves the mixing of aesthetic traditions in complex serials, a strategy that is greatly complemented by the generic mixing that is a feature of their concept design. In *The Sopranos*, aesthetic complexity is achieved through the intermixing of these generic and aesthetic components. Specifically, *The Sopranos* deploys a generic mix between family melodrama, the Mafia film and psycho-drama, pursuing this through a combination of realism (its primary aesthetic), touches of modernism (these usually rationalized as Tony's 'dream' sequences) and elements of postmodern textuality. Enhancing the aesthetic complexity of certain scenes and episodes (see, for example, 'Funhouse', 2:13), this combination allows for the construction and progression of a realist narrative, while allowing this same narrative to maintain and exhibit an awareness of its status as a fictional text. This aesthetic and generic mix, as observed in Chapter 5, is introduced in the opening minutes of the pilot episode, as Tony Soprano tells Dr. Jennifer Melfi about the sense of failure and futility that is contributing to the anxiety he feels. Tony's assertion that "the best is over'", as Glen Creeber (2002) observes, registers an awareness by the text itself of its lowly place in the distinguished trajectory of the Mafia movie. While Tony's assertions in this scene suggest a man experiencing mid-life crisis, they also point, self-reflexively, to the cultural status and aspirations of *The Sopranos* as a text to be something other than it is: a Hollywood movie rather than a long-format TV drama, specifically a gangster film in the tradition of *The Godfather*.

Complex serial dramas also foreground aesthetic complexity in their use of 'second-degree style' (Barrette and Picard, 2014). As a potential of postmodern textuality, this feature is facilitated not only by the shared interest of complex serials in visual storytelling but also by the extent to which, through self-reflexivity in particular, they acknowledge their own textuality. The potentials are strongly evident in *Breaking Bad*, a complex serial whose use of self-reflexivity gains additional importance in the context of the villainous and duplicitous character that Walter White becomes. Although there are other indicators of second-degree style in *Breaking Bad*, 'Face Off' (4:13), in which Walter denies his involvement in the attempted murder of a young boy, Brock, provides what is perhaps the most striking example in terms of narrative impact. By the end of this episode, the camera has become almost an animate contributor to the investigation of a truth that Walter has concealed. As a way to foreground the ire of the mute text itself, the camera finally asserts its own potential to control what viewers know. In this episode's final shot, the camera behaves almost as if it were a private detective hired by the text to ferret out the concealed truth and present it to viewers. In the absence of dialogue, it offers a slow pan left and zoom in to reveal the name of a potted plant at the side of Walter's swimming pool. Viewers learn that this is 'Lily-of-The-Valley', the very plant that was found to have been used in the poisoning that nearly killed Brock. The above image provides an audacious example of the capacities of self-reflexivity and second-degree style. As an aesthetic strategy with the capacity to disagree with and disavow other 'truth' claims in the text, the camera is enlisted to expose the truth as Walter demonstrates that his villainy knows no boundaries.

Final Remarks

Because of their untested concepts, morally ambiguous lead characters and sometimes confronting content, complex serials, to date at least, have been apt to reside at the niche-oriented margins rather than the broad-audience mainstream of American television. Their original concepts tend to transgress the boundaries of what commissioning executives consider as appropriate for the long-format TV drama that, if commissioned, will be crucial to supporting the articulation of their brand identities. For broadcast networks, complex serial concepts can seem problematic, not only because these are perceived to target narrow rather than broad audiences, but also because, as it is feared, there is the possibility that their more confronting depictions may offend some sectors of their established following. Yet, for non-broadcast, newly re-branded and/or newer networks looking for ways to target underserved niche or specialist audiences through the offer of distinctive programming, complex serial concepts have provided a sense of opportunity through risk-taking. The narrative foregrounding by complex serials of morally conflicted, potentially villainous characters has been a consistent concern to network executives because, as the human faces of these shows, such characters risk audience rejection. The deployment by these serials of complex narrative strategies – while this has itself allowed for the construction of some of the most multi-faceted, compelling characters ever created for American television – is a practice that defies casual viewing patterns. Instead these serials demand the focused attention of viewers, this sometimes extending to the re-watching of episodes so that all relevant details can be fully comprehended. Foregrounding the notable fit of complex serials with non-broadcast networks, as networks whose efforts to complement rather than compete with broadcast networks allows them to serve more specialized audiences, examples have been produced by HBO, FX, AMC, Showtime, Cinemax, Starz, Netflix, Amazon Prime and Hulu Plus, with additional networks also experimenting with the form. That complex serials have been so regularly produced is a testament, therefore, to the opportunities of television's multiplatform era – as one that offers an unprecedented number and range of networks to which writer-producers can take their ideas – and to the unprecedented appetite within non-broadcast American television for experimentation and commercial risk-taking in the particularly costly area of high-end drama.

Note

1 Complex serial drama has expanded significantly during the research and writing of this book. Testifying both to the diversity of examples being produced, current examples include HBO's *Game of Thrones* (2011–), Netflix's *House of Cards* (2013–) and *Orange Is the New Black* (2013–), A&E's *Bates Motel* (2013–17) and Hulu Plus's *The Handmaid's Tale* (2017–).

BIBLIOGRAPHY

Acuna, Kirsten (2013) "*Breaking Bad* Creator Vince Gilligan Says Show's Success Is Due To Netflix", *Business Insider*, 24 September. Retrieved from https://www.businessinsider.com.au/, May 24 2017.

Adgate, Brad (2013) "Broadcast Television Says Goodbye to a Most Disruptive Season", *Broadcasting and Cable*, 14 June, ID 114556. Accessed March 11 2014.

Akass, Kim and Janet McCabe (2008) "*Six Feet Under*", Chapter 4 in Gary R. Edgerton and Jeffrey P. Jones (eds.), *The Essential HBO Reader*, Lexington: University of Kentucky Press, pp. 71–81.

Albiniak, Paige (2010) "Can Cable Keep Making Big Off-Net Bets?", *Broadcasting and Cable*, 15 February, ID 36169. Accessed March 16 2014.

Allen, Robert (1987) "*The Guiding Light*: Soap Opera as Economic Product and Cultural Document" in Horace Newcomb (ed.), *Television: The Critical View*, Fourth Edition, Oxford: Oxford University Press, pp. 141–63.

Anderson, Chris (2008) "Producing an Aristocracy of Culture in American Television" in Gary R. Edgerton and Jeffrey. P. Jones (eds.), *The Essential HBO Reader*, Kentucky: University Press of Kentucky, pp. 23–41.

Ang, Ien (1993, orig. 1985) *Watching Dallas: Soap Opera and the Melodramatic Imagination*, London: Routledge.

Arango, Tim and David Carr (2010) "Netflix's Move on to the Web Stirs Rivalries", *The New York Times*, 24 November. Accessed February 20 2014.

Auster, Al (2005) "HBO's Approach to Generic Transformation", Chapter 10 in Gary R. Edgerton and Brian G. Rose (eds.), *Thinking Outside the Box: A Contemporary Television Genre Reader*, Lexington: University of Kentucky Press, pp. 226–46.

Ball, Alan (2013) TV Drama Writer, Producer and Showrunner, and the Creator, Showrunner and Co-Executive Producer of *Six Feet Under*, Interview with Trisha Dunleavy, 18 June.

Banet-Weiser, Sarah, Cynthia Chris, and Anthony Frietas (2007) (eds.), *Cable Visions: Television Beyond Broadcasting*, New York: New York University Press.

Barker, Chris (1997) *Global Television*, Oxford: Blackwell Publishers.

Barrette, Pierre and Yves Picard (2014) "Breaking the Waves", Chapter 7 in David P. Pierson (ed.), *Breaking Bad: Critical Essays on the Contexts, Politics, Style and Reception of the Television Series*, Lanham: Lexington Books, pp. 121–138.

Barthes, Roland (1977) *Image/Music/Text*, translated by Stephen Heath, New York: Hill and Wang.

Beail, Linda and Lilly J. Goren (2015) "*Mad Men* and Politics: Nostalgia and the Remaking of America", Chapter 1 in Lilly J. Goren and Linda Beail (eds.) *Mad Men and Politics: Nostalgia and the Remaking of Modern America*, New York: Bloomsbury, pp. 3–33.

Becker, Anne (2008) "Joshua Sapan", *Broadcasting and Cable*, 17 October 2008, ID 72918. Accessed March 11 2014.

Biskind, Peter (2007) "An American Family", *Vanity Fair*, 49.4 April. https://www.vanityfair.com/news/2007/04/sopranos200704. Accessed August 1 2015.

Boddy, William (1993) *Fifties Television: The Industry and Its Critics*, Urbana: University of Illinois Press.

Bonner, Frances (2003) *Ordinary Television: Analysing Popular TV*, London: Sage.

Brancato, Chris (2008) "It's a Mad, Mad, Mad, Mad Men World", *Writers Guild of America: West - The Journal of the Writers Guild of America*, February/March, pp. 36–43.

Brooker, Charlie (2013) GEITF 2013 - *Breaking Bad*: The Network & GEITF Joint Session Masterclass: Interview with *Breaking Bad* Creator/Showrunner Vince Gilligan, Edinburgh International Television Festival, https://www.youtube.com/watch?v=IXVJ8eRIRrc, 11 September. Accessed August 20 2015.

Brunsdon, Charlotte (1990) "Problems With Quality", *Screen*, Vol. 31 Issue 1, Spring, pp. 67–90.

Buchalter, Gail (1983) "His Animal Behaviour Puts Bruce Weitz on Top of the Heap", *People Magazine*, September 29, http://www.people.com/people/article. Accessed April 11 2014.

Butler, Jeremy G. (2010) *Television Style*, New York: Routledge.

Caldwell, John Thornton (1995) *Televisuality: Style, Crisis and Authority in American Television*, New Jersey: Rutgers University Press.

Caldwell, John Thornton (2008) *Production Culture: Industrial Reflexivity and Critical Practice in Film and Television*, Durham: Duke University Press.

Caldwell, John Thornton (2009) "The Writers' Room: An interview with Felicia D. Henderson" in Vicki Mayer, Miranda J. Banks, and John T. Caldwell (eds.), *Production Studies: Cultural Studies of Media Industries*, New York: Routledge, pp. 224–28.

Cardwell, Sarah (2006) "Television Aesthetics" in *Critical Studies in Television*, Vol 1. Issue 1, pp. 72–80.

Cardwell, Sarah (2015) "A Sense of Proportion: Aspect Ratio and the Framing of Television Space", *Critical Studies in Television*, Vol. 10, Issue. 3, pp. 84–100.

Carter, Bill (2002) "He Lit Up HBO. Now He Must Run It", *The New York Times*, 29 December, p. 3.1.

Carter, Bill (2012) "Showtime Is Gaining on HBO", *The New York Times*, 30 January, B1.

Caughie, John (1981) "Progressive Television and Documentary Drama" in Tony Bennett, Susan Boyd-Bowman, Colin Mercer, and Janet Woollacott (eds.), *Popular Television and Film*, London: British Film Institute, pp. 327–52.

Caughie, John (2000) *Television Drama: Realism, Modernism, and British Culture*, Oxford: Oxford University Press.

Caughie, John (2007) "Authors and Auteurs: The Uses of Theory" in James Donald and Michael Renov (eds.), *The Sage Handbook of Film Studies*, London: Sage, pp. 408–23.

Chatman, Seymour (1978) *Story and Discourse: Narrative Structure in Fiction and Film*, London: Methuen.

Chion, Michel (1995) *David Lynch*, translated by Robert Julian, London: British Film Institute.

Collins, Jim (1995) "Postmodernism and Television" in Robert C. Allen (ed.), *Channels of Discourse, Reassembled*, Second Edition, London: Routledge, pp. 327–53.

Collins, Jim (2000) "Television and Postmodernism" in Robert Stam and Toby Miller (eds.), *Film and Theory: An Anthology*, Massachusetts: Blackwell, pp. 758–73.

Connor, Jon (2014) "An Interview with *Breaking Bad* Writer Moira Walley-Beckett", Kessler University, http://www.kessleru.com/2014/01/an-interview-with-breaking-bad-writer-moira-walley-beckett/ January. Accessed August 30 2015.

Consoli, John (2011) "For Your Consideration", *Multichannel News*, Vol. 32, Issue 29, 25 July, pp. 12–14.

Cook, John (1998) *Dennis Potter: A Life on Screen*, Second Edition, Manchester: Manchester University Press.

Corner, John (1999) *Critical Studies in Television*, New York: Oxford University Press.

Creeber, Glen (2002) "'TV Ruined the Movies': Television, Tarantino, and the Intimate World of *The Sopranos*", in David Lavery (ed.), *This Thing of Ours: Investigating The Sopranos*, New York: Columbia University Press and Wallflower Press, pp. 124–34.

Creeber, Glen (2004) *Serial Television: Big Drama on the Small Screen*, London: British Film Institute.

Creeber, Glen (2013) *Small Screen Aesthetics: From TV to the Internet*, Basingstoke: Palgrave Macmillan on behalf of the British Film Institute.

Cuccinello, Hayley C. (2016) "*Game of Thrones* Season 6 Costs $10 million Per Episode Has Biggest Battle Scene Ever", 22 April 2016. https://www.forbes.com/sites/hayley cuccinello/2016/04/22/. Accessed May 10 2017.

Del Valle, Robert (2008) *The One-Hour Drama Series: Producing Episodic Television*, Beverly Hills: Silman-James Press.

Dempsey, John (2004) "Billion Dollar Baby: Cable Fees, DVDs Drive HBO's Profits" *Daily Variety*, 23 December, p. 1.

Drell, Cady (2016) "*Stranger Things*: The Secret CIA Programs That Inspired Hit Series", *Rolling Stone*, 5 August. www.rollingstone.com/culture/features/stranger-things-inside-shows-real-life-cia-inspirations-w432945. Accessed April 26 2017.

Dunleavy, Trisha (1995) "*Marlin Bay* and *Shortland Street*: Aspects of 'Localness' in Popular Television Drama", Masters' Thesis, Auckland: University of Auckland.

Dunleavy, Trisha (2009) *Television Drama: Form, Innovation, Agency*, Basingstoke: Palgrave Macmillan.

Dunleavy, Trisha (2016) "Crossing New Boundaries in Public TV Drama. The Transnational Success of Denmark's *Forbrydelsen*" in Gregory Ferrell Lowe and Nobuto Yamamoto (eds.), *Crossing Borders and Boundaries in Public Service Media*, Gothenberg: Nordicom, pp. 201–14.

Edgerton, Gary R. (2007) *The Columbia History of American Television*, New York: Columbia University Press.

Edgerton, Gary R. (2008) "Introduction: A Brief History of HBO" in Gary R. Edgerton and Jeffrey P. Jones (eds.), *The Essential HBO Reader*, Lexington: University of Kentucky Press, pp. 1–20.

Edgerton, Gary R. (2011a) "Introduction: When Our Parents Became Us", Introduction, in Gary R. Edgerton (ed.), *Mad Men: Dream Come True TV*, London and New York: I.B. Tauris, pp. xxi–xxxvi.

Edgerton, Gary R. (2011b) "*The Sopranos* as Tipping Point in the Second Coming of HBO" in David Lavery, Douglas L. Howard, and Paul Levinson (eds.), *The Essential Sopranos Reader*, Lexington: University of Kentucky Press, pp. 7–16.

Edgerton, Gary R. (2013) *The Sopranos*, Detroit: Wayne University Press.

Ellis, John (1982) *Visible Fictions: Cinema, Television, Video*, London and New York: Routledge.

Ellis, John (2000) *Seeing Things: Television in the Era of Uncertainty*, London: I.B. Tauris.

Emmy Legends (2011) *Archive of American Television*. Interview with Vince Gilligan, 9 August. http://emmytvlegends.org/interviews/people/vince-gilligan.

Ethridge, Blake (2008) "Baltimore on *The Wire*: The Tragic Moralism of David Simon", Chapter 8 in Marc Leverette, Brian L. Ott, and Cara Louise Buckley (eds.) *It's Not TV: Watching HBO in the Post-Television Era*, London and New York: Routledge, pp. 152–64.

Feuer, Jane (1984a) "MTM Enterprises: An Overview" in Jane Feuer, Paul Kerr, and Tise Vahimagi (eds.), *MTM 'Quality Television'*, London: British Film Institute, pp. 1–31.

Feuer, Jane (1984b) "The MTM Style" in Jane Feuer, Paul Kerr, and Tise Vahimagi (eds.), *MTM 'Quality Television'*, London: British Film Institute, pp. 32–60.

Feuer, Jane (1994) "Melodrama, Serial Form and Television Today" in Horace Newcomb (ed.) *Television: The Critical View*, Fifth Edition, New York and Oxford: Oxford University Press, pp. *Screen*, Vol. 25, No. 1, pp. 551–62.

Feuer, Jane (1995) *Seeing Through the Eighties: Television and Reaganism*, London: British Film Institute.

Feuer, Jane (2007) "HBO and the Concept of Quality TV", Chapter 11 in Janet McCabe and Akass (eds.), *Quality TV: Contemporary American Television and Beyond*, London and New York: I.B. Tauris, pp. 145–57.

Fiske, John (1987) *Television Culture*, New York and London: Routledge.

Follows, Stephen (2016) "Film vs. Digital –What Is Hollywood Shooting on?" *Stephen Follows' Film Data and Education*, 11 January. https://stephenfollows.com/film-vs-digital/. Accessed April 5 2017.

Fontana, Tom (2013) TV Drama Writer and Producer and the Creator, Showrunner and Co-Executive Producer (with Barry Levinson) of *Oz*, Interview with Trisha Dunleavy, 6 July.

Frazer, Bryant (2006) "HD Cinematography on Showtime's *Dexter*", *Studio Daily*, 18 October. www.studiodaily.com/2006/10. Accessed March 20 2017.

Friedman, Wayne (2007) "Ratings: *Sopranos* Finale OK, Whacks Tony Numbers", *Media Daily News*, 12 June, http://www.mediapost/co/publications, accessed March 1 2009.

Gardner, Carl and John Wyver (1983) "The Single Play from Reithian Reverence to Censorship and Cost Accounting", *Screen*, Vol. 24. Nos. 4-5, pp. 114–29.

Genette, Gérard (1997) *Paratexts: Thresholds of Interpretation*, translated by Jane E. Lewin, Cambridge: Cambridge University Press.

Geraghty, Christine (1991) *Women and the Soap Opera: A Study of Prime-Time Soaps*, Cambridge: Polity Press.

Girardot, Frank (2011) "*Breaking Bad* Creator Vince Gilligan Readies for End of Season", *Whittier Daily News*, 3 October. http://search.proquest.com.helicon.vuw.ac.nz/pqcentral/docview/895978944/fulltext/. Accessed July 22 2013.

Gitlin, Todd (1994) *Inside Prime Time*, Revised Edition, London and New York: Routledge.

Goldsmith, Jim (2002) "Milestone: HBO at 30: Ka-ching Cabler Helps Hurtin' AOL Stock", *Variety*, Vol. 388 (12) pp. A6, A32. Retrieved from https://search.proquest.com/docview/1895301?accountid=14782. Accessed February 2 2014.

Goldstein, Dana (2005) "FX Aims for HBO's Cachet", *Bloomberg Businessweek*, 18 September, ID 198186. http://web.a.ebscohost.com/ehost/pdfviewer/. Accessed March 5 2014.

Goodman, Tim (2005) "They Steal, They Cheat, They Lie and We Wouldn't Want It Any Other Way – The Timeless Appeal of the Anti-Hero", *San Francisco Chronicle*, 2 June http://www.sfgate.com/entrainment/article. Accessed November 2 2016.

Goren, Lilly J. (2015) "If You Don't Like What They Are Saying, Change the Conversation: The Grifter, Don Draper, and the Iconic American Hero", Chapter 2 in Lilly J. Goren and Linda Beail (eds.), *Mad Men and Politics: Nostalgia and the Remaking of Modern America*, London: Bloomsbury, pp. 35–61.

Gray, Jonathan (2006) *Watching With The Simpsons: Television, Parody and Intertextuality*, New York: Routledge.

Gray, Jonathan (2010) *Show Sold Separately: Promos, Spoilers, and Other Media Paratexts*, New York and London: New York University Press.

Green, Chris (2009) "Case Study: Matthew Weiner", *Produced By*, Vol. 10, Issue 2, pp. 10–18.

Gripsrud, Jostein (2002) *Understanding Media Culture*, London: Arnold.

Grow, Cory (2016) "*Stranger Things*: How Two Brothers Created Summer's Biggest TV Hit", *Rolling Stone*, 3 August. www.rollingstone.com/tv/features/stranger-things-creators-on-making-summers-biggest-tv-hit-w431735. Accessed April 26.

Guthrie, Marisa (2015) "Will HBO Go Digital in Foreign Markets: 'Take it Case by Case'", *The Hollywood Reporter*, 18 December, p. 26. Retrieved from https://search.proquest.com/docview/1752208774?accountid=14782. Accessed December 10 2016.

Hagedorn, Roger (1995) "Doubtless to Be Continued: A Brief History of Serial Narrative", Chapter 1 in Robert C. Allen (ed.), *To Be Continued... Soap Operas Around the World*, London: Routledge, pp. 27–48.

Haley, Kathy (2002) "The Way of Success", HBO 30th Anniversary Edition, *Multichannel News*, November, pp. 6A.

Hall, Jane (1984) "With NBC Still Rated No. 3, Grant Tinker Ponders His Own Decisions – and the Audience's", *People Magazine*, 14 May, www.people.com/people/article. Accessed March 26 2013.

Handy, Bruce (2009) "Don and Betty's Paradise Lost", *Vanity Fair*, 51 (9) http://www.vanityfair.com/news/2009/09/mad-men200909. Accessed February 2 2016.

Heffernan, Virginia (2004) "The Real Boss of *The Sopranos*", *New York Times*, 29 February. Retrieved from https://search.proquest.com/docview/432665591?accountid=14782. Accessed October 13 2014.

Heuring, David (2010) "Shooting *Boardwalk Empire* on Super 35", *Studio Daily*, 20 September. www.studiodaily.com/2010/09/shooting-boardwalk-empire-on-super-35/. Accessed April 5 2017.

Hibberd, James (2013) "*Dexter*: The Final Season", *Entertainment Weekly*, 7 June. http://www.ew.com/article/2013/06/07/dexter-final-season. Accessed December 15 2016.

Higgins, John (2006) "American TV Rebounds Worldwide", *Broadcasting and Cable*, 18 September, pp. 18–19.

Hill, John (1986) *Sex, Class and Realism: British Cinema 1956-1963*, London: British Film Institute.

Hilmes, Michele (2008) *Only Connect: A Cultural History of Broadcasting in the United States*, Belmont: Wadsworth Cengage.

Holloway, Daniel (2016) "*Stranger Things*' Ratings: Where Series Ranks Among Netflix's Most Watched", *Variety*, 25 August. http://variety.com/2016/tv/news/stranger-things-tv-ratings-netflix-most-watched-1201844081/. Accessed April 12 2017.

Hornaday, Ann (1993) "The ABC's of HBO: Original Programming Pushes Cable Station Past Networks at the Emmys", *San Francisco Chronicle*, 21 November, p. 49.

Hullfish, Steve (2016) "Art of the Cut With the Editors of *Stranger Things*", *Pro Video Coalition*, 25 November. https://www.provideocoalition.com/art-cut-editors-stranger-things/. Accessed March 12 2017.

Idov, Michael (2011) "The Zombies at AMC's Doorstep: Can the *Mad Men* Network Survive Its Own Success?" *New York*, 23 May. Retrieved from https://search.proquest.com/docview/866568867?accountid=14782. Accessed January 25 2012.

Inside the Writers' Room With Breaking Bad (2014) Writers Guild Foundation. Glen Mazzara interviews creator Vince Gilligan and writers Moira Walley-Beckett, Sam Catlin, Peter Gould, Thomas Schnauz, Gennifer Hutchison and George Mastras, 17 February., 17 February. https://www.youtube.com/watch?v=VOT1d4DC5tE. Accessed August 10 2015.

Jaramillo, Deborah (2012) "AMC Stumbling Toward a New Television Canon", *Television and New Media*, Published online, 20 April 2012. Downloaded 1 November, 2012.

Jaramillo, Deborah (2013) "Rescuing Television From 'the Cinematic': The Perils of Dismissing Television Style" in Jason Jacobs and Steven Peacock (eds.), *Television Aesthetics and Style*, New York: Bloomsbury, pp. 67–75.

Jarmusch, Jim (2013) "Things I've Learned: Jim Jarmusch", *MovieMaker*, 5 June. www.moviemaker.com/archives/series/things_learned/. Accessed April 17 2017.

Jenkins, Henry (2006) *Convergence Culture: Where Old and New Media Collide*, New York: New York University Press.

Jenkins, Steve (1984) "*Hill Street Blues*" in Jane Feuer, Paul Kerr, and Tise Vahimagi (eds.), *MTM 'Quality Television'*, London: British Film Institute, pp. 183–99.

Johnson, Ted (2003) "Great Expectations", *Variety*, 24 August. http://variety.com/2003/scene/markets-festivals/great-expectations. Accessed January 27 2016.

Kerr, Paul (1984) "The Making of (The) MTM (Show)" in Jane Feuer, Paul Kerr, and Tise Vahmagi (eds.), *MTM 'Quality Television'*, London: British Film Institute, pp. 61–68.

Lafayette, Jon (2009) "AMC Pursues a Good Break: *Breaking Bad* Is Next Original Bet for Cable Network", *Television Week*, 2 March, p.3.

Lafayette, Jon (2010) "The *Mad Men* Lesson: Buzz Lights up a Network", *Broadcasting and Cable*, 19 July, pp. 18–20.

Lafayette, Jon (2014) "Shrinking of Viewers in Dollar Demos a Growing Issue", *Broadcasting and Cable*, 24 June, p. 23.

Lafayette, Jon (2015) "Acura Decides It *Better Call Saul* for Sponsorship", *Broadcast and Cable*, 9 February, p. 21.

Lafayette, Jon (2016) "AT&T - Time Warner: Wall Street Not Buying Vertical Integration", *Broadcasting and Cable*, 24 October. http://www.broadcastingcable.com/news/currency/att-time-warner-wall-street-not-buying-vertical-integration/160587. Accessed December 14 2016.

Lavery, David (2005) "'It's Not Television, It's Magic Realism': The Mundane, the Grotesque and the Fantastic in *Six Feet Under*", Chapter 1 in Kim Akass and Janet McCabe (eds.), *Reading Six Feet Under: TV to Die For*, London and New York: I.B. Tauris, pp. 19–33.

Lavery, David (2012) "*Bad* Quality: *Breaking Bad* as Basic Cable Quality TV", *Telegenic* Blog, *Critical Studies in Television*, 22 November. http://cstonline.tv/category/telegenic, Accessed February 5 2016.

Lavery, David and Robert Thompson (2002), in David Lavery (ed.), *This Thing of Ours: Investigating The Sopranos*, New York: Wallflower Press and Columbia University Press, pp. 18–31.

Lawson, Mark (2007) "Mark Lawson Talks to David Chase", Chapter 14 in Janet McCabe and Kim Akass (eds.), *Quality TV: Contemporary American television and Beyond*, London: I.B. Tauris, pp. 185–220.

Levin, Gary (2003) "The Inside Story on HBO's *Oz*: True to Form Its Final Season Won't Be Pretty Either", *USA Today*, 1 January. http://usatoday30.usatoday.com/life/television/. Accessed March 10 2014.

Levy, Adam (2017) "HBO Now Subscriber Base Is Accelerating", *The Motley Fool*, 13 February. https://www.fool.com/investing/2017/02/13/. Accessed May 8 2017.

Liedtke, Michael (2017) "Netflix on the Verge of Hitting 100 Million Subscribers", *Boston Globe*, 17 April. https://www.bostonglobe.com/business/. Accessed May 8 2017.

Littleton, Cynthia (2015) "FX Networks Chief John Landgraf: 'There Is Simply Too Much Television'", *Variety*, 7 August. http://variety.com/2015/tv/news/. Accessed May 31 2017.

Lombardo, Michael (2014) President of HBO Original Programming, Personal Communication with Trisha Dunleavy, 7 January.

Lotz, Amanda D. (2006) *Redesigning Women: Television After the Network Era*, Urbana and Chicago: University of Illinois Press.

Lotz, Amanda D. (2007a) *The Television Will Be Revolutionised*, New York: New York University Press.

Lotz, Amanda D. (2007b) "If It's Not TV, What Is It? The Case of U.S. Subscription Television", Chapter 4 in Sarah Banet-Weiser, Cynthia Chris, and Anthony Freitas (eds.), *Cable Visions: Television Beyond Broadcasting*, New York, New York University Press, pp. 85–102.

Lotz, Amanda D. (2014) *Cable Guys: Television and Masculinities in the 21st Century*, New York: New York University Press.

Lotz, Amanda D. (2016) "The Paradigmatic Evolution of U.S. Television and the Emergence of Internet-Distributed Television", *Icono*, Vol. 14, Issue 2, pp. 122–42.

MacCabe, Colin (1981) "Realism and the Cinema: Notes on a Brechtian Thesis" in Tony Bennett, Susan Boyd-Bowman, Colin Mercer, and Janet Woollacott, (eds.), *Popular Television and Film*, London: British Film Institute, pp. 216–35.

McCabe, Janet (2013) "HBO Aesthetics, Quality Television, and *Boardwalk Empire*", Chapter 13 in Jason Jacobs and Steven Peacock (eds.), *Television Aesthetics and Style*, London and New York: Bloomsbury, pp. 186–97.

McDonald, Jim (2007) "*Sopranos*: One of the Most Popular TV Dramas of All Time", http://www.pr-usa.net, 10 June. Accessed March 15 2008.

Magid, Ron (2002) "Family Plots", *American Cinematographer*, Vol. 83, Issue 11, November, pp. 70–79.

Malach, Michele (2008) "*Oz*", Chapter 2 in Gary R. Edgerton and Jeffrey P. Jones (eds.), *The Essential HBO Reader*, Kentucky: The University Press of Kentucky, pp. 52–60.

Mann, Denise (2009) "It's Not TV, It's Brand Management TV: The Collective Author(s) of the *Lost* Franchise", Chapter 7 in Vicki Mayer, Miranda J. Banks, and John T. Caldwell (eds.), *Production Studies: Cultural Studies of Media Industries*, New York: Routledge, pp. 99–114.

Marc, David (2011) "*Mad Men*: A Roots Tale of the Information Age", Chapter 15 in Gary R. Edgerton (ed.), *Mad Men: Dream Come True TV*, London and New York: I.B. Tauris, pp. 226–38.

Martin, Brett (2007) *The Sopranos: The Complete Book*, New York: Time Home Entertainment.

Martin, Brett (2013) *Difficult Men. Behind the Scenes of a Creative Revolution: From The Sopranos and The Wire to Mad Men and Breaking Bad*, New York: The Penguin Press.

Martin, Troy Kennedy (1964) "Nats Go Home: First Statement of a New Drama for Television", *Encore*, No. 48, March/April, pp. 21–33.

Masters, Kim (2016) "HBO's High-Class Problems", *The Hollywood Reporter*, 4 March, p. 35.

Matisse, Nathan (2016) "Reboots be Damned, *Stranger Things* Shows a Better Way to Do Nostalgia", *Ars Technica*, 1 August. https://arstechnica.com/gaming/2016/. Accessed April 25 2017.

Meisler, Andy (1998) "Not Even Trying to Appeal to the Masses", *New York Times*, 4 October, 1998, p. AR 45, 48.

Mills, Brett (2013) "What Does It Mean To Call Television 'Cinematic'?", Chapter 3 in Jason Jacobs and Steven Peacock (eds.), *Television Aesthetics and Style*, New York and London: Bloomsbury, pp. 57–66.

Mitchell, Terry L. (2007) "Syndication vs. Network Broadcasts", *American Chronicle*, 10 May, www.americanchronicle.com. Accessed July 17 2008.

Mittell, Jason (2004) *Genre and Television: From Cop Shows to Cartoons in American Culture*, New York: Routledge.

Mittell, Jason (2006) "Narrative Complexity in Contemporary American Television", *The Velvet Light Trap* Vol. 58, No. 1, pp. 29–40.

Mittell, Jason (2013) "The Qualities of Complexity: Vast Versus Dense Seriality in Contemporary Television", Chapter 2 in Jason Jacobs and Steven Peacock (eds.), *Television Aesthetics and Style*, New York: Bloomsbury, pp. 45–56.

Mittell, Jason (2015) *Complex TV: The Poetics of Contemporary Television Storytelling*, New York and London: New York University Press.

Morabito, Andrea (2013) "CBS Tests New Model With *Under the Dome*", *Broadcasting and Cable*, 24 June, p. 24.

Motavalli, John (2002) "Albrecht: Life on the Edge", *Electronic Media*, 17 June, Vol. 21, Issue 24, p. 1.

Mullen, Megan (2003) *The Rise of Cable Programming in the United States: Revolution or Evolution?* Austin: University of Texas Press.

Mullen, Megan (2008) *Television in the Multichannel Age: A Brief History of Cable Television*, Malden: Blackwell Publishing.

Neale, Stephen (1981) "Genre and Cinema" in Tony Bennett, Susan Boyd-Bowman, Colin Mercer, and Janet Woollacott, (eds.), *Popular Television and Film*, London: British Film Institute, pp. 6–25.

Nelson, Robin (1997) *TV Drama in Transition: Forms, Values and Cultural Change*, Basingstoke: Macmillan.

Nelson, Robin (2004) *"Hill Street Blues"*, Chapter 21 in Glen Creeber (ed.) *Fifty Key Television Programmes*, New York: Edward Arnold, pp. 100–104.

Nelson, Robin (2007a) *State of Play: Contemporary "High-End" Drama*, Manchester and New York: Manchester University Press.

Nelson, Robin (2007b) "Quality TV Drama: Estimations and Influences Through Time and Space", Chapter 3 in Janet McCabe and Kim Akass (eds.) *Quality TV: Contemporary American Television and Beyond*, London: I.B. Tauris, pp. 38–51.

Nelson, Robin (2011) "Author(iz)ing Chase" in David Lavery, Douglas L. Howard, and Paul Levinson (eds.), *The Essential Sopranos Reader*, Lexington: University of Kentucky Press, pp. 41–53.

Newcomb, Horace (2007) "'This is Not Al Dente': *The Sopranos* and the New Meaning of Television" in Horace Newcomb (ed.), *Television: The Critical View*, Seventh Edition, Oxford: Oxford University Press, pp. 561–78.

Newcomb, Horace (2008) "*Deadwood*", Chapter 6 in Gary R. Edgerton and Jeffrey P. Jones (eds.), *The Essential HBO Reader*, Lexington: Kentucky University Press, pp. 92–102.

Newcomb, Horace and Robert S. Alley (1983) *The Producer's Medium: Conversations With Creators of American TV*, New York and London: Oxford University Press.

Newman, Michael and Elana Levine (2012) *Legitimating Television: Media Convergence and Cultural Status*, New York and London: Routledge.

Ott, Brian L. and Cameron Walter (2000) "Intertextuality: Interpretive Practice and Textual Strategy", *Critical Studies in Media Communication*, Vol. 17 No. 4, December, pp. 429–46.

Pearson, Roberta (2005) "The Writer/Producer in American Television", Chapter 1 in Michael Hammond and Lucy Mazdon (eds.), *The Contemporary Television Series*, Edinburgh: Edinburgh University Press, pp. 11–26.

Perren, Alisa (2003) "New U.S. Networks in the 1990s", in Michelle Hilmes and Jason Jacobs (eds.) *The Television History Book*, pp. 107–12.

Perren, Alisa (2011) "In Conversation: Creativity in the Contemporary Cable Industry", *Cinema Journal*, Vol. 50 No. 2, pp. 132–38.

Pierson, David P. (2014a) "Introduction" in David P. Pierson (ed.), *Breaking Bad: Critical Essays on the Contexts, Politics, Style, and Reception of the Television Series*, Lanham: Lexington Books, pp. 1–12.

Pierson, David P. (2014b) "Breaking Neoliberal? Contemporary Neoliberal Discourses and Policies in AMC's *Breaking Bad*", Chapter 1 in David P. Pierson (ed.), *Breaking Bad: Critical Essays on the Contexts, Politics, Style, and Reception of the Television Series*, Lanham and Plymouth: Lexington Books, pp. 15–31.

Porter, Michael J., Deborah L. Larson, Allison Harthcock, and Kelly B. Nellis, (2002) "Redefining Narrative Events: Examining Television Narrative Structure", *Journal of Popular Film and Television*, Vol. 30, No. 1, pp. 23–30.

Prys, Catrin (2006) "Issues in Television Authorship", in Glen Creeber (ed.), *Tele-Visions: An Introduction to Studying Television*, London: British Film Institute, pp. 20–25.

Pulver, Andrew (2017) "Martin Scorcese's *The Irishman* Bought by Netflix", *The Guardian*, 22 February. www.theguardian.com/film/2017/. Accessed April 8 2017.

Redvall, Eva Novrup (2013) *Writing and Producing Television Drama in Denmark*, Basingstoke: Palgrave Macmillan.

Reynolds, Mike (2001a) "FX Eyes Drama, Reality", *Cable World*, 29 January, p. 28.

Reynolds, Mike (2001b) "A Highly Original Interview with HBO's Albrecht", *Multichannel News*, 11 June, p. 124.

Rogers, Mark C., Michael Epstein, and Jimmie L. Reeves (2002) "*The Sopranos* as HBO Brand Equity: The Art of Commerce in An Age of Digital Reproduction", Chapter 6 in David Lavery (ed.), *This Thing of Ours: Investigating The Sopranos*, New York: Wallflower Press and Columbia University Press, pp. 42–57.

Romano, Allison (2002a) "Can *The Shield* Fix FX?" *Broadcast and Cable*, 11 March, p. 16.

Romano, Allison (2002b) "Rainbow Brightens Its Stripes", *Broadcasting and Cable*, 7 October, pp. 18-20. Retrieved from https://search.proquest.com/docview/225292207?accountid=14782. Accessed March 9 2014.

Romano, Allison (2004) "Leading the Charge", *Broadcasting and Cable*, 1 November, p. 16.

Rose, Brian (2011) "If It's Too Easy, Then Usually There's Something Wrong: An Interview with *Mad Men*'s Executive Producer Scott Hornbacher" in Gary R. Edgerton (ed.), *Mad Men: Dream Come True TV*, London: I.B. Tauris, pp. 25–41.

Ryan, Maureen (2016) "TV Peaks Again in 2016: Could It Hit 500 Shows in 2017?", *Variety*, 21 December. http://variety.com/2016/tv/news/. Accessed May 30 2017.

Sánchez-Baró, Rossend (2014) "Uncertain Beginnings: *Breaking Bad*'s Episodic Openings" in David P. Pierson (ed.), *Breaking Bad: Critical Essays on the Contexts, Politics, Style, and Reception of the Television Series*, Lanham: Lexington Books, pp. 139–53.

Santo, Avi (2008) "Para-Television and Discourses of Distinction: The Culture of Production at HBO" in Mark Leverette, Brian L. Ott, and Cara L. Buckley (eds.), *It's Not TV: Watching HBO in the Post-Television Era*, New York: Routledge, pp. 19–45.

Sconce, Jeffrey (2004) "What If? Charting Television's New Textual Boundaries" in Lynn Spigel and Jan Olsson (eds.), *Television After TV: Essays on a Medium in Transition*, Durham and London: Duke University Press, pp. 93–112.

Seitz, Matt Zoller (2015) *Mad Men Carousel: The Complete Critical Companion*, Abrams: New York.

Sepinwall, Alan (2012) *The Revolution Was Televised: The Cops, Crooks, Slingers, and Slayers Who Changed TV Drama Forever*, New York: Touchstone.

Shattuc, Jane M. (2005) "Television Production: Who Makes American TV?" in Janet Wasko (ed.), *A Companion to Television*. Malden, Oxford: Blackwell Publishing, pp. 142–56.

Shreger, Charles (2013) HBO President of International Programming, Interview with Trisha Dunleavy, 12 June.

Shaw, Lucas (2017) "Netflix Soars, Esquire Goes Dark as More TV Viewers Move Online", *Livemint*, 19 January. www.bloomberg.com/news/articles/. Accessed April 15, 2017.

Singer, Mark (2005) "The Misfit: How David Milch Got from *NYPD Blue* to *Deadwood* by Way of an Epistle of St. Paul", *The New Yorker*, 14 February. http://www.newyorker.com/archive/2005/02/14. Accessed March 17 2014.

Smith, Anthony (2013, orig. 2011) "Putting the Premium into Basic: Slow-Burn Narratives and the Loss-Leader Function of AMC's Original Drama Series", *Television and New Media*, Vol. 14, Issue 2, pp. 150–66.

Spangler, Todd (2015) "HBO Severs the Hold of the Pay-TV Bundle", *Variety*, 17 March, p. 11.

Spangler, Todd (2016) "Netflix Has 30 Original Series Today, Will Double That in 2017, Content Chief Ted Sarandos Says", *Variety*, 5 December. http://variety.com/2016/digital/news/netflix-ted-sarandos-original-series-scripted-unscripted-1201933645/. Accessed April 15, 2017.

Sparks, Richard (1993) "*Inspector Morse*: 'The Last Enemy' (Peter Buckman)", Chapter 5 in George W. Brandt (ed.), *British Television Drama in the 1980s*, Cambridge: Cambridge University Press, pp. 86–102.

Spigel, Lynn (1992) *Make Room for TV: Television and the Family Ideal in Postwar America*, Chicago: University of Chicago Press.

Stam, Robert (2000a) *Film Theory: An Introduction*, Malden and Oxford: Blackwell.

Stam, Robert (2000b) "Alternative Aesthetics", Introduction to Part IV in Robert Stam and Toby Miller (eds.), *Film and Theory: An Anthology*, Blackwell: Massachusetts and Oxford, pp. 257–64.

Stewart, Andrew and David Cohen (2013) "Filmmakers Lament Extinction of Film Prints" *Variety*, 16 April. http://variety.com/2013/film/news/. Accessed March 20 2017.

Straubhaar, Joseph D. (2007) *World Television: From Global to Local*, Los Angeles: Sage.

"The Game Is Real" (2007) Behind-the-Scenes documentary on *The Wire*, DVD Season 4.

Thompson, Derek (2016) "Hollywood Has a Huge Millennial Problem", *The Atlantic Daily*, 8 June. www.theatlantic.com/business/archive/2016/06/. Accessed March 19 2017.

Thompson, Robert J. (1996) *From Hill Street Blues to ER: Television's Second Golden Age*, New York: Syracuse University Press.

Thompson, Robert J. (2007) "Preface" in Janet McCabe and Kim Akass (eds.), *Quality TV: Contemporary American Television and Beyond*, pp. 145–57, pp. xvii–xx.

Thomson, Patricia (2010) "Mob Money", *American Cinematographer*, September. www.theasc. com/ac_magazine/September2010/BoardwalkEmpire/. Accessed March 20 2017.

Thomson, Patricia (2016) "It's Only Rock and Roll", *American Cinematographer*, March, Vol. 97, Issue 3, pp. 32–43.

Thorburn, David (1994, orig. 1976) "Television Melodrama" in Horace Newcomb (ed.), *Television: The Critical View*, Fifth Edition, Oxford and New York: Oxford University Press, pp. 537–50.

Thornham, Sue and Neville Purvis (2005) *Television Drama: Theories and Identities*, Basingstoke: Palgrave Macmillan.

Thrower, Emma (2016) "*Stranger Things*: The Duffer Brothers Share the Secrets of Their Hit Show", *Empire*, 27 July. www.empireonline.com/movies/features/. Accessed April 23 2017.

Tickle, Glen (2015) "Why the Frak Can't People Say 'Fuck' on Cable? It's All About the Money", *The Mary Sue*, 31 March. http://www.thenarysue.com/saying-fuck-on-television. Accessed February 2 2015.

Turner, Lexi (2009) "Bryan Cranston: From *Malcolm in the Middle* to America's Favourite Meth Dealer", *The Guardian*, 21 November. http://www.theguardian.com/tv-and-radio/2009/nov/21/bryan-cranston-breaking-bad. Accessed June 25 2015.

Vermeulen, Timotheus and Gry C. Rustad (2013) "Watching Television With Jacques Rancière: U.S. 'Quality Television', *Mad Men* and the 'Late Cut'", *Screen*, Vol. 54, No. 3, pp. 341–54.

Vine, Richard (2016) "The Secret LSD-Fuelled CIA Experiment that Inspired *Stranger Things*", *The Guardian*, 15 August. www.theguardian.com/tv-and-radio/. Accessed April 6 2017.

Vint, Sherryl (2013) *The Wire*, TV Milestone Series, Detroit: Wayne State University Press.

Weissmann, Elke (2012) *Transnational Television Drama: Special Relations and Mutual Influence Between the US and UK*, Basingstoke: Palgrave Macmillan.

Wells, John (1996) "Team Writing" in Julian Friedmann (eds.), *Writing a Long-Running Television Series: Lectures from the Second PILOTS Workshop*, Sitges, Catalonia: Fundacion Cultural Media, pp. 194–205.

Wells, Paul (2003) "Smarter than the Average Art Form: Animation in the Television Era", Chapter 1 in Carol A. Stabile and Mark Harrison (eds.), *Prime Time Animation: Television Animation and American Culture*, New York and London: Routledge, pp. 15–32.

Weprin, Alex (2009) "Premium Summer for Cable", *Broadcasting and Cable*, 22 August, p. 3.

Weinraub, Bernard (2001) "An Oscar Winner Returns to TV on New Terms", *New York Times*, March 4, http://www.nytimes.com. Accessed April 15 2014.

Willimon, Beau (2013) *TV Writer Podcast* 074, 23 June. http://blip.tv/tvwriterpodcast/watch. Accessed July 2 2015.

Winslow, George (2013) "Next TV Summit: TV Industry Faces Innovator's Dilemma", *Broadcasting and Cable*, 11 September. http://www.broadcastingcable.com/news/technology/. Accessed 6 March 2014.

Woodward, Richard B. (2011) "*Breaking Bad*: The Best Dramatic Show on TV Begins Another Season", *The Huffington Post*, 7 August. http://www.huffingtonpost.com/richard-b-woodward/breaking-bad Accessed July 20 2014.

Woolf, Michael (2015) "Sure, It's Television. But Don't Call It Television", *The Hollywood Reporter*, 22 May, p. 32.

INDEX